CANADIAN POLICING IN THE 21ST CENTURY

Canadian Policing in the 21st Century

A Frontline Officer on Challenges and Changes

ROBERT CHRISMAS

McGill-Queen's University Press
Montreal & Kingston • London • Ithaca

© McGill-Queen's University Press 2013

ISBN 978-0-7735-4274-7 (cloth)
ISBN 978-0-7735-8935-3 (ePDF)
ISBN 978-0-7735-8936-0 (ePUB)

Legal deposit third quarter 2013
Bibliothèque nationale du Québec

Printed in Canada on acid-free paper that is 100% ancient forest free
(100% post-consumer recycled), processed chlorine free

McGill-Queen's University Press acknowledges the support of the Canada
Council for the Arts for our publishing program. We also acknowledge
the financial support of the Government of Canada through the Canada
Book Fund for our publishing activities.

Library and Archives Canada Cataloguing in Publication

Chrismas, Robert, 1962–, author
    Canadian policing in the 21st century: a frontline officer on challenges
and changes / Robert Chrismas.

    Includes bibliographical references and index.
    Issued in print and electronic formats.
    ISBN 978-0-7735-4274-7 (bound). – ISBN 978-0-7735-8935-3 (ePDF). –
ISBN 978-0-7735-8936-0 (ePUB)

    1. Police – Canada. 2. Law enforcement – Canada. I. Title.

HV8157.C47 2013   363.20971   C2013-902562-6
                                            C2013-902563-4

This book was typeset by Interscript in 10.5/13 Sabon.

*This book is a testament to police officers everywhere,
in recognition of their dedication to protecting the vulnerable
and keeping communities safe in increasingly challenging times.
The weapons and battleground have changed over the past
two decades, but the values they fight for remain the same.*

Contents

Preface

In reflecting on my twenty-eight years of law enforcement, I realized that many of the stories from the pre-information age eras are fast disappearing. The policing profession has evolved in ways that were not imagined twenty years ago. Personal computers, smartphones, and social networking have become part of our new human experience. Increased access to information has transformed the public relationship with government agencies, including the police, and has changed the nature of accountability. Globalization and the complexity of today's social problems have created the need for more collaborative, multi-disciplinary approaches. Gender, race, and age diversity have also changed policing dramatically.

This book describes a frontline officer's perspective on how policing has evolved over the past two decades. It offers first-hand experiences and observations supported and complemented by a wide range of academic and professional sources. While it is not an account of all aspects of policing, this book describes two decades of unprecedented change. The views expressed in this book are my own and do not represent those of the Winnipeg Police Service.

Acknowledgments

Thanks go to my friends and colleagues Amanda Kerr Adam, Kimberly Carswell, Gabrielle Giroday, Shelley Hart, Gelareh Manghebati, Kevin Martell, Adrian May, Laura Normand, Christina Von Schindler, Ray Yuen, Melanie Zurba, and others for their generous donations of time and effort to edit and provide feedback on this work. Thank you to the anonymous experts who read earlier versions, providing insightful critiques and challenging me to improve the manuscript. I wish to extend a special thank-you to my editors, Joan Harcourt, Mark Abley, and Joan McGilvray, indexer Celia Braves, and the entire team at McGill-Queen's University Press for their insights, encouragement, and assistance in moving this book from draft to print. Any oversights are strictly mine.

Appreciation and love also go to my wife, Barb, and my children, Crystal, Chelsea, Brandi, and Bobby, for their patience and support during my graduate studies and the writing of this book, and for supporting my policing career and all that has come with it.

Abbreviations

AJI	Aboriginal Justice Inquiry
ASP	Brand name of a telescoping baton
CACP	Canadian Association of Chiefs of Police
CBA	Collective Bargaining Agreement
CBRNE	Chemical, Biological, Radiological, Nuclear, Explosive
CPA	Canadian Police Association
CPIC	Canadian Police Information Centre
CSIS	Canadian Security Intelligence Service
DNA	Deoxyribonucleic acid
ECD	Electrical Control Device
FASD	Fetal Alcohol Spectrum Disorder
FBI	Federal Bureau of Investigation
ICE	Integrated Child Exploitation
IPAC	Institute of Public Administration Canada
IPOC	Integrated Proceeds of Crime
ITO	Information to Obtain
JEPP	Joint Emergency Preparedness Program
LERA	Law Enforcement Review Agency
MDT	Mobile Data Terminal
MLAT	Mutual Legal Assistance Treaty
MPS	Metropolitan Police Service (London, England)
NGO	Nongovernment Organization
NML	National Microbiology Lab
NWMP	North West Mounted Police
NYPD	New York City Police Department
OC	Oleoresin Capsicum
OPP	Ontario Provincial Police

P3	Public Private Partnerships
PTSD	Post Traumatic Stress Disorder
RCMP	Royal Canadian Mounted Police
SQ	Sûreté du Québec
TRC	Truth and Reconciliation Commission
UCN	University College of the North
WPA	Winnipeg Police Association
WPS	Winnipeg Police Service

CANADIAN POLICING IN THE 21ST CENTURY

Introduction

Have technological advances and increased access to information helped government agencies like the police or have they overwhelmed them? The benefits and impacts of new technology are debatable, but the dramatic changes it has created cannot be overstated. In recent decades police agencies have changed in almost every aspect, from demographic composition to enforcement and prevention strategies to the roles they fulfill in society and the challenges they face. This book grew from my reflections on how policing has changed over the past twenty-five years of my career. In 1989 my recruit class in the Winnipeg Police Service (WPS) learned to write reports on manual typewriters, using little-remembered equipment such as carbon paper and white-out. Today, police officers cannot function without advanced skills in the use of sophisticated computers and communication devices. We now take for granted technologies that we could not have imagined twenty years ago.

In 2009, while on vacation in Florida, I used a smartphone to answer phone calls and e-mails from people in partner agencies who were assisting me on an important major investigation that I was overseeing. An issue that in the past would have had to wait until I returned from vacation was addressed without missing a beat. In 2012 my teenage children talk, Tweet, Facebook, and Skype in real time with people from all corners of the globe through Internet connections and video cameras built into their cell phones. Recently one of my daughters, who had misplaced her cell phone, used the computer in our kitchen and a global-positioning application to track it to a point in the opposite end of the city, where she had forgotten it in her boyfriend's truck. In somewhat the same way, smartphones now provide people with the tools to track other peoples' movements. Imagine this technology in the wrong hands. Some businesses are now operating without offices, with employees in opposite corners of the country or around the world meeting and operating as avatars in virtual office environments. Such changes affect interpersonal dynamics and relationships in fundamental ways. The technology that the police have to work with has advanced beyond our wildest imagining and yet organized criminals often still have the advantage, operating without the constraints that law enforcement agencies face, such as jurisdictional boundaries, laws, bureaucracy, and operational costs.

Criminal sophistication, advancements in technology, and changing societal demands have created continuously increasing challenges for frontline, middle management, and executive-level police officers. Terrorism, organized crime, Internet-based child exploitation and human trafficking, international fraud, and a host of other emerging criminal activities have redefined traditional boundaries and drawn policing into a new, borderless universe. Effective police work now requires interagency cooperation and information and resource sharing on an entirely new level.

Law enforcement agencies are undergoing fundamental shifts in strategy. Historically, the police have been largely reactive, responding to crime without being overly concerned about its root causes. Now, approaches that focus on preventing crime rather than just reacting to it are preferred. However, shifting strategies and redeploying resources that are already stretched thin can be difficult. In addition, police officers everywhere are attempting to ensure that their work is based on evidence and not merely past practices, which can also add to operational demands.

Within the police, mass baby boomer retirements are resulting in a critical loss of institutional memory and shifting demographics, forcing police services to focus on recruitment, retention, and succession planning. Twenty years ago Canadian police agencies were made up of white Anglo-Saxon males, a far cry from the gender, ethnic, and age-diverse workforces of today. This new dynamic requires a different set of management and leadership competencies.

In the past twenty years most Canadian police agencies have changed their names from "Force" to "Service" (Templeton 1998) in an attempt to cast off the traditional bunker mentality, wherein police forces worked in isolation from other service industries, in favour of an increased focus on partnerships with stakeholders and community resources. Today's law enforcement issues are so broad and complex that no one agency can manage any of them in isolation.

Geographic boundaries and communication barriers are collapsing so rapidly and dramatically that we risk failing to recognize the impact of these changes and learning how to respond most effectively. With the evolution of the Internet and portable communication devices, the average citizen now has instant access to information that only senior government officials were privy to in the past. Technology is advancing so quickly that civil servants now risk becoming like the metaphorical frog in the pot of water which, because the water comes to a boil very gradually, is not aware of the need to take action. The fast pace of the modern work environment may distract us from realizing the full effects of continuous technological change in law enforcement and thus finding means to keep up with increasingly complex organized crime and ever-changing technology.

This book examines twenty years of change in Canadian policing. I have tried to present a credible, balanced, and sourced account, corroborated by my own twenty-eight years of law enforcement experience. Prior to joining the WPS in 1989, I worked as a Manitoba sheriff's officer. I have also worked in Manitoba's courts and travelled to the North, gaining insights into the Canadian justice system and social justice issues, particularly as they relate to Aboriginal peoples.

In the past twenty-three years with the WPS I have worked in four of Winnipeg's six uniform patrol divisions and numerous specialty units: the Anti-Crime Tactical Unit, targeting serial break-and-enter gangs; the Major Crimes Unit, investigating commercial robberies, shootings, and major offences; the Child Abuse Unit, investigating child deaths and maltreatment; district detectives, investigating general crimes; the Integrated Child Exploitation Unit, investigating Internet-based child exploitation through pornography; and as a sex-crimes analyst. I was a founding member of the Arson Strike Force during the 1999 arson crisis in Winnipeg. I recently helped the Missing Persons Unit develop new prevention-oriented multidisciplinary strategies to intervene in the lives of self-destructive and exploited high-risk youth. As a staff sergeant in the duty office, I oversaw frontline police operations for the City of Winnipeg. I also have twenty years of experience in numerous extra-duty teams, such as the riot squad, disaster management, and peer support. This experience, along with my graduate level university education, first in public administration and then in peace and conflict studies, provides the background for this book.

Over the course of centuries policing has taken many forms, but it is the principles set out by British Home Secretary Sir Robert Peel in 1829 in establishing London's Metropolitan Police Force (Lentz and Chaires 2007) that became the model for police forces in Canada and throughout most of the British Empire. These principles remain apposite today, despite the changes that have occurred in policing and society in recent decades. Peel's nine principles of policing are:

1 The basic mission of the police is to prevent crime and disorder.
2 The ability of the police to perform their duties is dependent upon public approval of police actions.
3 Police must secure the willing cooperation of the public in voluntary observation of the law to be able to obtain and maintain the respect of the public.
4 The degree of cooperation from the public diminishes proportionately the need for the use of physical force.
5 Police seek and preserve public favour not by catering to public opinion but by constantly demonstrating absolute and impartial service to the law.
6 Police use physical force to the extent necessary to secure observance of the law or to restore order only when the exercise of persuasion, advice, and warning is found to be insufficient.
7 Police, at all times, should maintain a relationship with the public that gives reality to the historic tradition that the police are the public and the public are the police; the police being only members of the public who are paid to give full-time attention to duties that are incumbent upon every citizen in the interests of community welfare and existence.
8 Police should always direct their action strictly towards their function, and never appear to usurp the powers of the judiciary.
9 The test of police efficiency is the absence of crime and disorder, not the visible evidence of police action in dealing with it. (Peel 1829)

Despite shifting demands, these principles are still the goal of good policing. This book describes trends and issues that are similar across the broad spectrum of Canadian policing: the impacts of rapid and continuous technological advances, increased accountability, and the gamut of changing demands are experienced from region to region. New demands call for continual re-evaluation and innovative strategies. In the final analysis, however, I find that the underlying principles remain relevant. The battleground and the weapons have changed, but the fight to provide safe communities remains the same.

1

Some Policing History

In the pre-industrial era parents played a more substantial role in the upbringing and development of their children. As industry progressed and people left the house for work, much of the responsibility for child-care was shifted to public schools. Public institutions have also taken on greater roles in security, safety, justice, and social regulation. Today, some people look to child welfare agencies and the police to solve problems that would historically have been handled in the home. A joke passed around law enforcement agencies for many years involved an answering machine message with multiple choices, one of which was, "If you want us to raise your kids for you, press one." People now ask the police for assistance with very different matters from those that were seen as their responsibility at the turn of the century. On many occasions, while working in uniform patrol, I responded to public calls for assistance that turned out to be minor disputes and often found myself at a kitchen table in a private home mediating domestic arguments or sibling rivalry. If even a small segment of society has unrealistic expectations of service providers like the police, their calls for attention can be overwhelming. People often turn to the police when other community resources are unavailable or not readily accessible; everyone knows how to dial 911. Our child welfare systems are chronically overwhelmed by serious issues and limited resources, leaving the police as the service that people think of first when they are desperate for advice or help during a crisis.

Popular media often suggest that the police or government agencies are responsible for the failure to correct social problems. Rarely is the focus on the root causes of problems or the social structures that perpetuate them. The reality is that no amount of money could make government agencies, such as the police, so effective that they can correct major societal ills alone. We must recognize that the entire community needs to work together to address complex problems. While, as I discuss later in the book, there has been a recent shift to multisystem approaches and public engagement, reliance on government to deal with social problems has driven police mandates and strategies for decades.

While the first Canadian police officers are said to have patrolled Quebec City as early as 1651, most of Canada's early municipal police forces were not established until the mid 1800s. After Confederation in 1867, the Constitution Act of 1867 gave each of Canada's provinces the authority to establish police forces within their jurisdictions and law enforcement remains a provincial responsibility (Ross 1995).

The earliest law enforcement systems followed French and English traditions. They were also greatly influenced by the practices of our American neighbours (Ross 1995). In the west, the Hudson's Bay Company, which played a large part in Canada's settlement, had its own legal system and regulations that served as a body of Canadian laws until they were replaced by Federal statutes in 1869, following the seizure of Manitoba's Fort Garry by Lois Riel (Brown 2002; Duhaime 2008).

Sir John A. Macdonald established the North-West Mounted Police (NWMP) in 1873. The powers and discipline of the red-coated NWMP troops differed from those of the British military traditions from which they had been born: they had a system of military structure and discipline, but constables acted as both police and magistrates, enforcing the laws and also acting as prosecutors (Brown 2002). This was a marked departure from the system that had been established in the early 1800s in eastern Canada, whereby citizens were appointed magistrates and the military were called on during rare times of civil unrest when force was needed (Brown 2002). Sir John A. Macdonald defended the NWMP structure as needed in the wild expanses of western Canada that the NWMP had to patrol. In 1904 the NWMP were granted the "Royal" prefix and were renamed the Royal Canadian Mounted Police (RCMP) (History of the Royal Canadian Mounted Police 2012). The RCMP was meant to be a temporary force but the model was so successful that in 1905 the new provinces of Alberta and Saskatchewan convinced

Prime Minister Wilfrid Laurier to leave the NWMP in place. Its jurisdiction was extended to Manitoba in 1912 and to British Columbia
in 1918 (Brown 2002).

The RCMP provide federal enforcement across Canada and continue to be involved in provincial law enforcement in all provinces
except Ontario and Quebec. The Ontario Provincial Police, Sûreté
du Québec, and Royal Newfoundland Constabulary are the only
provincial police forces in Canada. In Ontario and Quebec the
RCMP serves only federal functions such as national security and
smaller municipalities often contract police services from provincial
agencies, while larger ones maintain their own forces. Newfoundland's
provincial police force is responsible only for its larger urban areas;
the province has contracted the RCMP to patrol the rest of the province (Statistics Canada 2011a). In other provinces, the RCMP han-
dles policing except where regional forces have been set up. For
instance, in Manitoba, the RCMP is contracted by municipalities
to police most rural regions outside of the cities of Winnipeg and
Brandon. Several towns have opted to create their own small stand-
alone police services, and the Dakota Ojibway Police Service polices
several reserves.

Many First Nations Communities have their own police forces,
often called peacekeepers, funded through tripartite agreements
between the Government of Canada, the provinces, and First Nations
communities. Currently Aboriginal policing is supported through
168 policing service agreements for the policing of 408 First Nations
communities in Canada (Public Safety Canada 2012).

Canada's economic development sheds light on the historical
establishment and evolution of its justice system and the philosophy
behind it. Canada's staple-based economy grew out of European
demand for beaver pelts (Innis 1930). Therefore, it is not surprising
that our legal system evolved, to a great extent, around protection of
ownership and control of property. Among the first Canadian laws
enacted were those that authorized the Hudson's Bay Company to
control beaver trapping throughout central Canada and to export
pelts to Europe (Duhaime 2008).

Canada's colonization began with the exploitation of its natural
resources. Indigenous peoples were an important part of early trapping and trading networks and Canada's original political boundaries were defined by trade routes set up between the European settlers
and indigenous peoples to gather beaver pelts for the European

market (Innis 1930). The effects of colonization are still felt by the people who were displaced. Indigenous peoples are often marginalized in mainstream Canadian communities and are over-represented in our prison systems. Colonization and the residential school policy disrupted connections between Aboriginal people and their culture and have resulted in serious intergenerational problems, including widespread substance abuse and lack of parenting skills (Canada, Indian and Northern Affairs 1996; Comack et al. 2009; Hallet, Thornton, and Stewart 2006). Aboriginal people continue to face the barriers of low-income, racism, and the destructive impacts of colonization (McCracken and Michell 2006).

In addition to colonization, the European influence on Canada's justice system is expressed in the principle of imprisonment as a social punishment and crime deterrent. Various forms of imprisonment have been used throughout history, including debtors' prisons, which were used primarily in Europe. The first prison in North America, in the modern sense of the term, was established in Philadelphia in 1790 (Takagi 1974). Canada's first federal penitentiary was founded in Kingston in 1933 (Correctional Service of Canada 2008). The idea of imprisonment and loss of freedom as a deterrent is a cornerstone of modern North American justice paradigms.

Another cornerstone of Canadian justice is the belief, also of European origin, in professionalized police services with authority and responsibility for keeping the peace. Peel's principles of police authority and powers have remained an important part of Canada's social fabric (Kelling 1999). Traditions of using police as regulatory agents, coupled with imprisonment as a deterrent to crime, have resulted in Canada's justice system developing a culture that is not only reactive rather than preventative but very expensive to maintain. I examine these issues in more detail in the next chapter on the costs of justice.

Each police organization also has a unique culture that is moulded by its specific circumstances, history, regional characteristics, and cultural context. The WPS, for instance, is over one hundred years old. Winnipeg has a long labour movement history, dating back to the 1919 General Strike that gave the city an international reputation for fighting for human rights and planted the seeds of the Canadian labour movement. The Winnipeg Police Association evolved in that rich labour culture, which may explain in part why it became one of Canada's most active police unions.

For a four-year period in my career, I was on the board of the Winnipeg Police Association. At one point, I attended the Canadian Police College in Ottawa for a two-week labour relations course with officers from across the country. We all brought copies of our collective bargaining agreements (CBAs). Winnipeg's CBA was (is) about sixty pages long and outlines everything from minimum street strengths for the start of every shift to the equipment that every officer is entitled to and the amount of notice required to alter officers' work shifts. The CBAs of some other police services, such as Edmonton's, are much thinner and define much less. This is the result of a different organizational cultures and attitudes among police officers' union representatives, senior bureaucrats, and politicians in other cities. In some cities, grievances are more likely to be settled before the need for formal adjudicated hearings that entrench the issues in CBAs. There have, however, been some intense work-to-rule campaigns in other jurisdictions, including Toronto and Montreal.

Work stoppage is generally not an option for police officers in Canada as essential service workers have, historically, been quickly legislated back to work during work stoppages. The cost of the one-week strike by the Montreal Police in 1969 was said to be six bank robberies, one hundred shops looted, twelve fires, $3 million in property damage, and two men shot to death (Time Magazine 1969). In most, if not all, regions of Canada the police are now restricted by law from striking and must take disputes to binding arbitration. These mediation processes generally end with decisions that become entrenched in collective bargaining agreements.

Winnipeg has seen a number of changes since 1974, when six surrounding municipalities were amalgamated with the City of Winnipeg. Six separate police departments, each with different organizational characteristics, were integrated into the original Winnipeg Police Department (as it was then known), which had jurisdiction over the downtown neighbourhoods. The new Winnipeg Police Service was now responsible for the primarily French-speaking community of St Boniface, the downtown area, suburban and middle- to upper-class River Heights, Fort Garry, Charleswood, Tuxedo, and the North End, which had been primarily settled by European immigrants – a mosaic of cultural and socio-economic diversity. Increasing immigration from other countries and urbanization of Aboriginal peoples also enhance this diversity, which affects virtually every aspect of police work and police leadership.

The amalgamation that occurred in Winnipeg in 1974 reflects a trend that has occurred in numerous jurisdictions across Canada where regional forces have been created. In Ontario, the Peel Regional Police was established in 1974, following the creation of the Regional Municipality of Peel, which incorporated the former police services of Mississauga, Port Credit, Streetsville, Brampton, and Chinguacousy, creating the largest municipal police force in Ontario (Peel Regional Police 2012). Other regions, such as Vancouver, BC, have not yet adopted the regional police model, preferring to maintain their stand-alone municipal agencies (Pablo 2009).

As Canadian cities have grown, so too have municipal police forces. Currently Canada's 222 police organizations include one federal police force (the RCMP), three provincial police forces, 150 municipal police services, over 50 First Nations Police Services, and some special agencies such as the two railway police services. These police organizations are comprised of 12 police services with over 1,000 employees, 15 large-sized police services with 300-999 employees, 27 medium-sized police services with 100-299 employees, and 65 small police services with 25-99 employees. There are 103 small police services employing fewer than 25 employees. In Canada there are 61,050 police officers and 23,391 civilian support staff, which amounts to one officer for every 528 Canadian citizens (Police Sector Council 2012).

As populations in urban centres grow, the cost-benefit analysis of contracting with large regional police services is inevitably assessed against the value of creating or maintaining one's own stand-alone police agency. Similarly, as multiple agencies evolve in close proximity to each other, the question inevitably arises whether amalgamation of agencies would be more efficient. For police departments, amalgamation can create opportunities by centralizing shared resources. For example, one large centralized identification unit may serve numerous police agencies more efficiently than if each agency maintained its own unit.

The downside of amalgamating police agencies lies in how resources are deployed. The Winnipeg amalgamation in 1974, for example, caused most of the resources of the outlying police departments to be drawn into the city's core and precipitated a reduction in services to the suburbs. Before the amalgamation, the residents of the middle-class suburbs of St James and Fort Garry had their own police forces, which provided good service to their small jurisdictions. Post-amalgamation, taxes remained the same and services were changed, except in the more impoverished neighbourhoods where they were arguably increased. The downtown core and areas of the North End are the most impoverished neighbourhoods in the city and, from a frontline police officer's perspective, seem to consume more emergency, social service resources, and other government services, per capita, than any of the outlying neighbourhoods.

Certainly the issues in the impoverished neighbourhoods are serious and need focused attention and resources and it is in the nature of public services, which manage the most difficult of society's problems, to attempt to deal with these actively. However, as I will argue later in the book, I believe the focus should be on preventing violence and crime rather than continually pouring more resources into dealing with them without addressing, or at least analyzing, the root causes of the problems.

The average citizen would be shocked to experience the stress of trying to meet high demands with limited resources. For instance, not many activities are more stressful than being on the phone with a distraught person who has called 911 for help but having difficulty finding available police units to send. I have the highest respect for dispatchers who manage this stress with discipline that defines the ultimate concept of professionalism and dedication.

It is useful in understanding the stress caused by limited resources to explore how the costs of justice have continued to increase. The next chapter explores some justice system costs and how the police role in the justice system has changed.

2

Police Roles and the Costs of Justice

CHANGING EXPECTATIONS

Police agencies, and many sub-units within them, tend to vacillate between being silos, operating in isolation from other stakeholder agencies, and, at the other end of the spectrum, being community-based team players. These shifts often occur in about ten-year cycles, so police officers can experience several of them in the course of a career. A respected colleague recently retired after over thirty years in policing, half of which were at a mid- to upper-management level rank with the RCMP. When I asked her if she had any doubts about retiring she said "No," explaining that when she saw the same issues come around for the second or third time she knew it was time to step aside and let someone else take up the cause.

In the late 1990s, Edmonton was a leader in community-based policing. During that time David Cassels, a former deputy chief in Edmonton, became Winnipeg's police chief, appointed mainly to implement this new cutting-edge policing structure that placed officers in storefronts, back on the beat, and in closer interaction with the public. It was an attempt to return to a time when people knew the names of the police who worked in their neighbourhoods – a reinvention of Peel's British policing model (Chacko and Nancoo 1993; Gayder 2008). In 1829, Peel established a structured police force in London, comprised of citizens who would walk the beat, preserve order, and guard public safety. These professional police officers later became known as Bobbies or, in Ireland, Peelers, after Sir Robert (Bobby) Peel. The origin of the modern slang term "cop" or "copper" has been debated. Some argue that the term derives from the copper helmets that Bobbies wore, which was then short-ened to "cop." Other sources refer to "constable on patrol," while yet others claim that the term originated from the fact that the police "cop" or catch people, as in the Latin *capere*, and therefore are "cop-pers" (Officer.com 2012). Bobbies walked beats and knew their neighbourhoods. It is little surprise that the idea resonates in modern times when police agencies have often been seen as isolated, reactionary forces, responding to complaints in cars and without connections with the neighbourhoods in which they serve.

In policing, reinvention and repetition of past strategies are often viewed as the answer to emerging problems. Having more officers on the beat is a good thing, and is consistent with the greatest traditions of policing. Beat officers have a chance to slow down and get to know people, rather than racing from call to call. They also have the opportunity to learn and take ownership of neighbourhood problems and to recognize and keep tabs on criminals. However, increasing the number of officers in one area inevitably creates shortages in other areas. In Winnipeg we ended up with virtually two police departments, one "community-based" (proactive) and one "primary response" (reactive) and found it challenging to run both with optimal effectiveness. It is difficult to find a balance between retaining the ability to effectively respond to emergency calls while engaging in crime prevention programs.

Some modern policing innovations would never have been considered two decades ago, illustrating dramatic departures from the conservative ethos that has dominated much of policing in the past. One example is government-supervised injection sites such as those that were established in British Columbia. Vancouver's notorious East Side, the home of one of Canada's largest illegal drug trade problems, was a likely site for an innovative new approach. The city implemented legal drug injection sites, with a view to reducing negative long-term health effects and healthcare costs associated with illicit drug use (Bayoumi and Zaric 2008). Drug users could take illegal drugs to a government facility where they would be given clean needles and a safe injection room in which to take the drugs. Analysis after the first ten years of the program revealed that there were healthcare savings involving HIV AIDS and hepatitis C, mainly due to increased awareness of the negative effects of street drug use and of the role of clean drug paraphernalia in limiting the spread of diseases (ibid.).

Another innovative approach to an old problem is the "Fugitive Return Program" – otherwise known as "Con Air" – which was developed in response to the problem caused by many of Canada's wanted criminals congregating in Vancouver. When a person in any province or territory is wanted on a warrant, a return radius stamp is put on the warrant, indicating how much the province is willing to spend to bring that person back to their jurisdictions for trial or sentencing. Only major offences are given a "Canada-wide" radius. Lesser crimes warrant a return radius such as within Manitoba or within 100 kilometres of Winnipeg. When I was on duty as a police supervisor in Winnipeg, I received a call from the Vancouver police. They had a person on one of our warrants and, as has been done for decades, asked if we wished to return him. Since the offence was not serious, I said no. The sergeant on the other end of the phone said "That's O K, we'll return him for you." By the first half of 2012 the Province of British Columbia had paid $100,000 to send ninety-eight fugitives back to their home provinces (Austin 2012). There is obviously a discussion to be had about shifting a problem from one jurisdiction to another, but this policy cost British Columbia far less than would otherwise have been spent on court and prison costs. Con Air is an example, like the legal injection sites, of an innovative approach based on economic justifications. The next section explores economic aspects of the justice system in more detail.

JUSTICE ECONOMICS

The modern prison system is based largely on the assumption that people are deterred from committing crime by the threat of the loss of freedom (Rubenstein 1995). The model proposes that people balance the potential benefits of committing crimes against the potential costs, which include the possibility of prison sentences, fines, and social embarrassment. The problems created by criminal records include such things as difficulty getting jobs and restrictions on travel across international borders. This economic, cost-benefit based, principle of deterrence has been adopted to a greater extent in the United States than in Canada: imprisonment is used more extensively in the United States and the resulting costs of maintaining the justice system are exponentially higher (Donohue 2007).

Understanding the economic principles on which our prison systems were founded helps explain how and why there has been a focus on decreasing crime rates but increasing costs of justice in recent decades. Cost-benefit analyses of crime prevention and the costs of crime are quite complex. For instance, which costs society more, large numbers of petty thieves or small numbers of large-scale thieves? Who is being victimized and which crimes should we focus on deterring? Should we put more resources into investigating and deterring crimes against property or into crimes of violence committed against people?

It is easy to put a value on property-related crimes and a value on their deterrence: we can put an accurate dollar value on property that is damaged, defrauded, or stolen. Determining the cost of crimes against persons, however, requires value judgments. How much is closure worth for the family of a murder victim? What is the value of preventing rape, child abuse, Internet child exploitation, or gang involvement? These questions drive the evaluation processes of police managers who must determine when and how to refocus resources from one area to another. Understanding this value-laden decision-making process is critical and is explored in more depth in later chapters.

One very broad way in which the overall cost of the justice system can be measured is in terms of gross aggregate numbers (Fellows et al. 1997). The Gross Domestic Product for one year minus the cost of the entire justice system for the same year is one way of determining the costs and measuring change. However, gross aggregate numbers have limited usefulness in measuring justice system performance, because the justice system, and policing in particular, fulfills a much broader mandate than just responding to crime. The justice system also provides public safety functions such as emergency response, rescue, public education, and deterrence. I will argue later that policing should play a greater role in leading social change and collaboration because such proactive strategies are more effective than responding to crimes after they have been committed. But, if police agencies take a lead role in improving community resilience to crime, how can the resulting costs and benefits be measured? Far too often, system effectiveness is measured by a very limited focus on issues such as a reduction of one particular category of crime. To give a simple example of a complex problem, the police can eradicate curb-side prostitution by flooding an area with officers. However, the inevitable reduction in reported prostitution may well mean that the sex-trade was just pushed out of sight, into online human trafficking networks or brothels.

The benefits of crime prevention are also extremely difficult to measure. Some argue that the optimal level of prevention that should be targeted is the level at which the benefits of crime prevention equal the costs (Fellows et al. 1997). Complete suppression of a particular crime problem may be possible; the question is whether it is worth the cost. For instance, theoretically, all, or nearly all, vehicle speeding could be stopped if enough resources were assigned to that problem. But placing unlimited resources into one area of enforcement would, of course, neglect other priorities.

In 2005 I learned a lesson about constraints involved in police and resource deployment. I had been working as a child abuse investigator when I was transferred into the new position of sex-crimes analyst. The Child Abuse Unit is chronically overworked, yet a patrol sergeant could not be spared from anywhere in the police service to fill my vacated position in child abuse. Every patrol sergeant position in the police service was accounted for and no one could be released from their duties to move into Child Abuse, at least not until the next round of promotions. Then a stray bullet killed an innocent teenager during a gang-related shooting in downtown Winnipeg. As a result of this tragic incident a new Street Crime Unit was created by redeploying fifty members of various ranks from throughout the service (Dehn 2008). The Street Crimes Unit was freed from regular dispatch work to target specific problems, such as hot spots for gang activity and street violence. The unit's creation illustrates that, with the right catalyst, resources can be found and directed to a particular area of concern. The need, however, must be sufficient to justify reducing services in other areas.

The speeding example also suggests another aspect of policing that must be considered in deploying resources – that sporadic enforcement has a deterrent effect. When officers are deployed to an area only periodically, the public never knows when the traffic officers are present and prepared to enforce the laws and therefore they slow down. In economic terms, equilibrium (maximum efficiency) is achieved when the amount of resources deployed provide optimum deterrence and avoid excess deployment to the point of diminishing returns. The same principles apply to virtually any aspect of police enforcement strategies. Limited police resources cannot be deployed in one area without reducing services in others. In the case of driver safety and speeding, we need to assign sufficient resources to deter speeding, through awareness of enforcement (people need to think they may get caught and therefore should not speed) and public education, but without focusing so many resources on this area that others are neglected. The policing dilemma is that reduced resources and attention in one area inevitably result in other problems resurfacing. This is the dynamic that creates cycles wherein we revisit the same strategies every few years. If we reduce the number of narcotics officers in order to augment traffic enforcement, the old problems will eventually recur and we will need to reinvest in narcotics. The cycle, as I will argue later, is only disrupted permanently if the root causes of the problems change. Ultimately, it comes down to a discussion about where to assign resources and how to remain aligned with community values.

In my policing career, I have frequently witnessed and participated in the debate over resource deployment. Members of small specialized units invariably, and correctly, argue that they could do a great deal more with just one more team of investigators. They often ask why the police service has a mounted horse patrol or a bicycle patrol when so much more could be done with one more team of detectives to investigate homicides or Internet crime or a host of other emerging priorities. On the other hand, mounted horse patrols, for instance, have substantial value in public relations and education. Police executives have an extremely difficult job balancing the numerous and varied community demands with basic frontline emergency services, all within the confines of finite resources.

The effectiveness of imprisonment as a deterrent to crime can also be looked at as a balance. The threat of prison is only effective up to a point, after which its returns diminish. The "Becker Model" is the concept upon which the modern prison system was largely constructed; it is based on the premise that people weigh the costs against the benefits in their decision to commit crimes. This theory assumes that the possibility of imprisonment will be a deterrent to crime (Donohue 2007). Some people, however, are not deterred by the threat of prison and prison sentences do not always deter individuals from committing crimes once they are released.

In my experience, once a youth has been to the Manitoba Youth Centre the threat of imprisonment is dissipated and he or she is less afraid of getting caught committing crimes in the future. In May 2011, the Government of Manitoba reported that 90 percent of young offenders are re-arrested within two years after release from in-custody sentences. The adult recidivism rate is almost as abysmal, at 71 percent (Owen 2011a). The Youth Criminal Justice Act, enacted in 2003, was designed to protect young offenders from the negative effects of the criminal justice system by allowing warnings instead of charges (Canada, Department of Justice 2012a). For example, a youth with no record can be cautioned instead of being charged with shoplifting, the idea being that a warning will avoid the negative effects resulting from a criminal record. For many youths, however, the deterrent effect wears off after several warnings. Some youth are far beyond feeling threatened by a short sentence in the Manitoba Youth Centre or by probation.

For five years in the 1980s, I worked my way through university as a sheriff's officer, escorting prisoners from communities all over Manitoba, including First Nations reserves, to the Manitoba Youth Centre in Winnipeg. The criminal justice system was (and still is) a very expensive operation, requiring that youth be tried in courts within the community in which their crimes were committed while the only provincial youth holding facility is the Manitoba Youth Centre in Winnipeg. Youth in custody are also entitled, as is any citizen, to be remanded in front of a judge every couple of weeks in the jurisdiction where their alleged offences occurred to argue for their release and receive judgement on whether they must remain in custody. This system resulted in a lot of travel – it often meant a trip up north once or twice a month for a two-minute remand appearance. I made a living escorting young people who had been placed in custody back and forth between the Manitoba Youth Centre and rural courts all over Manitoba. Sometimes I drove but some communities were fly-in only. Those cases required a commercial flight into a larger centre like Thompson or The Pas, and then a drive to a neighbouring community. I got a lot of studying towards my first university degree done on those flights.

During this time many of the youth told me they had committed crimes just to get a free trip into Winnipeg for a stay at the Manitoba Youth Centre. Their remands meant that they would get a trip home to see their families on court day. One sixteen-year-old boy, who had been involved in a gunfight with high-powered rifles with other boys on the First Nations reserve where he lived, told me that his father was an inmate in Stony Mountain, Manitoba's federal prison, and his uncle was in Headingley, the largest provincial jail. He was hoping for federal time (a sentence of two years or more is served in a federal prison), in order to be with his father. What can you say to a child who is forced to live in a system that offers such limited prospects?

During this time I also met many adults who deliberately sought to increase their prison sentences in order to get into federal prison, which has better resources and programs, and better prospects for parole than the provincial prison system. Many experienced recidivist inmates have told me that they will plead guilty to a more substantial offence in order to make their sentence two years plus a day. Others preferred a "deuce less" (two years less a day), which makes it a provincial sentence and keeps them closer to their home community. During plea-bargaining, many experienced criminals manipulate the system to ensure that they end up sentenced to the system they prefer.

Police officers are aware that some youth, and adults for that matter, occasionally commit crimes with the hope of ending up in jail. In Manitoba, where temperatures can drop to minus 40 degrees Celsius in the winter, we get "snowbirds," street people who commit crimes in order to get into jail so that they have food and shelter during the harsh winter months. I recall an incident in which a homeless person threw a brick through the window of a downtown department store, waited for the police to come and pick him up, and then asked to remain in custody.

In the 1980s I worked for several years in Regina House, a halfway house for federal inmates run by the highly respected Native Clan Organization. It was heartbreaking to see the torment that some inmates with long-term or life sentences went through as they got "short," meaning their sentences were almost completed and they would be asked to leave the system and fend for themselves. Many knew, either consciously or subconsciously, that they had become institutionalized and needed the structure of the prison system to survive, recognizing that they did not have the discipline to find and keep the sort of jobs they would be offered. Institutionalization is a well-known phenomenon in the prison system and perhaps one of the worst by-products of the prison model of deterrence (Haney 2001).

Some criminal behaviour is driven by emotion or substance abuse that overrides reason. When I worked in the robbery squad I found that most people committed gas bar robberies out of desperation, with very little regard for the risks. The power of addiction is well recognized. For a while back in the early 1990s, the flavour of the day was "T and Rs" (Talwin and Ritalin). In recent years the trend has been drugstore robberies, not for money but for the narcotic

Oxycontin. These substances can be so addictive that people will risk years in prison for one bottle.

In December 2010, three men were arrested for a string of armed robberies of pharmacies in which they were only after Oxycontin (Giroday 2010). In my role on the Policing with Aboriginal Peoples committee of the Canadian Association of Chiefs of Police (CACP), I learned that in many remote First Nations reserves a single pill of Oxycontin 80 (which contains 80 milligrams of the active ingredient, Oxycodone) now sells on the underground market for as much as $500. Prescription drug abuse is a top priority on the national agenda for Aboriginal police chiefs in 2012.

The street drug trade is an ever-increasing threat as well. "Crack" (cocaine) and "meth" (methamphetamines) can be so addictive that even a single dose can lead to addiction for some people. It is said that people, from all walks of life, often become obsessed with trying to recreate the high that they experienced the first time they used the drug. Knowing this, drug dealers will create demand by simply giving away samples of their street drugs. Then, once a few samples are consumed and the person has become addicted, he or she will start demanding a steadily increasing supply of drugs. Street level dealers are often groomed this way as well, when they suddenly find themselves indebted to a dealer who is one or two steps up the marketing chain. Young girls are often manipulated into being sexually exploited through drugs. Their "boyfriend" provides them with drugs, they become addicted, and then they suddenly have a huge drug debt. They are then forced into the sex trade to repay the debt, becoming part of the cycle of drug use and prostitution. This is how organized human trafficking often begins. The threat of arrest or prison is not a significant deterrent in any of these activities.

The threat of prison does not enter the minds of many people during violent outbursts precipitated by high emotion. Some experts agree that only 15 percent of prison inmates need to be imprisoned for reasons of public safety (Donohue 2007). The other 85 percent are apparently sentenced on a basis other than true public safety concerns: additional reasons can include a sense of justice for the victim, deterrence of other potential offenders, or perceived rehabilitative resources that a presiding judge may believe the prison system can provide for an offender.

Some, like Donohue (2007), have argued that funding is better spent on crime prevention than prison. The Becker model has, however, influenced the American philosophy of corrections which now calls for mandatory sentences for serious crimes and longer periods of incarceration than is generally the case in Canada (Rubenstein 1995). In their book *Three Strikes and You're Out: Vengeance as Public Policy*, Schicor and Sechrest (1996) describe how repeat offenders statutes have contributed to the massive costs associated with incarceration, the courts, and policing in the United States. The American philosophy of lengthy prison terms is described by some as the main difference between the United Sates and Canadian approaches to justice (ibid.).

The American criminal justice system has evolved into a massive industry, particularly since the late 1980s. Sheldon (2001) describes how the justice system has targeted people in lower socio-economic strata, perpetuating existing hierarchies of class, gender, and race. One could argue that the same is occurring in Canada, where Aboriginal peoples are substantial consumers of justice system services and grossly overrepresented in the prison system. Hallet et al. (2006) found that the proportion of Aboriginal people in Manitoba prisons increased dramatically from 10 percent in 1950 to approximately 60 percent in 2000. Some have attributed these increases in part to the rapid urbanization of Canada's Aboriginal peoples (ibid.). Regardless of the reasons, the financial and social costs are unsustainable and should encourage assignment of resources with a focus on improved crime prevention and addressing the root causes of crime in Aboriginal communities in the coming decades.

Not only do increased sentences not appear to deter crime – paradoxically, they may increase the severity of some criminal activity. The high number of American police officers killed in the line of duty may be linked to attempts to avoid capture and the lengthier prison terms in the United States. Whittingham (1984) and Parsons (2004) found that Canada's rate of murdered police officers is lower than that of the United States. Officers are more frequently killed intentionally rather than accidentally in the United States (Boylen and Little 1990). Substantial research has identified policing as a high-risk occupation (Brown and Langan 2001; Castillo and Jenkins 1994; Kraus 1987). Sheriffs, police officers, and their supervisors are among the top five of the twelve highest-risk occupations (Castillo and Jenkins 1994). Federal Bureau of Investigation (FBI) statistics reveal that between 1976 and 1998 an average of seventy-nine police officers were murdered each year in the line of duty in the United States (Brown and Langan 2001).

Some researchers have found that police officer homicide is decreasing, most likely due to improved training and increased use of body armour (Boylen and Little 1990; Hill and Clawson 1988; Kraus 1987; Southwick 1998). Over the past twenty years there has been continuous improvement in the training police officers receive in how to survive physical attacks (Duran 2003; Lesce 1988). Extensive research has led to changes in close-quarter combat and shooting techniques so that the modern day officer has a much better tactical arsenal.

Felons (an American term for convicted persons) who murdered police officers in the United States have been found to be predominantly between eighteen to thirty years of age; an overwhelming majority are male and have prior criminal convictions (Boylen and Little 1990; Brown and Langan 2001). Talk among experienced police officers often involves the observation that criminals are getting younger. In fact, what police officers are observing is that they themselves are aging while the age of the criminal population generally remains the same. It is rare to find a fifty-five-year-old man who is still committing break and enters. This is partly because people are rarely so entrenched in criminal behaviour that they continue committing the same crimes as they age. Most people eventually get tired of returning to prison and outgrow the life of chronic reoffending.

From the perspective of police officers, it is easy to hypothesize why police homicide occurs more frequently in the United States than in Canada. A criminal in the United States who, if caught, can expect a forty-year prison sentence because it is his or her "third strike" is more likely to make desperate attempts to evade capture. The consequences of leading the police on a dangerous high-speed chase or engaging in a shoot-out may be seen as an acceptable risk, even for a relatively minor offence, when facing a lengthy third-strike prison term. In 2005 alone, fifty-five American police officers were murdered in the line of duty (United States Department of Justice 2005a).

The jeopardy of life-ending prison sentences does not exist in Canada and may explain why relatively fewer officers are killed in the line of duty (Whittingham 1984). In Canada, life in prison generally means twenty-five years, because almost all "lifers" (people sentenced for murder) are released on parole after twenty-five years. The death penalty was abolished in Canada in 1976 and in the same year the "faint hope clause" (Section 746.6 of the Criminal Code) was enacted, which permitted Canadian inmates to apply for parole from a life sentence after fifteen years of their sentence had been served. This opportunity was seen by many as undermining the intention of prison sentences, but allowing application for parole after fifteen years is consistent with the practice in Australia, Belgium, Denmark, England, Scotland, Switzerland, and New Zealand (Stein and Antonowicz 2001). Juries, comprised of people from the community, judged these applications for parole and, of the average six cases that are heard each year, about 85 percent of applicants had their sentences reduced (ibid.).

Canada's faint hope clause was the subject of much debate in recent years. Both the CACP and the Canadian Police Association (CPA) lobbied Parliament to repeal the clause, arguing that it undermined justice by watering down punishments and making sentences less meaningful (Department of Justice, Canada 2011) and that victims felt they had not received justice if the person who had committed a crime against them received a prison sentence and was then let out on parole or early release.

In response to public pressure for more truth in sentencing, the Canadian Government finally repealed the faint hope clause and it is no longer available to offenders who committed their crimes after 2 December 2011 (Seymour 2012). This means the maximum prison sentence a person can receive in Canada, for premeditated first-degree murder, is life with the opportunity for parole after twenty-five years.

The 2011 election of a majority Conservative government has brought about changes to Canadian justice. Prime Minister Harper's government promised that, within one hundred days of being elected, they would pass into law a series of crime reforms that included a crack-down on organized crime, house arrest for violent criminals, and longer prison sentences for certain crimes, such as sexual child abuse (Mayeda and Kennedy 2011). Bill C-10, the omnibus crime bill, was passed into law in March 2012 (Ballingall 2012). How these justice reforms will play out will be interesting to see. It is easy to legislate longer prison sentences but, if sufficient resources are not deployed to support them, longer sentences will likely have little effect on crime rates. Longer prison sentences, without sufficient accompanying programs, might even have the paradoxical effect of increasing recidivism, as the effects of institutionalization increase the chances of recidivism, as mentioned earlier (Haney 2001).

In 2011 the federal and provincial governments debated who would pay the costs associated with the new federal omnibus crime bill (Owen 2011b). It is recognized that imprisoning people does not in itself rehabilitate them (Baum 1934; Owen 2011b) and longer prison sentences without corresponding resources to reduce recidivism amounts to warehousing people at ever increasing costs. Ontario Premier Dalton McGuinty argued that the federal government should pay for the costs of building additional provincial prisons and hiring staff required as a result of the new bill and the Quebec premier at the time, Jean Charest, stated his province would not pay for the added prison costs (Kennedy 2011). The provinces of Newfoundland and Labrador, Quebec, Ontario, British Columbia, and New Brunswick have all spoken out against the bill, saying they cannot afford to pay its associated costs (Canadian Centre for Policy Alternatives 2011). The John Howard Society of Manitoba calculates the total (federal and provincial) costs of the new bill to be approximately $2 billion annually, or $1,400 per taxpayer (ibid.). Only time will reveal whether the effectiveness of the new measures are worth the costs of this crime bill.

Many argue that prison is over-used and that placing people, impressionable youth in particular, in prison, all of whom will eventually be released, only creates more accomplished and hardened criminals (Comack et al. 2010). Complacency or unwillingness to adapt to evolving community needs is often a significant weakness of our justice system. High recidivism rates call for better analysis and flexibility. They also require recognizing and letting go of old practices that are no longer effective.

VALUE AND COST OF PREVENTION

Research has demonstrated the long-term benefits of crime prevention measures in offsetting the long-term costs of the justice system (Aos et al. 2001). At the same time, the decreasing usefulness of imprisonment as a deterrent to crime has not been fully understood. Research shows that, despite a reduction in reported overall crime in Canada over the past thirty years, investments in the justice system have consistently increased in Canada (Statistics Canada 2010) and prison costs in the United States have exploded (Warren 2008).

One percent of all American citizens are currently imprisoned and the overall cost of the prison system in that country has risen an astounding 315 percent over the past twenty years (Warren 2008). Canada has over 25,000 people incarcerated in the federal penitentiary system and the same number of provincial inmates at any given time (Correctional Service of Canada 2008) – about one percent of the Canadian population. Prison sentences, however, are dramatically shorter across the spectrum of offences in Canada, whereas in the United States many states routinely hand down prison sentences of fifty years or more.

For prison to be truly effective, inmates' behaviour problems need to be corrected before they are released and this is often an expensive proposition (Baum 1934; Owen 2011a). This is a major argument against the sort of privatization that is increasingly taking place in the United States, as warehousing people in prisons should be only the beginning of the system: the programs that occur behind the prison walls to correct behavioural problems and reduce recidivism are the important and expensive component of the system. The previous discussion of the new Omnibus Crime Bill further highlights the importance of investing in programs to accompany longer sentences and help reduce recidivism (Mayeda and Kennedy 2011; Kennedy 2011; Haney 2001; Owen 2011b). Sentencing people to longer prison sentences without effectively addressing the root causes of the problems that put them in prison ensures that the cost of the system will soar upward.

"Dead time" is another topic that has caused much consternation in the police community and among the public at large. Dead time is the time spent in custody, pending trial and/or conviction. People are remanded in custody when they do not meet the conditions of the Bail Reform Act, which determines if an arrested person is detained in jail or released pending court. People have a right to be released except in certain circumstances, such as serious charges, being a flight risk, having no home address, having a permanent address that is far from the jurisdiction they are arrested in, posing a risk of continuing to commit the offences with which they are charged, or posing a danger to witnesses. When the charges are serious, for instance, or the accused person is a danger to the public or not likely to show up in court, they will be remanded in custody. Time spent in remand is not a sentence, but is considered time served in sentencing. For decades, the Canadian courts considered remand time to be worth double the normal prison sentence (Conway 2011). Two years in remand was therefore worth four years at sentencing. The rationale was that dead time was hard for prisoners because in remand there were almost no programs such as school, vocational training, and life skills development. Dead time also offered very little recreational activity because the remand process was meant to be short-term.

Some people preferred to stay in remand and accumulate dead time rather than enter the prison system for their full sentence. I have seen many cases where people deliberately delayed court processes, firing their lawyers, telling the courts they were unprepared to defend themselves, asking the courts for time extensions, all in efforts to remain in remand longer before their case went to trial. They then pled guilty and were sentenced to "time served" because their sentence was completed when calculated as double time. "Truth in sentencing" had been a hotly debated topic for many years. In 2010 the Canadian laws were amended and the practice of accounting for dead time calculations in sentencing was no longer allowed (Conway 2011).

In spite of massive government downsizing in the 1980s, the Canadian justice system saw a continued expansion of resources (Borins 2002). While crime rates rose slightly during the recession of the 1980s, they dropped consistently during the 1990s (Fellows et al. 1997). In other words, crime decreased while the costs of the justice system increased.

Statistics Canada reported expenditures of $11 billion, or $362 per Canadian, on policing and the courts in 2000–01 (Taylor-Butts 2000). In 2006, expenditures on policing alone increased 4.4 percent over the previous year, costing each Canadian $303 for policing alone (excluding the costs of the courts). Statistics Canada reported an average 3 percent annual increase in policing budgets over the ten years leading up to 2007 (Beattie and Mole 2007).

Some researchers argue that justice agencies and politicians are prone to reporting alarming crime rates in order to maximize their budgets and sustain current financing (ibid.). Crime reporting is a fine balance for police agencies, which need to project needs and set budgets while also showing that they are reducing crime. Increased costs in the justice system may be a good thing, if the money is going to programs that reduce crime and recidivism in the long run. However, program performance must be monitored and evaluated diligently to ensure that programs are achieving the best possible outcomes.

Canada's highly controversial long-gun registry is a case in point. Hundreds of millions of dollars have been spent on regulating gun owners, yet gang violence involving firearms has continued to rise

(Woodcock 2011). There is room to question the value and return on such a massive investment while weapons-related offences are on the increase (Statistics Canada 2011b). The Firearms Act was enacted in 1995, requiring registration of firearms. Initially the cost of the program was estimated at $119 million, with $2 million being recovered through the cost of registration fees. By 2001, the estimated cost of the program was $529 million, due in large part to increased costs in developing the computer system. By 2002, Auditor General Sheila Fraser released a report projecting costs of the system at $1 billion once it was complete, with registration fees covering $140 million. Fraser also expressed concerns that the costs were being kept secret by the government (Global News 2012). By 2011, the government responded to public pressure and introduced bills to cancel the program, despite CACP endorsement of the national firearms registry. On 6 April 2012, Bill C-19 ended the requirement that all non-restricted weapons be registered and mandated that the registration records be destroyed (Canada Gazette 2012). However, the process was delayed as a result of a pending court ruling in Quebec, which would like to keep the part of the registry that pertains to its jurisdiction (Global News 2012). One billion dollars could permit a lot of good work in a variety of areas. Such massive expenditures should, therefore, be given careful thought and ongoing program performance measurement, evaluation, and analysis to ensure the best value is being achieved. Many police officers have mixed feelings on firearms regulation.

The number of police officers per capita in Canada has increased continuously over the past thirty years; a 2.7 percent increase in 2007 brought Canada's police population to over 64,000 officers (Beattie and Mole 2007). The number of total officers increased by 2,000 in 2009 bringing the total in 2010 to 69,299. This 2 percent increase in 2010 represented the sixth consecutive year of increased numbers of police officers (Statistics Canada 2010). These trends of ever-increasing costs for policing are coupled with parallel increases in the private sector security services (Forst 2000).

The Canadian courts alone required more than $1 billion in 2000 to employ 2,000 judges and 10,000 support staff (Taylor-Butts 2000). In the same year, Statistics Canada reported that adult corrections were costing $2.5 billion. In 2000, housing an inmate cost $189 per day in a federal penitentiary and $137 per day in a provincial institution, which usually have fewer programming costs. The legal aid budget increased 6 percent between 1997 and 2001, to $593 million (for 511,000 applications) in 2001. Legal Aid budgets have increased at a proportionally slower rate than other components of the legal system (Statistics Canada 2010).

In 2008–09 there were almost 371,800 adults admitted to Canadian correctional services and admissions to community supervision increased from the previous year, driven by a 3 percent increase in probation and a 4 percent increase in conditional sentences. The number of conditional sentences (no prison) grew for the second consecutive year to 18,400 for adults (Calverley 2010).

The operating costs of Canadian correctional services, including prison, community supervision, administration, and parole totalled almost $3.9 billion in 2008–09, a 7 percent increase from the previous year. Operating costs increased by 6 percent provincially and 7 percent nationally. The cost of housing a federal prison inmate has continually increased over the past decade. In 2008–09 the cost had reached $323 per day (ibid.).

The cycle of recidivism is another major contributor to the costs of running the justice system. In 1934, Baum published *The Canadian Criminal Justice System: Discount Justice*, in which he describes how society ultimately pays a large price for incarcerating prisoners without rehabilitating them. Looking at his work today raises questions about what we have learned since the 1930s. The concept of reducing recidivism plays an important role in determining the effectiveness of the multifaceted justice system. The high incidence of recidivism, among Aboriginal offenders in particular, supports the argument that crime reduction in those communities should be a high priority for Canadian governments (Owen 2011a).

In the United States, the problem of increasing prison costs is more pronounced. In 2008, budget officers' reports from each state revealed that the overall costs of the prison system had risen from $10.6 to $44 billion between 1987 and 2007 (Warren 2008). In the United States there is currently a projected need for three new prisons by 2030, each of which will cost $250 million to build and $45 million per year to run (Aldhous 2007).

In both Canada and the United States, an increase in prison terms has coincided with decreased crime rates in some categories of crime over the past fifteen years (Donohue 2007). Statistics can be misleading: in policing we are astounded at the increase in gang involvement and street violence and general disrespect for laws and law enforcement in Canada over the past twenty years. The impression among many frontline police officers is that more violence is occurring. Statistics Canada (2011b) reports that, based on police-reported crime, between 2008 and 2009 attempted murder charges increased by 10 percent and firearms-related offences increased by 15 percent.

When I started policing in 1989 a shooting in the street was a high profile case that would have generated a public outcry. In 2012, shooting-related incidents occur in Winnipeg with such regularity that they are often not reported by the media and do not raise much public attention. In July 2012 Toronto saw twenty-five shootings and four killings in three days. These acts of violence were particularly disturbing as many occurred in public spaces such as parks, malls, and playgrounds that are normally considered safe (Paperny 2012).

It is possible that many people are becoming desensitized due to continuous media reports of violence. After a triple shooting in August 2011, police officials attributed at least fourteen drive-by shootings and fire bombings between June and August of 2011 to gang-related battles over Winnipeg's drug trade (Germano, McIntyre, and Giroday 2011). One particular triple shooting involved a battle between the Hells Angels and the Rock Machine outlaw motorcycle gangs (ibid.). But violence is occurring on a much more routine basis within and between Aboriginal youth gangs.

Working in uniform patrol, I have seen first hand the increased levels of violence over the past twenty years. From 2005 to 2010 I was assigned to plainclothes detective work in the Crime Division, working in child abuse, in sex crimes as a major sex crime analyst, and then developing the Missing Persons Unit. I was then promoted and returned to frontline uniform patrol in 2010 as a staff sergeant, overseeing frontline policing operations. I was surprised at the dramatic increase in levels of violence and gunplay that had occurred over the five-year period of my absence. Much of the violence appears to occur within and between street gangs, which is consistent with research that has attributed much street level violence to fighting over drug trade turfs (Blackwell 2010; Bolan 2009). How to intervene in these cycles of violence is complex and challenging, but the need to do so is critical.

Research on the economic benefits of crime prevention is still surprisingly limited. Aldhous (2007) found that several programs dealing with youth crime deterrence and drug addiction treatments could potentially save the American government $1.4 billion by 2030. DeRiviere (2005) conducted research on sex-trade workers in and around Winnipeg, examining the financial impacts of life in the sex-trade on the justice, medical, and social welfare systems. She found strong evidence that money spent on prevention is a far better investment than traditional reactive strategies that do little to address the root problems associated with high-risk or criminal activity.

Even where the value of preventative strategies is understood, such strategies are difficult to put into place. The challenge we face in policing is finding ways to take resources that are fully engaged – and often overwhelmed in simply reacting to crime – and redeploy them into preventative strategies that can take years to yield measurable results. How can you send officers to participate in public education and crime prevention programs when there is a backlog of new calls for service awaiting dispatch?

As the WPS Missing Persons Unit Coordinator for several years I attempted to implement more preventive strategies to protect high-risk youth. The police executive supported increasing the unit from two temporary investigators to five full-time detectives with three civilian support staff. Working with social workers, we identified high-risk youth who had been using thousands of police officer hours and hundreds of child welfare contacts each year. These children were being victimized and sexually exploited, were highly self-destructive, and in several tragic cases were murdered (Amnesty International 2004; Dedel 2006; Hedges 2002; Highway of Tears 2012; Joyce 2003; Lanning 2001; Skelton 2005; Winnipeg Police Service 2008).

Analysis of those cases where young girls were exploited and murdered revealed gaps within and between child welfare and police agencies that had overlapping mandates (Guy 2008). My argument, when meeting with the numerous agencies with responsibility for the safety of these troubled youth, was that everyone in these various agencies was doing their job, yet children were still being victimized. The police were fulfilling their mandates and so were child welfare and protection agencies. Consequently, our approaches and responsibilities needed adjustment. Mandates needed to be blended so that agencies worked together rather than in isolation. We needed to become victim-centred and focus on the needs of at-risk children rather than following practices that were proving inadequate and ineffective.

Historically, with a runaway child, the police would put the child in custody and the child's assigned social worker would direct that the child be taken back to their placement. The child would be delivered back to the foster or group home and, in many cases, would run out the back door and into harm's way again. We – the police – started questioning this and in some cases resisted the direction of social workers by going over their heads to their executives in the child welfare system in order to protect vulnerable children. When we dealt with children who were chronically running away, abusing substances, engaging in prostitution, and displaying other high-risk behaviour, we began to lobby for new placements and different resources. If a facility was unable to hold high-risk youth and was then constantly calling the police to look for run-aways, we started refusing to take such youth back to the same ineffective facilities. We did not ignore the workers' problems but, rather than following previous procedures, contacted senior bureaucrats and executives with whom we were partnered in the leadership of the child welfare system. These people were able to authorize resources for such things as hiring social workers to work with a specific child, making room in existing facilities with better resources, or, in some cases, moving a child to another province to remove them from the people who were hurting or exploiting them.

Resources in the Missing Persons Unit were initially increased to decrease the burden on frontline uniform operations of responding to chronic runaways. However, we quickly realized that there was a population of chronic high-risk youth who needed multidisciplinary, intensive, preventative approaches. The police and child welfare agencies were operating in isolation from each other and as a result children were being victimized. We focused on working together in multidisciplinary teams to fix system gaps that previously had been unaddressed. In doing so we charted a new path by collaborating and working with social workers and performing roles that previous generations of police had rarely taken. For example, officers met with social workers in multisystem conferences, contributing to safety plans. This gave police a voice in the child welfare system and an effective way to participate in these multidisciplinary teams.

Officers began to establish relationships with the vulnerable youth and to earn their trust so that they would be willing to provide the necessary intelligence for successful prosecution of the people who were exploiting them. Much of this model was learned by looking at the proactive approach that had been developed in the Dallas (Texas) Police Department Child Exploitation Unit (Dallas Police 2011). For instance, they tracked missing persons reports and connected with chronic runaways, knowing that predators and pimps often target such individuals. When I travelled to Dallas to learn from their experience, I was struck by how advanced Canada is in the area of child welfare. In Texas, child welfare agencies would not intervene with teenage girls who were being exploited in the sex-trade. The police, therefore, had to take the lead in creating changes in the system.

In Winnipeg, we have had success in partnering police and child welfare workers and have received positive feedback from social workers, family members, and the youth themselves, who were impressed by this new police interest. The youth were motivated to cooperate more with the system that was trying to protect them – some of these troubled teens even said they did not want to let their assigned detectives down. Among the proudest moments in my policing career were those when social workers took me aside and told me that taking this approach had saved lives. This is the core value in policing, protecting the vulnerable.

We knew instinctively that this was the right approach to take with high-risk youth, although it increased the workload for the police service and required realignment of resources. For instance, because officers in the Missing Persons Unit were focussing their attention on the high-risk victims, there was less time for work on complex long-term missing persons and interprovincial and international abduction cases. This created some stress for investigators who were deeply committed to all of these causes and felt pulled in several directions at once. We were committed to protecting vulnerable young people from victimization, sexual exploitation, and self-harm, but also knew that we were the only team dedicated to providing closure for the families of long-term missing persons. We spent much time and energy in discussion of these issues, trying to figure out how we could get more than twenty-four hours into a day. I believe that the average citizen does not realize the burden that many police officers carry, striving to do justice to the issues they are tackling. In the first six months or so of the development phase of the high-risk victim strategy we fielded calls twenty-four hours a day, seven days a week, from victims, family members, police officers, media, and partner agencies, driven by the principle that saving just one life would justify the whole program.

Other Canadian police agencies are experiencing the same troubles with overlapping issues around high-risk youth, child exploitation, missing persons, and human trafficking, and many are emulating what we created in Winnipeg. After presentations to the Ontario Provincial Police (OPP) Commanders Conference, the Canadian Police College Gang Prevention and Diversion course, Saskatoon Police Service, and Thompson RCMP, numerous police commanders from across Canada committed themselves to moving in this direction, creating a nation-wide movement towards more multidisciplinary, collaborative policing approaches to working with high-risk youth. Numerous programs to intervene are underway in many agencies – I have highlighted Winnipeg's high risk youth strategy as an example of how innovation can spread across agencies.

The Winnipeg Auto Theft Suppression Strategy, which started in 2005, is a similar program that identifies high-risk auto-thieves and monitors them intensely (Paul 2011). Between 2004 and 2009 this program was credited with reducing Winnipeg's auto thefts by 70 percent (Winnipeg Police Service 2011), largely through collaborative multi-agency efforts. In 2010 the International Association of Chiefs of Police awarded the WPS with the Motorola Webber Seavey Award for Quality in Law Enforcement for this initiative.

In response to the violent crime wave described earlier, the Toronto Police Service is adapting a successful multi-agency model for high-risk youth intervention like the one that has been active in the Prince Albert Police Service since 2007. Prince Albert adopted their program from a program started in Scotland, basically identifying high-risk youth and bringing together whatever community resources are required to stabilize and support them (Paperney 2012).

Another interesting multidisciplinary team with which I was involved was Winnipeg's Arson Strike Force, a joint task force consisting of police, firefighters, and fire commissioner's investigators established in 2000 to address a rash of arsons that were occurring in Winnipeg. A dozen of us were instructed to meet in an empty office in the basement of Fire Paramedic Station Number One in downtown Winnipeg. Our new commander, Inspector Keith McCaskill (later Winnipeg's chief of police) told us we were the Arson Strike Force and we went to work. We set up the office, gathered computers, phones, and stationery, and then set about trying to determine who was setting fires in businesses, vacant homes, dumpsters, and landmark buildings across Winnipeg.

We knew that the arsonists would probably attend the fires they set because part of the thrill is in seeing emergency equipment respond. For about four months I took a cruiser car home and slept with a police radio, a fire department radio, a cell phone, and a pager. They would go off at all hours of the day and night and I would be on my way to the newest fire scene. We worked around the clock, arrested dozens of people, and laid hundreds of charges in those months (Nicol 2000).

Many police officers work like this because they appreciate that they are entrusted with unique responsibilities and opportunities to serve the community. Specialty units such as homicide, vice, child abuse, and sex crimes require a commitment from officers that they are willing to be on call and come to work on a moment's notice, never knowing when their workday will run into long hours of over-time and often missing family gatherings and special events. Despite their efforts to fit more hours into the day, the police often cannot meet all of the rising expectations of the public. Some of these gaps are being filled, in part, by the private sector.

CAPACITY AND PRIVATIZATION

Increased demands have exceeded the supply of some services pro-vided by government and by traditional policing and have precipi-tated massive growth in the private sector. The escalation of demand is a result, at least in part, of sudden catastrophic events, such as the terrorist attacks of 9/11, and of increasingly complex social prob-lems such as substance abuse, including the age-old scourge of liquor, illicit drug trades that seem to be increasing, and a relatively new and growing problem with prescription drug abuse. Major events like 9/11 heighten public awareness about security issues and increase people's expectations for public services like the police.

In many cases, citizens in North America favour the privatization of some services as it offers the promise of more direct control than is possible with government agencies. Public sector services are accountable to the greater public good and often cannot cater to the specific wishes of individuals. Gated residential communities or pri-vate firms often want enhanced security measures or special services beyond what the local constabulary are capable of or are willing to provide. Forst (2000) provides an overview of police privatization over the past thirty years, showing that some functions that were entirely in the mandate of professional police agencies until the 1960s are now supplemented by private industry, with over $300 billion spent annually on privately contracted security in the United States.

In 2001, Sheldon estimated that 57,000 private security firms in the United States employed the equivalent of two security guards for every police and correctional officer (Sheldon 2001). In 2008, Statistics Canada reported that the number of people employed in private security firms in Canada rose from 80,000 in 1991 to over 100,000 in 2006 (Li 2008). Statistics Canada reported that policing is now carried out by mutually supportive networks of private security and public police (ibid.). While some mandates overlap, police officers generally must have much higher educational degrees and receive much more job-related training and higher pay than private security personnel. Police careers in Canada generally start with a minimum of six months of recruit class followed by a period of mentoring and come with an average salary of $53,795, which is $20,000 more than private investigators earn and more than double the average income of security guards (Swol 1997).

Many private investigators and security positions have historically been filled by retired police officers, meaning that the industry has been able to obtain workers who are already trained and skilled. However, the private security industry is undergoing the same demographic shifts as the police: a workforce that is becoming younger due to mass retirements, increasing the need for training for the growing numbers of young people entering the workforce. Over the past twenty years my experience suggests that there are increasing numbers of security academies and programs, which tend to be training grounds for prospective police officers. Research is needed to confirm what effects this has on police forces.

When private industry provides public goods, such as public safety, there is a risk that a democratic deficit will be created or increased. Governments are elected on the understanding that they will represent the values and interests of the public that voted for them. If responsibility for sensitive public services such as policing is contracted out to the lowest bidder, how can government be held accountable for protecting the public interest? When government responsibilities for justice, corrections, and social welfare are contracted out, we must guard against developing a justice system that protects only those who can pay for the services.

Fair and equitable treatment for all citizens is a Canadian value that underpins the vision of most public organizations. That impartiality is questionable when the person being investigated also signs the investigators' pay cheques. Remaining impartial is even more difficult for private investigators who are not sworn to protect the public interests but instead are paid to protect their employer's interests. Healthy debates also exist over the question of whether private agencies are more or less efficient than government agencies.

Research has shown that, over the past century, private industry has steadily increased its role in providing public services that were historically provided by government alone (Rosen, Dahlby, and Smith 2003). This is a major shift in public attitudes that historically held that certain public services should not be contracted out to private firms. Privatization raises questions about accountability and mandates. At the 2007 national conference of the Institute of Public Administration Canada (IPAC), federal Minister Vic Toews said that it is increasingly difficult to retain accountability over the $30 billion that is spent by the federal government on services that are contracted to the private sector each year (Toews 2007).

Public sector agencies deal with the nasty tasks in society, such as the most challenging social problems, which private industry has historically been reluctant to take on. Senge (2006) describes a study that found one third of all Fortune 500 corporations that existed in 1970 had vanished by 1983. It seems likely that most of these highly successful corporations got out while they could, when the profit margins were high. This is perhaps the key difference between private and public corporations: public agencies, like police services, cannot quit when things get rough. They have to ride out the ebbs and flows of public opinion and controversy and carry on providing services regardless of whether they are meeting, exceeding, or failing to meet continually changing public demands.

Private corporations are guided by corporate boards that have a duty to seek profit. It is technically illegal for a private corporation to run at a financial loss, even if it is providing a good service to the public (Bakan 2004). Public agencies, on the other hand, have a duty to provide the best service possible with finite resources, and they cannot quit. Maintaining public trust is therefore a crucial priority for public services such as the police (Flexon, Lurigio and Greenleaf 2009; Goldsmith 2005; Hohl, Bradford and Stanko 2010; Jackson and Bradford 2010; Peel 1829; Tyler 2005; Westmarland 2010).

Quickly evolving technology also raises challenges and questions about private contracting. Private firms can often perform functions, such as computer analysis or laboratory examination of criminal evidence, at a lower cost than the police can. It is also a challenge to keep officers trained and abreast of evolving technology. In the joint R C M P / W P S / Brandon Police Service Integrated Child Exploitation Unit, we had technicians who were sworn police officers who continually trained in order to keep up with evolving technology. Training involves travel and expense, as well as sizeable time commitments that take officers away from the roles they are fulfilling.

However, contracted services bring a completely new set of challenges. A technician in a private firm is generally not trained in gathering evidence, proving the chain of continuity, and testifying effectively in court. Bringing evidence into court does not just entail a person's describing what they did. They must also prove that the evidence was secured and was not tampered with by anyone. So, a facility needs to be secure and anyone having access to the area where the evidence was stored may be a compellable witness, required to testify that they did not alter it. Proving continuity can be a very tricky business if several people performed different analyses on an item. Police processes are designed around these needs but a private firm may require an extensive and cost-prohibitive process and facility changes in order to be prepared for the trial process.

Competence in court testimony can only be developed to a limited extent in the classroom. We have found that officers need real experience and exposure in order to improve these competencies, although I have seen D N A (deoxyribonucleic acid) experts doing an extremely professional and polished job when testifying.

Use of contracted services also leads to questions around the security of sensitive investigations and the protection of confidential information. The Criminal Code prohibits people, other than sworn police officers in the execution of their duties, from possession of illegal items such as prohibited weapons, illegal drugs, and child pornography. You cannot hire a computer expert to investigate child pornography without addressing these legal requirements. If we allow civilian contractors to handle child pornography without making them peace officers or changing the law, we are parties to a criminal possession offence. It is not simply a matter of swearing in a person and calling them a police officer. Being a sworn police officer brings with it a host of duties and responsibilities that require training, the most obvious being the duty to act. Citizens are not required to intervene in a crime when they see it in progress. Peace officers, on the other hand, have a duty to act in such a circumstance.

Technological changes create great challenges for modern policing. Civilians are appropriate for some functions but not suited for
others. For instance, a highly educated specialist can be hired for less
than the cost of a sworn police officer, perform many functions better, and can continue to develop expertise and skills over a long
period of time. The RCMP is advanced in their utilization of civilian
support staff; they often hire highly educated people as analysts.
Those civilian analysts stay in positions for long periods or throughout an entire career, developing a high level of expertise that is
a great support to investigators, whereas sworn police officers are
periodically reassigned.

Officers are subject to regular transfers in most areas in order for
them to retain generalist-policing skills, share the knowledge they
obtain in special assignments, and allow opportunities for other officers to learn new skills. Young officers in uniform patrol gain a great
deal from working around experienced officers who have transferred
back from specialty units. For example, an officer returning to uniform operations after an assignment in the drug unit can teach young
officers how to work with confidential informants and do drug
search warrants; an experienced officer can mentor less experienced
officers through major investigations. When officers with experience
are not around, opportunities for knowledge transfer and mentorship can be lost.

In high-demand environments, police officers have no problem
with private security firms protecting property or investigating issues
the police do not have the resources for, as long as they do not inter-
fere with police mandates. For instance, having private security firms
responding to alarms and doing lock-fast property checks is wel-
comed by the police.

People who are responsible for a property, such as a security guard
who has been hired to protect a building or prevent theft in stores,
have a right to eject people from the property or apprehend them,
using reasonable force. They can detain persons who have committed a crime, turning them over to a police officer as soon as possible.
Problems can arise when they detain a person for long periods of
time before turning them over to the police as it can become a question of whether the person's constitutional rights have been breached.

Tiered policing is another trend that has evolved in response to
ever-increasing demands. Many agencies have specialty officers who
have limited powers and specific mandates that are much narrower

than those of a full-fledged constable. For instance many large police forces have a parking authority that takes care of traffic-related issues. In 2011 the WPS created a cadet corps that quickly became a great resource in support of uniform operations. Members of this corps receive lower wages and free police officers from many time-consuming activities. WPS management and the Winnipeg Police Association (WPA) negotiated the types of calls for which cadets could be used and how they would be supervised. They escort and guard prisoners, conduct traffic duty, guard crime scenes, and provide a range of other activities.

Some police services that work primarily within Aboriginal communities have instituted "peacekeepers" to provide support to regular constables. The Manitoulin Anishinabek police in Ontario, for example, has peacekeepers for a wide range of services, including prisoner escort and guard duties. The innovation is in their connection with the community and with traditional Aboriginal culture. United Chiefs and Council Manitoulin Anishnaabe Police Chief Rodney Nahwegahbow described the program in a presentation to the First Nations Chiefs of Police Conference in Winnipeg, in May 2012, noting that the peacekeepers are heavily involved in almost all cultural events and foster a great connection between the police and the community.

The effective solution to all of today's pressing challenges is in finding a balance that meets the current needs while retaining the flexibility required to change with evolving demands. The key to optimum effectiveness lies not in reacting over-quickly to changes but in predicting future trends, planning for them, and acting strategically. It calls for attention to succession planning, in particular in an environment marked by changing demographics. Police services are now largely comprised of officers approaching retirement and larger numbers of younger and less experienced officers.

Highly specialized areas aside, new police recruits now have their hands full learning the basics, which are far more involved and demanding than they were twenty years ago. The next chapter examines how some demands on policing have changed over the past twenty years, starting with the new recruits.

3

Changing Demands in Policing

TRAINING AND CONTEXT

Thirty years ago a new constable starting with the WPS was expected to learn on the job. Recruit classes came later for advanced lessons and training in order to receive a firearm. Members who started their service during that era often laugh when they reminisce about how they carried a banana or some other snack in their holsters for the first few months until they had the firearms training that allowed them to receive their service weapon. Police officers today are fully equipped and trained in recruit classes and are able to hit the street running.

Two decades ago, in Winnipeg, the patrol sergeant on each platoon was considered the training officer and he (there were very few women on the job back then) worked with new recruits. Field trainers and patrol sergeants generally had at least ten to fifteen years or more of experience. Now, officers with two years on the job are considered seasoned and are often assigned as field trainers, mentoring new members.

Two decades ago, officers with less than two years combined experience would rarely be assigned together to a patrol car. Now, members with only a few years of street experience are routinely asked to act in a higher rank as street supervisors, managing platoons of up to twenty-five members, overseeing high-risk incidents, and handling sensitive administrative issues. Officers with less experience are required to do more demanding work in environments that are increasingly challenging.

Police work has also become more intellectually demanding. The Canadian Charter of Rights and Freedoms was enacted in 1982 and changed Canadian policing significantly. Police officers must now have a highly developed understanding of the Charter, of constitutional rights, and of a wide range of case law that affects the constraints placed on police officers in the execution of their duties.

Before the Charter was enacted, police officers arrested and processed people with little concern for their right to legal counsel, to be free of arbitrary search and seizure, and not be arbitrarily detained. At court, it would be enough justification for an arrest for an arresting officer to state, "My sergeant instructed me to arrest them." This all changed with the Charter, which now protects people against laws that infringe on fundamental rights to counsel, the right to not self-incriminate, and the right to be free of arbitrary detention, random searches, and breaches of privacy. Scrutiny of police by the courts jumped to an entirely different level after the Charter was enacted. Just as advancing technology (especially complex computer-based reporting software developed in the mid 1990s) motivated the retirement of some police officers, the Charter may have played a significant part in prompting others to retire.

Case law affecting issues such as evidence handling, disclosure for court, and search and seizure demands a higher level of knowledge than was required by police officers twenty years ago (Malm et al. 2005). The standards and requirements of the justice community have substantially expanded. Richard Wolson QC, a respected Winnipeg defence lawyer with over thirty years of experience in criminal law, remarked at a Canadian Homicide Investigators Conference in Winnipeg in 2006, that police officers used to have automatic credibility in court simply by virtue of being police officers. This is no longer the case.

Today, police officers must establish their credibility in every single court case. They must articulate the reasons for every action they have taken, demonstrating detailed knowledge of the laws, pertinent court decisions and constitutional rights, policies, and best practices. They must substantiate their actions with meticulous notes backed by audio and/or videotaped evidence if possible and through investigations using a wide range of support services that previous generations of officers never had at their disposal; officers today must prove what they say with evidence. In many cases, as far as the court is concerned, if it is not written in your police notebook, it did not happen.

In police reports and in court, officers must now articulate the use of force policies and how their actions and any weapons used were appropriate to the level of resistance, force, or aggression offered by offenders. As the number of tools on police officers' utility belts has increased, justifying force has become much more complicated. Prior to the 1980s, police used "billy clubs," which were short clubs. Another favourite in that earlier era was a small, eight-inch long, leather pouch with lead weights in the end and a spring in the handle. Hitting a person in the head with either of these could be considered to be using lethal force. In 1989 we were issued a firearm and a club – the "Tonfa" – a weapon that evolved in Asia and has a handle that sticks out to the side so it can be swung with force. The Tonfa was an awkward weapon to carry but effective if you trained with it. It also looked intimidating as when police officers went to a call they would take the Tonfa out of the car door and drop it like a sword into a loop on their service belt. (I used to joke that the main reason I carried the Tonfa was to use it to push that awkward and hard to reach button at the prisoner carport entrance of the Provincial Remand Centre.) In recent years, the Tonfa has been replaced by the expanding tactical baton – a collapsible metal baton that can be easily carried on a service belt. Armament Systems and Procedures, Inc. is a large producer of tactical batons, which are therefore often referred to as ASP batons. They are small enough that detectives can carry one, unlike the Tonfa, which was large and bulky.

Over the past twenty years other tools have been added, which can complicate the choices made during highly stressful and even life-threatening events. We now have pepper spray or oleoresin capsicum (aka OC), a finely ground, concentrated cayenne pepper carried in a solution that is sprayed from a can. More recently the electronic control device (ECD) was added. These devices are often referred to as Tasers; Taser is the brand name of one ECD commonly used across North America.

The force continuum is highly complex, compared to the knowledge we worked with twenty years ago. While it is a common perception that added tools in the service belt have complicated the decision-making process in use of force, the research and literature does not support this commonly held belief. Research suggests that these complicated scenarios can be mastered with training and experience (Klein 1998). The fact remains, however, that the complexity and accountability have increased substantially over previous decades.

In the first years of my policing career when police reports commonly read, "A brief scuffle ensued and the accused was placed under arrest." Now we must articulate in detail the level of resistance offered and the resulting force that was utilized, starting with presence, verbal commands, soft and then hard empty-hand control, pressure-point control tactics, intermediate control devices, right up to the threat of lethal force. Such matters are all subject to disclosure to defence lawyers, who may show up in court with policy manuals and regulations, prepared to cross-examine officers about whether their actions complied with policy.

In court, police officers are now often subjected to intense cross-examination about their justification for using force. They may be asked why they used pepper spray instead of hard or soft empty-hand pressure-point control techniques, or why they resorted to lethal force options instead of attempting control of a subject with an ECD or ASP baton. Officers must be prepared to answer questions about why they resorted to the use of weapons and why they chose one over the other in a split second when their life and safety, or the life and safety of others, may have been at stake.

The requirement of accurate notes and corroborating evidence is partly justified by increasing delays before cases go to court. Historically, it was rare for cases to take months or even years to get to court. Now, many cases are much more complex and the court system is so chronically backlogged that cases rarely reach court within a few months. A common experience now is for cases, especially those with serious charges, to reach trial four or more years after the original charge was laid. Officers need good notes to remember what happened during an incident that occurred that long ago.

The requirements for police officers to testify in court have also changed. For instance, twenty years ago it was rare for shift supervisors to be called to testify in a case. Usually, it was the officers who were directly involved and very few other witnesses. In recent years, however, shift supervisors are often called as witnesses when charges are serious. I have been called as a witness in a number of cases where people were arrested for serious offences while I was the sergeant in charge of the station. These cases often involved my testifying that I was in the police station, that I signed a prisoner in and out, and that I recall nothing else about the event. More often now, unlike the past, defence lawyers will not agree to release such witnesses: they want to see them in court, just in case there is something they can use for their client's defence.

When court trials take place years after initial charges are laid, it is not beneficial for the victims, the accused, or the community. The victim experiences re-victimization on the witness stand and may feel no sense of justice being served when participating in a trial for an offence that occurred many years before. The accused learns little from being punished years after committing a crime. The deterrent effect of justice is also watered down by such long delays. When people see that a person is being sentenced for something they were charged with years earlier, the deterrent effect loses its immediacy; people may not even associate the sentence with the idea of deterrence because the event is so far removed in time. There is also the issue of the presumption of innocence and the effect on people of having charges hanging over their heads for years.

Although the right to a speedy trial is guaranteed by law, charges are often not dropped after years of delays because it is the accused who is causing the postponements; accused individuals often deliberately stall court processes in order to avoid facing the courts and answering to the charges. Sometimes this is done in order to deliberately accumulate dead time, as described earlier.

Slow court processes do not ensure justice. In fact, recent discoveries of wrongful convictions have shown the justice system to be a blunt instrument that sometimes convicts the wrong person. It also allows many guilty people to go unpunished. The Government of Canada, Office for Ministerial Review of Miscarriages of Justice, has found several potentially wrongful convictions in the last few years across Canada (Canada, Department of Justice, Canada 2006, 2011a). Many cases sent back to provincial justice ministers for review are investigations that were flawed by systemic problems such as insufficient disclosure at trial and investigations flawed by tunnel vision on the part of the investigators (Janis 1971).

In 2005 the "Report on the Prevention of Miscarriages of Justice" by the Federal, Provincial, and Territorial Prosecutions Committee Working Group urged changes across Canada to combat issues in the justice system that have lead to wrongful convictions. Some of the main causes of wrongful convictions include police tunnel vision, mistaken eye witness identifications, unreliable jailhouse informants, and misleading evidence by experts in forensic sciences. The report recommended that a full review take place in five years

(Bellemare and Finlayson 2004). The follow-up report is titled "The Path to Justice: Preventing Wrongful Convictions Report of the Federal/Provincial/Territorial Heads of Prosecutions Subcommittee on the Prevention of Wrongful Convictions (Federal/Provincial/Territorial Heads of Prosecutions Subcommittee 2011). These committees are comprised of senior police officers and prosecutors from across Canada and both groups emphasize that vigilance is required throughout the justice system to avoid pitfalls such as tunnel vision.

The ministerial justice group was formed as a result of the case of Thomas Sophonow, who was convicted in Winnipeg for a murder that he did not commit. After sixteen-year-old Barbara Stoppel was viciously murdered in December 1981 in the donut shop where she worked in the quiet, predominantly French neighbourhood of St Boniface, the public outcry for justice and closure was loud. The resulting investigation was a textbook case of tunnel vision.

Sophonow was charged and then endured a series of trials and appeals that were unprecedented at the time. The first trial jury was unable to reach a unanimous verdict. At the second trial, Sophonow was convicted and Manitoba's Appeal Court overturned the conviction, ordering a third trial. As a sheriff's officer I was sworn to guard Sophonow's third jury. I was sequestered with them twenty-four hours per day for three weeks in one of the longest jury deliberations in Canadian history, sitting outside the jury room as they debated Sophonow's fate. Sophonow was acquitted but continued to seek exoneration, insisting he was innocent. In 1998, the WPS reinvestigated Barbara Stoppel's murder and found flaws in its own investigative processes as well as identifying another suspect in the murder (Manitoba Government 2012a).

In June of 2000, then Police Chief Jack Ewatski announced that Thomas Sophonow was innocent of the murder of Barbara Stoppel. On that same day, the Manitoba Attorney General publicly apologized to Sophonow for his having to spend forty-five months in jail and endure three jury trials for an offence he did not commit. A subsequent public inquiry found that the police conducting the initial murder investigation had been influenced by tunnel vision that had caused them to focus on Sophonow to the exclusion of other evidence. Many lessons were learned and policies amended, which make the process and management of major investigations very different now than they were twenty years ago (Buiza and Thompson 2003). For instance, investigators now often focus on eliminating suspects rather than focusing on one suspect and then discounting any evidence that does not support that person's guilt. Psychological phenomena such as tunnel vision and groupthink are now better understood and practices have been incorporated to avoid these pitfalls.

DNA is the scientific advance that has cleared and continues to clear many wrongfully convicted people. Fortunately evidence from murder cases is kept indefinitely, because physical evidence that was relied on heavily in previous court trials may be reinterpreted later through new technological lenses. Guy Paul Morin was convicted twice for the 1984 murder of Christine Jessop in Ontario and later exonerated through DNA evidence in 1995 (Tyler 2005). Kyle Unger is the victim of another famous case of wrongful conviction; he was acquitted in 2009, after fourteen years in prison, for his wrongful 1990 conviction for the murder of Bridgette Grenier in rural Manitoba. DNA, again, was the main evidence that eventually cleared him (Winnipeg Free Press 2011).

In a precedent-setting case, Canada's Supreme Court ruled in 2007 that the police could be sued for their role in wrongful convictions (Skurka 2007). Thomas Sophonow's settlement was $2.3 million (Canadian Press 2003); this ensures that there is a motivation beyond seeking justice in seeing that investigations and trials are managed properly. But a question remains as to how many wrongful convictions there are. Graham Zellick, chairman of Great Britain's Criminal Cases Review Commission, told an international gathering in 1995 that Canada's process of identifying and correcting wrongful convictions was insufficient. (The United Kingdom was then receiving about 1,000 applications annually, whereas Canada was considering only thirty-five.) In Canada, allegations of miscarriages of justice go to the federal justice department and, if errors are detected in the original investigations or trials, are then assigned to provincial justice ministers to decide whether any action should be taken. This differs from the British system in which a commission decides which cases should be re-examined (Tibbetts 2005).

Higher standards of accountability, more stringent procedures, and increased police education have been implemented since the previously mentioned federal, provincial, and territorial prosecutors' reports and help decrease the potential for future injustices (Criminal Law Quarterly 2007). Much has been researched and written in recent decades on the phenomenon of wrongful convictions and the literature is useful in helping practitioners avoid investigative pitfalls (Cotler 2010; Denov and Campbell 2005; Kassin 2010; Manishen 2006; Staples 2003; Thorne 2005; Tyler 2005).

As technology advances and accountability continues to increase, so too must training and education for police officers. Designing and conducting training results in logistical challenges. For example, the WPS currently requires that every sworn officer have a full day of firearms training and qualification each year. First aid and police vehicle operations training are each full-day courses and are required every three years for all officers. Use-of-force training must also be completed every two years. The logistics of coordinating this training for 1,400 police officers working shifts around the clock as well as those assigned to various detective shifts and task forces with special work-hours is complex. It also exposes police agencies to possible legal problems because it may be questioned whether incidents of lethal force or severe injury were caused by officers in the lawful and proper execution of their duties if officers have not completed their regular training in the use of weapons, tactics, and case law.

Officers can have difficulty completing mandatory training, especially if they are active investigators and are often required to be in court. Court is often a challenge for officers. After working nightshift, it can be extremely taxing to sit on those hard wooden benches in the courthouse hallways all day long waiting to be called to testify. I recall one time I was called on an urgent basis to a trial for which I had not been subpoenaed; it was a murder trial and I was working surveillance. I was working in "grubs," a police term for undercover dress. I was called to attend court immediately. I explained that I didn't have a suit and the crown attorney said it was not a problem as it was urgent in order to counteract some argument a defence lawyer was making. So, half an hour later I ended up testifying in front of a jury in the court of Queen's Bench unshaven and in jeans.

The opposite case of being prepared and then not called to testify is far more common, even routine. This is a point of contention between prosecutors and police officers. Police officers take hours or days to prepare to testify, then cases are often cancelled due to delays or plea-bargaining. Prosecutors want officers to prepare in the event they are needed, but officers often have difficulty getting motivated to do the work to prepare when they know that they are likely to be dismissed without testifying. Imagine preparing for a two-, six-, or ten-hour long presentation and then not being called to provide it because a plea-bargain has been struck (as happens in most cases).

The flipside is when an officer takes a risk and does not prepare and then a case goes ahead. That is why the most professional officers do the painstakingly tedious work of preparing for each and every case.

In addition to regular annual standard training, there is a fairly regular occurrence of unique issues that require extra training for the entire police service. For example, when we started using Taser ECDs, a full day of training was required for every officer. Other examples include mental health training, wellness training, and training in use of new computer systems as they come online. After the Aboriginal Justice Inquiry, the entire WPS attended several days of cultural diversity sensitivity training (Hamilton and Sinclair 1991).

Officer training in police sciences and techniques is continuous, as is ongoing education in case law, legal rights, and policy. Major case management is another aspect of policing that is continually evolving and requires constant attention, learning, and change. Historically, a lead investigator on a major case would also simultaneously act as the analyst, file and disclosure coordinator, logistics officer, and Crown liaison. Experience has taught that asking officers to take on such tasks simultaneously is a recipe for failure. Current best practice policy is to assign a separate officer for each of these critical roles during major investigations (Canadian Police College 2002). This is where theory diverges from reality – police agencies do not have numerous teams of officers available to assign to such tasks for anything short of the highest profile major cases. Standards are improving, however. Officers are increasingly aware of how to avoid pitfalls such as tunnel vision and are getting better at making full use of advancing police sciences.

The police/prosecution relationship also needs constant attention. This arranged marriage often suffers from domestic tension, in particular when high-profile cases fail. In recent years, one of the deepest and most common points of contention has been over issues of disclosure. Prosecutors often complain that the police fail to disclose good evidence early enough. On the other hand, police continually ask prosecutors to do more with less. For instance, in Manitoba we negotiated with prosecution to provide notes only on the highlights of video-taped statements rather than a transcription of the entire narrative. This saves the police a great deal of work but can make the prosecutors' jobs slightly more difficult. Either way, the system fails if both sides are unable to work together effectively and gain convictions in court. Another look across the border to the south offers interesting comparisons.

In 2009, I visited the Dallas Police Child Exploitation Unit to learn how they are combatting the sexual exploitation of children. As luck would have it, at the time of my visit, my Dallas police colleagues were testifying at the trial of a man they had arrested for facilitating prostitution. A sixteen-year-old girl had been groomed and then "put out" (exploited as a prostitute) on the street by a twenty-five-year-old male pimp. I was impressed by the speed of their court process. A jury was selected, opening statements were made, the victim and police witnesses were questioned and cross-examined, legal arguments were completed, and final summations were all done within a day and a half. By the end of the second day the accused had been convicted and sentenced to forty years in prison.

I was also struck by the apparent informality of their court process. The judge chatted with the sixteen-year-old victim/witness before court and talked informally with the defence and district attorneys and the trial began without ceremony. I was barely able to determine when the informal chatting transitioned into the formal trial process.

In Canada, there would have been a preliminary hearing of approximately a week, followed, usually a year or more later, by a Queen's Bench jury trial lasting from one to several weeks. A Canadian Queen's Bench judge would never speak with a witness before court, for fear of being accused of tainting their testimony. The whole process would be significantly longer than what I observed in Texas, as well as more expensive, and the sentence in Canada for such an offence would be closer to forty days than forty years. This is not to say the American system is better, but it is clearly different.

Investigations require more work than they did twenty years ago, primarily because the justice system, laws, and court decisions demand more from the police. The amount of time needed for a police officer to manage a case from the initial call for service to final disclosure to prosecution has increased over the past thirty years by around 60 percent for break-and-enters and thefts to almost 1,000 percent for a domestic assault file (Malm et al. 2005). The fact that a criminal investigation takes longer to process means that units making arrests are now less frequently on the street patrolling. The challenge of getting out of the office is further increased by the higher priority now given cases such as domestic assault, which were lower priority service calls twenty years ago. Investigations now take longer and there are more of them.

The intensity of police work has also increased. Criminal violence, increased weapon use, dangerous drugs, and general lack of respect for the law and law enforcement officers have made police work more challenging and demanding than it was twenty years ago. Officers are more frequently involved in shootings, high-risk incidents, work-related injuries, and trauma. Research has also found that officers face increasing exposure to physical, chemical, biological, and psychosocial hazards (Parsons 2004).

In 2010, the Toronto Police Union grieved the service's plan to make officers wear nametags (Kives 2011). This demonstrates how threatened officers feel on the street – they would prefer to have their names concealed from the public. Toronto officers cited violence committed against Winnipeg police officers by the Hells Angels motorcycle gang as a reason to not make officers' names more accessible. In Winnipeg, there have been documented instances of harassment of officers in public and even at family gatherings. In some cases, there have been physical attacks and assaults on police officers' homes by gang members. It is increasingly common for officers to catch criminals stalking police facilities and following officers home as well as checking parked cars around police buildings and recording licence plates. For this reason, in Winnipeg and many other jurisdictions, most officers wear only a badge number and rank insignia for identification while on duty. Visible numbers are provided so that citizens can identify police officers for the purposes of legitimate complaints.

The volume of police work has also increased exponentially. Fifteen years ago, a uniformed patrol officer in Winnipeg would receive some sort of commendation from their supervisor for recovering a stolen car or finding a building that had been broken into. These types of events are now considered minor. Since 2000, the wps has handled well over 220,000 calls for service each year. Rare is the occasion when there are no calls pending dispatch; on those rare occasions when the queue does reach zero pending calls, the lull generally lasts for only a few minutes. Police officers in previous decades had only a fraction of the work volume handled by officers in the new millennium. Malm et al. (2005) found that police work-loads in Canada increased 700 percent between 1962 and 2003 and there is every indication that they have continued to rise.

The nature and type of offences changes with societal problems, priorities, and ever-evolving crime trends; frauds are one example. My first assignment to "plainclothes," back in the early 1990s, was with the district detective office in the Fort Garry district. In Winnipeg, each of the six districts had a "back office" with a small unit of detectives who handled major or complex cases that would have taken a uniform crew off the road for too long if they had continued to deal with the investigation. I was assigned to frauds and spent a great deal of time investigating fraudulent cheques and "empty envelopes." The latter is a type of theft in which people indicate they are depositing money in a bank machine, put an empty envelope into the machine, and then immediately withdraw the money they had supposedly deposited. Empty envelopes were easy investigations, as we would often have security camera pictures of the suspects making the transactions. We used to complain that the banks made it too easy for people to steal, but it was their prerogative to offer easy access to cash despite some peoples' inability to resist the temptation to steal. Sometimes the envelope would even contain a note saying, "sorry, I needed the money."

When we started out, theft was theft, but by the early to mid 1990s we were only investigating larger thefts – empty envelopes and fraudulent cheques over a certain amount. Frauds are any form of theft through deceit and may include bad cheques (known in policing as "hanging paper") as well as increasingly complex schemes such as international credit card scams. Most fraud investigations are quite complex and labour intensive, leading to an emphasis on prioritizing investigations.

Eventually our priority became investigating only frauds over a certain amount (not disclosed here). These changes occurred partly because the banks did not wish to pay the cost of processing the security camera pictures or the costs of the investigation, as well as the high number of cases; it is just not worth it for a theft of a small amount. The disturbing aspect of this was seeing the people who are victimized by such policies. An elderly person on a fixed income who has been defrauded of $100 is much more deeply victimized that a business that has taken a bad cheque for $3,000.

When the Integrated Proceeds of Crime units (IPOC) were set up across Canada in 2005, they held great promise of being able to hit organized criminals where it hurts, taking drug traffickers' toys and money away from them (Public Safety Canada 2011). IPOC units are a great example of integrated policing, drawing on a wide range of resources, municipal and federal police officers, forensic accountants, and tax evasion experts. The IPOC program has done great work taking down major drug dealers and organized criminals who are laundering money. The downside, as I see it, is also the result of the program's strength. It was run as a business, going after the largest criminals, targeting those with the largest amounts of money that could be seized. The downside is that the small players escape investigation because they do not have large enough assets to hit IPOC's radar. As an investigator I was disappointed when in some instances I brought cases to IPOC that they deemed too small for them to take on.

This gap was later addressed, at least in part, through new legislation, such as the Manitoba's Criminal Property Forfeiture Act (Manitoba 2011). This legislation allows the authorities to seize property used for organized crime. One of the first enforcement actions was the seizure of the Hells Angels clubhouse in Winnipeg (Ashley 2010). It was a small victory reminiscent of the time in the mid-1990s when an astute WPS detective noticed that the corporate name of the Spartans motorcycle gang had expired. The detective ran down to the Corporations Branch and registered the name as a club; the gang was then served notice that they could no longer be the "Spartans" because their name had been legally registered by someone else.

Fraud is one area of policing that has evolved due to increasing volume. However, this is one small part of the broad mandate that police agencies fulfill and of the wide range of continually shifting priorities. For the first ten years of my career we prosecuted people for simple possession of marijuana, even if it was only a gram or one "joint" (rolled cigarette). Now small amounts are generally not prosecuted, mainly due to the costs of testing it for prosecution purposes.

As a duty officer overseeing frontline police operations for the WPS, I have seen the way increased intensity and volume has challenged police in responding to and investigating crimes. Because of a backlog of calls-for-service needing dispatch, uniform police crews now have limited time for proactive patrolling. As soon as they clear one call, they are dispatched to the next. Police dispatchers are under relentless pressure to send units and clear calls. Because of the continuous influx of high priority service calls, some lower priority calls await dispatch for hours and even days. The queue is a fact of life in policing. The only way to reduce it is either to reduce service (not respond to some types of events) or streamline processes. In Winnipeg we have chosen to reduce services very little. Consequently, there is a constant demand on frontline uniform officers to take the next call.

Ten years ago police officers got the thirty minute lunch break to which they are entitled in each ten hour shift – they would send a request for dispatchers to assign them to lunch. Today they normally never ask. Officers do not put dispatchers in the awkward position of having to deny them lunch because there are always calls awaiting dispatch. So, most often officers grab a bite to eat while they are still assigned to a service call.

In 2011, on busy nights it was common for the WPS to be managing over one hundred calls for service. This is an improvement from the three hundred calls pending service that was often reached in 2007. The Police Service addressed that problem by identifying the types of calls that were taking the most resources and finding efficiencies to reduce the time spent on certain types of calls. For example, the WPS was still responding to commercial burglar alarms at a time when other major centres across Canada had stopped responding to calls from businesses that had contracted with private companies to monitor and respond to alarms. This policy was re-evaluated in Winnipeg and we stopped going to commercial alarms, except when they are suspicious in nature, significantly reducing officer-hours that had previously been spent on alarms.

Several types of investigation were streamlined to reduce the time required for police officers to write reports. At the same time, as previously mentioned, investigations take much longer now than they did in the past because of increasing complexity and higher demands by the courts. Research by Malm et al. (2005) has found that in the new millennium report writing for Canadian police officers takes four times longer than it did in the 1970s. Some services have reduced this demand by hiring civilian staff to support the reporting requirements. For instance, in the WPS we implemented direct voice entry, which allowed officers to dictate reports by telephone from the cruiser car to civilian staff in an office. The impact of these processes is a subject for potential research.

Police officers used to have more time available to patrol. If a uniform crew got involved in a major incident, they could continue the investigation through to conclusion. My mentors taught me early in my career to take pride in finishing investigations. I rarely, if ever, handed over an investigation unless I was ordered to do so. In particular, I would never willingly hand over an arrest to another crew or unit unless absolutely necessary. Now, frontline uniformed officers have continuous pressure to clear each call as quickly as possible and get onto the next one. Therefore, they have less time to get involved in complex investigations and to develop detective skills. On top of increased work volume, officers also have less opportunity to be mentored by seasoned investigators, an aspect covered in later chapters. When discussing work volume one needs to be cognizant of the statistics that are relied upon to guide decisions and to remember that statistics can be misleading.

ABOUT CRIME STATISTICS

Crime statistics are a complex tool for attempting to discover truth, because they can be interpreted in numerous ways. The way that data is gathered and decisions over what data to gather can drastically affect the results before the interpretation even begins. For instance, an increase in certain classes of crime could actually indicate that service has improved. If a police agency had not been responding to commercial burglar alarms and then began to do so, reporting in the first year following the decision would show a huge increase in calls resulting from burglar alarms. In fact, the number of alarms may have remained the same; the only thing that changed would be that police are now responding to and/or reporting them. Similarly, a large spike in the number of domestic violence reports could simply mean that a policy change resulted in more charges or that more people reported domestic assaults, while the incidence of the actual behaviour was constant. Statistics Canada acknowledges that there are many legitimate ways of reporting crime and whichever one is chosen affects the outcomes (Crowley 2011a).

Compounding the challenges of defining and quantifying crime is the fact that only a certain percentage of most crimes are reported. In the "General Social Survey – Victimization" released in September

2009, Statistics Canada reported that in the previous year only 31 percent of victims had reported crimes in which they were victimized to the police. That is a substantial drop from a decade ago, in which the same survey found that 40 percent of people had reported crimes (Newark 2011). This is a disturbing trend if it indicates a lack of confidence that the police and the justice system can or will do anything about victimization.

Where the statistics are obtained also makes a difference. The police may report statistics according to the label assigned for dispatch purposes, which may differ from what the suspect is convicted of at the end of the court process. Charges are often changed throughout the pre-trial process, or when a person pleads guilty to a lesser offence. For instance, assault with a weapon or aggravated assault are often plea-bargained to simple assault in order to show a conviction while avoiding a costly trial. Statistics reported by the courts thus often differ from those reported by the police.

This reporting problem applies to many different offences and presents great opportunities for manipulation. Winston Churchill highlighted the importance of scrutinizing statistics and how they can be manipulated to create a particular perception. He said that when he asked for a statistic on infant mortality he was seeking numbers that proved that fewer babies died when he was prime minister. That, according to Churchill, is a "political statistic" (Churchill 2011). Statistics can be interpreted to say almost anything you want.

In 2011–12 there is much debate among and between scholars, politicians, and those in the Canadian justice community as to whether crime has increased or decreased. I contend that, regardless of the statistical interpretation of increasing or decreasing crime trends, on the street we are seeing a higher incidence of weapon use and severe violence.

There seems to be agreement that overall crime rates have continually declined since 1991 (Corbelia 2010). Statistics Canada data reflects a national decline in violent crime over the past decade; however, these recent numbers do not reflect significant increases that have occurred over the past half century. In 1962 Canadians reported 221 violent crimes per 100,000 population; in 1992 the number was 1,084 per 100,000, a 500 percent increase (Lee 2011). The 2005 Statistics Canada General Survey reported that 92 percent of sexual assaults, 61 percent of physical assaults, and 54 percent of robberies were not reported to the police (ibid.). If these violent crimes are reported less frequently and reported crime is declining, does this indicate a decrease in actual crime or just a decrease in reported crime?

Statistics Canada surveys differ from police-reported crime as well. Police-reported crime statistics in Canada showed that violent crimes, including murder, serious assaults, and robbery, declined in 2009. However, increases were reported in attempted murder, extortion, firearms offences, and criminal harassment (Dauvergne and Turner 2010). The same study by Dauvergne and Turner found that the youth crime severity index had declined continually since 2001; However, in 2009 it was still 10 percent higher than a decade earlier. Winnipeg showed a 15 percent increase in violent crime severity in 2009, which can be attributed in part to increased youth street gangs and gang activity.

Some scholars have identified a relationship between crime trends and the changing size of the youth population. University of Ottawa criminologist and research advisory chair for the Federal Police Sector Council Ron Melchers has suggested that the 1992–93 high crime rates corresponded to the crest of the baby-boom bulge of youth aged sixteen to twenty-four. Overall, crime has slowly declined with the decrease in the size of the youth demographic. However, the numbers for some violent crimes have grown with the increase in youth gangs in many areas across Canada (Steve 2011).

Melchers cited other possible explanations for the decline in some crimes, such as tougher locks and security systems on cars and homes to deter thieves, fewer people reporting crime, and "maybe, that Canada has become a more peaceful place over the years" (Steve 2011, 1).

In his controversial paper entitled, "Why Canadian Crime Statistics Don't Add Up: Not the Whole Truth," Newark (2011) critiques Statistics Canada's methods of gathering crime data, stating, "Many of the most common conclusions that are drawn about crime in Canada are in fact incorrect or badly distorted." Newark argues these problems are linked to the ways that Statistics Canada collects and interprets crime data (Newark 2011, 1). He also challenges reports about crime reduction over the past two decades, supporting my anecdotal observations that we are seeing more serious and violent crimes on the street. Newark argues that violent crime is increasing and that flawed statistical methodology has resulted in reported reductions in some classes of crime. He recommends complete modernization and a change in design of Canada's crime data gathering systems, including greater involvement by law enforcement in development of the process (ibid.).

Some scholars have suggested that the problem in Newark's argument is that his focus is more on crime volume and the total number of crimes committed than crime rates, which are the number of crimes per 100,000 people (Crowley 2011b).

So, what does this mean from a policing perspective? One interpretation is that the reduction in overall crime in the past two decades corresponds to increased police budgets. But it is a mistake to judge police performance and costs in terms of crime rates alone. Melchers argues that more police officers do not necessarily mean less crime as active crime fighting is a relatively small part of the job (Macleod 2011). Others have found that about half of police work involves traffic duties. The other half is comprised of work in patrol and public order, and investigating crimes (ibid.).

Melchers points out that the massive costs resulting from traffic-related accidents more than justify investments of police resources. Police operating costs of $12.3 billion nationwide are well over double what they were in 1985. Melchers, however, suggests that if you look at police costs as an investment in reducing traffic-related accidents rather than just in terms of crime reduction, they provide good value for Canadian dollars (Macleod 2011).

From a frontline policing perspective, crime statistics are only part of the picture with respect to public safety and police performance measurement. From the perspective of those of us on the frontline, the chances of encountering someone armed with a gun or having to struggle with someone who is violent towards the police or resisting arrest are higher now than they were two decades ago, regardless of the various interpretations of statistical data. Another major change that has occurred is increased accountability.

INCREASED ACCOUNTABILITY

Today, frontline police officers routinely make decisions that twenty years ago were made by those higher up the chain of command. For example, in the early to mid 1990s, WPS officers would take a police report and then call the crime division sergeant for direction as to whether a person should be arrested, which charges should be laid, and whether the accused person should be detained in custody or released with a court date. Now, as a result of increased call volumes and changes to organizational structure, these decisions are routinely made by officers at the scene of a crime or in consultation with their immediate supervisors, not by specialized sergeants. This places a higher burden of responsibility on officers and frontline supervisors.

High numbers of retirements are resulting in an overall younger police demographic. At the same time, officers are required to take on more responsibility, with less experience, in more hostile, high-risk environments and under greater scrutiny from a public that has more access to information. Increasing scrutiny and higher demands by the courts, the public, and police oversight agencies compound the accountability and responsibility of modern-day police officers.

Leadership in policing is also more demanding than it was twenty years ago. As criminal sophistication has increased and community-based problems have become more complex, police administrators are required to be more innovative. Old paradigms need to be challenged. In his article "Evidence-Based Policing," Sherman provides insight into how paradigms in the profession of medicine, as in policing, have caused resistance to change. He estimated that 85 percent of medical decisions at the time were based on subjective opinions and experience, not on scientifically tested results. He shows that this has parallels with the situation in policing, where decisions were often based on past practice rather than scientifically proven and supported facts (Sherman 1998). However, since Sherman's research in 1998, policing has become much more evidence-based and transparent.

The new focus on evidence-based policing has brought with it new levels of accountability in management. Communities are increasingly questioning the rationale for police programs and the choices that are made in the deployment of limited resources. It is no longer acceptable for police to say to the public, "This is how we do it," unless we can provide the reasons behind the decision. This means managers need to be knowledgeable not only about police policies but also about the rationale behind the policies. They need to be flexible in collaborating with the community in order to foster teamwork and develop effective, evidence-based solutions.

Walsh and Conway describe the challenges of police governance and accountability as having increased immensely over the past fifty years in response to "an increasingly diverse, technological, urbanized, globalized, mobile, sophisticated, rights-conscious and knowledge-based society." They found that the shift towards "intelligence-based, problem-oriented, proactive strategies" has increased specialization within agencies, which now have heavily armed tactical units, more specialized investigative units, and specialists for a much broader spectrum of tasks (Walsh and Conway 2011, 61).

Policing the police is an ongoing challenge and a hotly debated topic with respect to police governance and accountability. In 2009, the RCMP Commission for Public Complaints Against the RCMP released a report entitled "Police Investigating Police – Final Public Report" that provided results of the examination of police oversight models ranging from the municipal level in Chicago to regional equivalents in South Australia and country-wide in Great Britain (Kennedy 2009). Kennedy found that in those countries, all of which have police systems that originated in the British tradition, there are currently three different models of police oversight.

The dependent model involves police investigating another police force. The interdependent model, utilized in British Columbia, Saskatchewan, Alberta, Yukon, New Zealand, the United Kingdom, and South Australia, introduces civilian involvement into criminal investigations of police officers (Kennedy 2009). In the interdependent model, civilian observers monitor police investigations to be sure they are conducted with impartiality or may conduct investigations in collaboration with the police. This model combines police investigative experience and civilian independence. The independent model involves civilians or police officers with no ties to the agency under investigation. Ontario's Special Investigation Unit uses this model. The key advantage of an independent oversight body is that it offers an appearance of total independence and objectivity. Ultimately Kennedy finds that there are benefits, such as independence and objectivity, as well as cost constraints tied to these varied models. There is no one configuration that stands out as the best for all of Canada (ibid.).

Regardless of the oversight model, police executives and frontline officers are all under increasing pressure to ensure accountability and transparency. The following section examines how professional accountability has continued to increase, often creating situations of multiple jeopardy for individual officers.

QUADRUPLE JEOPARDY

Police officers today are accountable to the public and to their direct chain of police command. They are also held to account by internal professional standards investigations, external oversight agencies, and the courts, all of which look for and vigorously investigate any suggestion of misconduct. Most police oversight falls within four categories: the public (including media), internal, the courts, and oversight bodies. Together they are a source of quadruple jeopardy for those in the police that far exceeds the oversight and accountability required of most other professions.

Almost every officer goes through a rite of passage when they have to testify at a court case and worry that a defence lawyer will focus his or her cross-examination on something the officer should or should not have done during the investigation. It is challenging for officers to recall all the details of an incident recorded four years earlier while under stress.

Officers are subjected to relentless media coverage that often focuses on alleged police misconduct. This sort of publicity is difficult for officers because they are acutely aware that their children, spouse, extended family, and friends will suffer from the stress and embarrassment caused by such allegations. Members of the public are able to make allegations and say anything they wish to the media, while officers are bound by strict rules of confidentiality that do not allow them to speak publicly about aspects of police business or investigations. Police issues pose a difficult challenge for reporters as well. They need to report on incidents that interest the public, such as alleged police misconduct, while also attempting to be objective (hopefully) and maintain positive relationships with the police, whom they rely on for information about high-profile police activities, stories of public interest, and public safety announcements.

In the second year of my career, I was entangled in a major internal investigation over alleged misconduct (with the emphasis on alleged) in the handling of a confidential informant. It involved things that occurred while I was being trained in the field and was accompanying senior officers who had brought me along to learn about working informants. I was young and starting out in a career that I loved. I had worked hard in recruit class and had been selected as the recipient of the Don Gove Memorial Award, named after a respected police academy instructor and given to one constable in each recruit class that peers and teachers believe has the character of the ideal police officer. (I mention this as it suggests how committed I was to a career in policing.)

An informant alleged that certain officers were committing criminal acts by encouraging another informant to set up crimes in order to allow the police to catch the criminals involved. The result was a massive investigation that resulted in the arrest of over half a dozen officers. One day I picked up a newspaper and saw that an officer that I had worked with and been trained by had been arrested and detained in the Provincial Remand Center. I quickly realized that the detention had to do with some of the incidents I had been involved with while I was being trained. That is when the high-stress weight-loss program began for me and about twenty colleagues.

When I was also charged, four months into the investigation, my name made the front page of newspapers and was televised nation-wide. I knew that I had done nothing wrong and continued to maintain this until I was finally vindicated. It was, however an excruciatingly stressful experience that lasted for several years until the slow wheels of justice finally resolved the matter.

The news reports seen by family members and friends were probably the most embarrassing and nerve-racking aspect of that entire experience. When the charges were dropped and my colleagues and I were vindicated, the story was buried in the back pages of the news outlets and was barely reported in the other news media. It certainly did not run in huge block letters on the front pages of newspapers across the nation, as the stories on the initial allegation had. The Winnipeg Police Association paid for our legal fees, which were later recovered from the City of Winnipeg after years of protracted litigation. If the association had not done this, the legal fees alone would have bankrupted most of the officers who were involved.

Long drawn-out court processes are severely stressful for officers who are the subject of allegations. In one case, two Winnipeg police officers were sued for $1 million over their 1999 arrest of a man for domestic assault. It was a straightforward case that did not allege wrongdoing on the part of the officers but instead challenged the grounds for arrest, which were tied to the w p s and Manitoba Justice Department's zero tolerance policy on domestic violence. In other words, the officers were compelled by policy to make the arrest. The domestic assault charges were later stayed and it was decided not to proceed with charges; however, the man who had been arrested sued the police over the alleged zero tolerance policy, arguing that the police should not have intervened in the first place. The civil suit was finally settled and the officers were exonerated twelve years later, in 2011 (McIntyre 2011). Imagine spending twelve years of your life conducting criminal investigations and arresting people while you have a million dollar lawsuit resulting from an arrest you made hanging over your head.

These cases highlight the importance of having a union's protection in cases of professional jeopardies. After I was charged and later cleared, I sought and was elected to serve on the WPA board for four years. I was the youngest officer to ever serve on the WPA board, but I had learned from that early experience that the policing profession is full of risks, and in many ways the Police Association provides our only indemnification against them. Police have no access to professional liability insurance such as that purchased by doctors, and yet we are in the business of conflict, interfering with people's victimization of each other for the good of the community. It is a recipe for complaints as every arrest has at least one party who is unhappy about what has transpired.

An experience of being the subject of allegations also increases the strong bond among officers as well as the realization that we are isolated within our communities. Neighbours usually remember who you are once they learn that you are a police officer. Police officers' children carry this burden as well because other school children always remind them that their parent is a police officer. This can be a badge of pride but also a cause of stress, depending on who they associate with.

Officers are simultaneously dedicated to community service and singled out in their personal lives as police officers. People often treat you differently when they find out you are a police officer. Many officers eventually have only police friends, because they get tired of hearing a story about how they were speeding and got a ticket from everyone they meet. However it is vitally important for officers to resist the tendency to associate only with other police officers. Good mental health requires that they remain connected with the world outside policing, as it affects one's sense of identity and ability to serve with sensitivity. This takes awareness and a concentrated effort.

In recent years the WPS has brought in experts to provide seminars on these topics, teaching officers and their spouses about the stresses inherent in the profession and how to manage them. But this only started in the past decade – twenty years ago the rule of thumb was to leave your problems at home and not bring them to work. The new awareness about mental health is based on the acknowledgement that some of the problems at home originate at work. The sense that police officers are public figures and are answerable to any citizen at any time is a reality that they must learn to live with. Public office carries responsibilities and in many ways it is a burden. My brother, Doug, just finished a twenty-seven-year career with the Calgary Police Service. He is proud of his career, and he should be, but he also described the sense of relief he felt on the day he handed in his gun and badge and became a private citizen.

For the last few years of his career Doug worked in the Calgary Police Service arrest-processing unit, a job that involves presenting charges to the on-duty magistrate and either opposing or agreeing with bail for the person in custody. In one case in or around 2006, a Calgary police officer was arrested for an off-duty matter and had to appear before a magistrate for bail on the alleged charges. Doug argued for a publication ban on the hearing, citing the multiple jeopardies that police officers are subjected to. He argued that the officer was subject to internal investigation, his job would be in jeopardy, and the media would place more emphasis on covering the case because the accused person was a police officer. The magistrate agreed and ordered the publication ban. Some police executive members, however, were not impressed, as they wanted the media to report on the internal accountability they had shown by arresting the officer.

People accused of crimes have been known to make false complaints against officers in the hopes of having their own charges dropped. Such cases require a fine balance on the part of police executives. The public must feel confident that complaints will be investigated thoroughly and taken seriously. At the same time, individuals need to be deterred from making false allegations and police officers need to see false complaints rooted out as a matter of maintaining high morale. Technology has improved these investigations and allowed for quicker and more definitive closure in many cases. Global Positioning System (GPS) devices, which are now in many cruiser cars, have made it possible to disprove many false allegations. Police records management and computer-aided dispatch systems are so accurate now that in most cases the police crew that is the subject of any allegation is easily identified. The GPS from their unit reveals exactly where they drove, within inches. An investigation into allegations of misconduct that might have taken months and involved numerous interviews with potential witnesses may now, in some cases, be cleared up in minutes utilizing GPS technology.

In December 2010, a young Aboriginal man made an allegation to local media outlets that WPS officers had dumped him at the city's edge and threatened him with a stun gun (CBC News 2010). Several different outlets ran the story, interested particularly because of the previous "starlight tour" scandals in Saskatchewan, in which police had driven marginalized individuals to the outskirts of town and abandoned them (Brass 2004). The 2010 allegation threatened to damage police-Aboriginal relations in Winnipeg. Fortunately the GPS in the police unit that had had contact with the man could be used to prove that the allegation was false and a video from the bus he was riding at the time of the alleged event also provided support. The individual was charged with public mischief and, in a rare move, Grand Chief Ron Evans of the Assembly of Manitoba Chiefs stood beside Police Chief Keith McCaskill to affirm that the allegation was false (CBC News 2010). Of course, the same technology could also be used to corroborate true allegations against the police, a positive effect that is desired and supported by police management.

Manitoba's Law Enforcement Review Agency (LERA) is the provincial police oversight body that investigates allegations of police misconduct. LERA conducted over five hundred investigations into allegations of police misconduct between 2004 and 2008 (Manitoba Law Enforcement Review Agency 2010). That number does not reflect the number of internal investigations conducted independently by police services into allegations of criminal offences by their officers, as LERA generally does not investigate criminal allegations. The bulk of the LERA complaints in Manitoba are against members of the WPS, as Winnipeg is the largest city in Manitoba. There are a large number of complaints made to LERA, but very little comes of them. Many complaints are dismissed as frivolous and unsubstantiated after the LERA investigator speaks to the complainant and the involved officers and learns the details of what actually occurred during an incident. When I was on the Winnipeg Police Association board, representing members' interests, I used to voice my concerns about the process and how long it takes. Even when complaints are false and unsubstantiated, police officers can have allegations hanging over their heads, and in the back of their minds, for years before they are resolved.

In my career I have only had one LERA complaint and it took three years to resolve. The complaint was that my unit, the Anti-Crime Tactical Unit, had disordered a woman's house while executing a search warrant for marijuana. We were also accused of being insensitive because we had looked at a video that was in a camera while searching for evidence of drug dealing. (This was embarrassing for the complainant because the video was of her and her partner having sex.) In this case, we had turned out some drawers, placing the clothes in piles on the floor, and had turned over bed mattresses. We left things in that state, as it would be inappropriate for police officers to start trying to sort out someone's clothes and put them back into drawers. We did not find the illegal drugs we were expecting, but this is not uncommon, as drugs tend to disappear quickly when an experienced dealer is involved. We believed that the information on which the search warrant was based was very likely to be true – we had executed numerous successful search warrants based on the same source of information and had taken illegal weapons and large amounts of illegal drugs off the street and recovered hundreds of thousands of dollars worth of stolen property for return to its rightful owners. We did look at the video in question, but for the purpose of acquiring evidence. In the execution of previous search warrants, our unit had found cameras that contained pictures of suspects with stolen property, weapons, and drugs.

There were about ten of us in the unit and we were all named in the complaint. I took responsibility, however, as it was my information and my search warrant that led us to that house and charges against everyone else in the unit were dismissed. Three years later, when I finally had the opportunity to sit down with the complainant and the LERA commissioner, I explained to the complainant that I would have been happy to explain our position and even apologize for any insensitivity or misunderstanding at the time of the warrant, if she had not gone straight to the media and to LERA with allegations of misconduct. I explained that once she had gone to LERA it was inappropriate for me to contact her and as a result, she had to wait for three years to talk with me about what had happened. Once she and the LERA commissioner learned about the drug dealing that we were investigating and trying to eliminate from the neighbourhood, the complaint was dropped.

The duty of answering public complaints is part of the police experience and a stress that many officers have to deal with as part of their career. Our outlaw motorcycle gang officer held the record. He had hundreds of LERA complaints filed against him by bike gang members, who, with the assistance of their lawyers, were filing such complaints in an attempt to frustrate police efforts against their criminal activities in and around Winnipeg. The outlaw bikers even attempted to get a restraining order to keep this officer away from them – an action that was seen by many as an indication of his passion for regulating outlaw motorcycle gangs.

Officers also learn early in their careers which things need to be documented to prevent their coming back and biting. One example that comes to mind is a domestic call that I attended at the outset of my career. I was a new officer, maybe one year on the job, and working with a senior officer with about eighteen years of experience. We went to a domestic fight in a small North End house where we found a frightened young woman, perhaps five feet tall. The first glance in her eyes when she opened the door told us that she was scared and that something had happened. She was restrained and did not say a word. Then her boyfriend stepped out from the kitchen and we could see why she was not speaking. He was a barrel-chested lumberjack, six feet tall and three hundred pounds, who had spent most of his life in the woods doing hard manual labour. He was older, maybe close to sixty, but still strong as an ox and also a man of few words.

We tried to separate them in order to find out why she had called the police. He refused to budge, and she would not say anything with him in the room. I finally herded him around the corner and into the kitchen so that my partner could talk to her privately. It is common practice, in fact policy, to separate parties so that the victim is not intimidated by the aggressor. After a few minutes my partner learned that the man was a new acquaintance who had started becoming aggressive after consuming liquor and now she just wanted him out of her house. No assault had occurred but she was scared of him, so we needed to remove him from the residence.

He had been drinking but was not completely intoxicated. We told him he had to leave and that we would drive him anywhere he liked. He refused and said he wasn't going anywhere. Then the fight was on; both my partner and I weighed two hundred pounds each, but he threw us around the kitchen like a couple of rag dolls. It eventually took two sets of handcuffs to restrain him, hooking one set to the other, because he was so thick-boned and muscular that we could not bring his arms together behind his back. The young lady thanked us profusely for helping her and getting him out.

Once the scuffle was over, he became more of a gentleman and asked if we could drive him to his brother's place. We decided to write off the incident as an indiscretion on the logger's part, give him the benefit of the doubt, and just drop him off instead of arresting him for assaulting us. We could have charged him with assault of a peace officer or a raft of other charges, but instead we gave him a break. We dropped him off and carried on to the next call.

When we arrived back at the district station, no more than three hours later, our sergeant said the logger had been in complaining that we had assaulted him. He had been to the hospital and had documented proof of his injuries. Because we had not arrested him it could look as if we had something to hide. Nothing came of it, but it could have been difficult if he had proceeded with a formal complaint. Instead, he was apparently satisfied, as people often are, with just talking to a supervisor. From that experience, I learned that if there is a fight and grounds exist for charges, someone is getting arrested.

Freedom of information and increased accountability and transparency in the courts also adds an element of jeopardy for officers. The 2009 Supreme Court of Canada *McNeil* decision requires police agencies to disclosure an officer's serious relevant misconduct to prosecutors (Supreme Court of Canada 2009). McNeil was a police officer with the Barrie Police Service in Ontario. An individual he had arrested for drug-related offences learned, after his conviction but before his sentencing, that McNeil was under internal and criminal investigation in relation to allegations of drug-related misconduct. The accused appealed to the Supreme Court, arguing that he could have helped his defence if he had known that the key witness for the prosecution had been charged with drug-related offences. The resulting Supreme Court decision says that prosecutors may disclose allegations of misconduct in which an officer has been involved. As a result, an officer who has been convicted of a charge may have to answer questions about it, under cross-examination, for the rest of their career, even if the incident took place many years before.

The *McNeil* decision builds upon the previous 1991 Supreme Court *Stinchcombe* decision. That ruling dramatically changed Canadian policing forever. In the 1980s Calgary lawyer William Stinchcombe was arrested for misappropriating $1.6 million. During his trial, the prosecutors were upheld by the judge in their refusal to disclose to the defence a witness statement that had been used at the preliminary inquiry but was not used in the trial. Stinchcombe appealed to the Supreme Court after starting his nine-year sentence and was released on bail. Justice John Sopinka of the Supreme Court wrote in the ruling of the court that "the Crown has a legal duty to disclose all relevant information to the defence" (Supreme Court of Canada 1991). Stinchcombe's conviction and nine-year sentence were overturned and his licence to practise law was reinstated (Marshall 2011).

The *Stinchcombe* decision took away the element of surprise during court cases, which had existed historically. In the first few years of my career, police notes made by officers were not disclosed; they were just brought to court. Often there were bits of information in officers' notes that never made their way into the police reports but only the reports, written statements, and other evidence were submitted to prosecutors for disclosure, not the notes. For example, the police report might having included that the accused was intoxicated by alcohol. In the notes, however, the officer may have had information not in the report, such as the fact that the accused had defecated or urinated in their clothing, vomited, or was acting obnoxiously when arrested. The defence would not find out about this additional information until they were in court, which sometimes resulting in a last minute plea-bargain to avoid having that information testified to in open court. After *Stinchcombe*, officers' notes had to be submitted to the defence along with the police reports and any other evidence that had been gathered. It changed the way notes were written, making them more like reports, as officers knew that others would be reading them. This brought an entirely new level of transparency to policing.

In 2006, over one hundred RCMP and WPS police officers and numerous specialty units executed search warrants on suspected arms dealers' homes in the Interlake area of central Manitoba. Dozens of Sten submachine guns, two cannons, a homemade .50-calibre rifle, and three exotic solid steel pen guns were seized. On the eve of trial, prosecutors learned of a 2006 police interview with an inmate who claimed to have provided the information that made some of the seizures possible. The late disclosure caused a mistrial (Marshall

2011). These court decisions have moulded practice over the past two decades and have significantly changed the way police work is now done.

Such transparency is necessary to ensure that people accused of crimes can mount their defence properly. Nonetheless, it is an added stressor and level of accountability that officers must maintain in a profession with ever-increasing demands. Technology and increased access to information have also intensified the demands on modern-day police officers even as they have given them new tools.

4

Technology: How the Tools Have Changed

THE BREADTH OF CHANGE

Modern police officers must contend with and seek to make the best use of continually changing technology. In 1989 my WPS recruit class used manual typewriters to write reports. When electronic typewriters were introduced in the early 1990s, they seemed to be a major advance. I recall some senior officers refusing to use the new electronic gadgets, favouring the manual typewriters they were used to. When computers were introduced, it was too much for some to handle and some police officers have cited technology as a major factor in their decision to retire. (Retirements due to technological challenges are an area for potential future research.) Now, peers from my 1989 recruit class routinely use a wide range of advanced computer technologies in performing their daily duties.

The idea that technology would make work easier has not worked out as many anticipated. Research on the effects of changing technology on Canadian police services over the last thirty years has revealed that in some cases it actually creates more work.

Greater disclosure requirements and the need for use of complex computer software has increased the administrative burden on officers. Report writing that took officers an average of an hour and a half per day to complete in the 1970s took over four hours by 2005; approximately 40 percent of their workday (Malm et al. 2005). Now, the police routinely need search warrants and arrests warrants, which take a great deal of time to create. Detaining a person in jail on new charges took three minutes of paperwork two decades ago. We would decide on the charges, take them to jail, and fill out a very brief form with their name and crime report numbers and that was it. Granted, reports needed to be done at some point, but we would often put off report writing until quiet times, when front line police units were not required for high call volumes. Nowadays, detaining a person in jail on charges takes hours of paperwork. All of these increased administrative requirements for police officers mean less time on patrol responding to calls for service. A major challenge for modern police managers is to find ways to reduce such burdens on officers, so that they can be out of the office policing.

When my partner and I were involved in a complex investigation into a local crime ring that had committed nearly two hundred break and enters and thefts, we had one major administrative task on our hands: we had to get technical support to alter the WPS reporting system so it could accommodate more than one hundred charges (previously it would only link ninety-nine offences). The reporting/disclosure process was so complex and involved we had to have a clerk assigned to us full-time for six months. However, in the routine day-to-day business of policing, officers are their own clerks. So much time and effort are spent writing reports that it is a continual source of tension. Dispatch is always looking for units to take calls for service, and officers want to get out and take calls, but are instead grinding out the required reports. As previously described, case law, such as *Stinchcombe*, requires timely disclosure; without this prosecutors become frustrated and the charges can be stayed. (If charges are withdrawn, prosecution of those charges is finished. If they are stayed, they can be "brought back to life" within one year of the day on which they were stayed.)

Complacency is another enemy of police officers. It is truly challenging to focus on creating high-quality notes and reports, knowing that most cases are plea-bargained and many of the reports will not be read. This is a particular frustration for officers working in detective units where large volumes of highly complex material must be put into case files. Some police reports are works of art in which detectives have skilfully pulled together and presented large amounts of information and evidence in a way that can be presented in court. Fraud investigations, for instance, can involve hundreds of victims and thousands of documents as evidence. Often, officers will work on major cases for many months and create detailed reports on large complex investigations, only to be told at court by a crown attorney that the accused had pleaded guilty to a lesser charge and there will be no trial.

The case described earlier, regarding two hundred break-ins, involved consolidating two hundred reports with complainant interviews, witness statements, insurance claims, search warrants, property dispositions, reports to justices on disposition of seized property, and arrest reports on the apprehension of twelve people who had all committed various offences. The matrix of suspects and the evidence against each of the individuals was complex.

One of our suspects had obtained a jailhouse confession from a person who had committed a murder and ultimately received immunity on the two hundred break-ins in exchange for his testimony at the murder trial. Our work on the break and enters helped solve a murder as it motivated the suspect/informant to talk, although he wasn't prosecuted as part of our investigation. We did, however, get closure for a number of victims by solving the cases and recovering a large amount of stolen property so it could be returned to its rightful owners. And we were proud of doing a thorough job on a major case.

Ironically, the newest version of reporting software is no more environmentally friendly that the old manual method. It was showcased as a "paperless" system but, as a result of court disclosure requirements, this paperless system has not resulted in a substantial saving of paper. Officers are now required to copy original documents and send the copy to the Direct Voice Entry Unit for scanning and subsequent destruction. Reports are also printed in hard copy and sent to public prosecutions for court processes. The Crown prosecutor, in turn, makes copies for each accused (and his or her attorney). I have worked on criminal cases that required three or four three-inch binders to hold all the disclosure materials. If there are multiple accused, a complete copy is supplied for every accused, so what often ends up in court is a room full of boxes and binders full of paper.

The court system has historically been environmentally unfriendly, using a significant amount of paper; however, incremental gains are being made in the use of technology for electronic disclosure. Lengthy videotaped interviews and electronic evidence are now disclosed on DVDs with a written synopsis of the highlights. This is a substantial gain, saving both paper and the time officers used to spend transcribing and typing the full content of recorded statements. How I wish I could have back all the time I've spent during my career typing hand-written statements and transcribing recorded ones! Through continuous negotiation with Crown prosecutors we are slowly gaining concessions about submitting reports electronically. Much of the hold-up is in the courts, which are often not equipped for the electronic presentation of evidence. Technological advances in court disclosure and presentation are in various states of evolution across the country but change is happening everywhere.

A step forward was achieved when I was in the Integrated Child Exploitation (ICE) Unit in 2005. This was a joint RCMP/WPS unit mandated with investigating Internet-based child exploitation through child pornography. We seized computer systems in every case and had to show the electronic evidence in court. Disclosure of electronic images for court presentation, and for defence and Crown prosecutors, was problematic. Disclosing the evidence to defence lawyers was a challenge because it is illegal for anyone other than a police officer engaged in an investigation to have possession of child pornography. It is legal for lawyers to view the evidence in preparation of a client's defence, but we were concerned about illegal materials being shared with the clients they had been seized from or with copies of the illegal materials and child pornography remaining on hard drives after cases were disposed of.

The principle by which we operated was that child pornography is recorded evidence of child abuse and every time someone views images of child abuse the child is re-victimized. In many cases hundreds of thousands of images were seized and became evidence of charges. Members in the ICE unit created a tamper-proof computer tower that nothing could be copied from and that could be loaned to defence lawyers with the evidence and with a signed contract that it would be used only for purposes of defending their clients. For court, ICE unit members put together a portable system with four monitors that could be transported in a large car trunk. This way the judge, defence, Crown prosecutor, and jury could all see evidence as it was presented. It all seemed a bit awkward and backwards, but it was incrementally bringing the rest of the justice system into the twenty-first century and facilitated the education of many lawyers and judges on these technically complex, leading-edge cases.

Pre-trial, we spent many hours in the office showing and explaining the evidence to prosecutors and defence lawyers so that they could prosecute and defend their clients effectively.

Software and reporting systems differ between and within each police agency across the country. For example, specialty units and task forces often develop reporting systems that meet their specialized needs and reporting systems are often incompatible between units or agencies. Standardization of systems would enable agencies to communicate more effectively across Canada or even around the world. Considering the incredible technological advances that have occurred over the past twenty years, worldwide compatible reporting software in the coming years is now easy to envision. However, it is not likely to become a reality anytime soon.

A major obstacle to sharing information is political, not technological, as many agencies are still very territorial about their information. In many cases "holdback" information is carefully guarded and is not shared between units internally, let alone between agencies. Holdback information is kept secret so that investigators can test the veracity of intelligence from informants or in confessions. For example, a homicide unit may withhold information such as the fact that a person was shot by a .38 calibre bullet. Then, when an informant asks for a reward and states he knows who stabbed the victim, or shot them with a shotgun, investigators know immediately that the information is inaccurate. If a suspect admits to a serious offence under interrogation, it is hard for him or her to say they were coerced if they provide information that only the perpetrator could know. Holdback information is thus important for prosecutions and is guarded closely. This type of required secrecy is both a legitimate barrier and a challenge to full disclosure.

Other types of information could be shared more openly, however, for the greater good. For example, child pornography seized around the world should be shared between investigative agencies. If this information was shared and analyzed properly it could result in the identification and location of more victims and suspects. The logistics of sharing this information, unfortunately, are substantial. Software and equipment capable of analyzing the seized images are cutting-edge new technology and therefore expensive. The only way such sharing could happen is if hundreds of agencies agreed to purchase and operate compatible tools.

Technological advances are, without a doubt, offering limitless opportunities for improved effectiveness in policing. They have connected people in ways that were unimagined two decades ago, creating connected networks that span the globe seamlessly and instantaneously. Technology also has negative effects, as people are constantly distracted and may be losing their ability to communicate effectively. A Time Magazine article, "Help! I've Lost My Focus" describes how electronic devices have damaged the ability of professionals to focus on their work, arguing that constant interruptions from e-mail, cell phones, pagers, and other electronic devices create an attention deficit that reduces the overall quality and volume of work. A study of a New York City firm with 1,000 employees revealed that answering messages generated by electronic devices consumed 28 percent of the average employee's workday. This represents 2.1 person hours per day, not counting the recovery time required after every interruption before the interrupted task can be resumed. It has been estimated that such interruptions cost the United States economy $588 billion per year (Wallis and Steptoe 2006).

Wallis and Steptoe also describe a modern phenomenon, in which employees send copies of e-mails to their supervisors as a protective strategy. Supervisors must check such e-mails because the one that they ignore could be the one that has important information. Such tasks can feel like enslavement and can cause a sense of powerlessness. In 2005, one WPS sergeant, with thirty years of experience, commented to me on his sense of loss of control caused by an overwhelming number of technological changes, noting that it made him feel "less like a police officer than ever before," a sentiment echoed by many current-day police officers.

The increasing use of smartphones also tethers employees to the workplace. Carrying a smartphone results in many employees working numerous extra hours each week while away from the workplace. Many government employees, and those in the private sector as well, are required to carry smartphones, although some resist it in an attempt to preserve work-life balance. Cell phone and Internet technology provide instant access at any time, even while on vacation. In policing, this is an advantage as we have officers with expertise available 24/7 for consultation or direction. From my own experience, carrying a smartphone has extended the workday, blending work and home life. A text or e-mail can be sent at any time, to multiple people, regardless of where they are around the world. The increase in speed and volume of shared data has also created a work environment in which many people are overwhelmed with information and prioritizing and managing it takes a substantial part of each workday.

Work-life balance will need to become a focus of leadership in the coming decades. Communication protocols need to be further developed as well, as it has become difficult to have a meeting or a discussion without individuals checking electronic devices for messages while they are speaking with you. These devices are also changing communication patterns for developing children and young adults. My teenage kids all have cell phones, because we like having instant access to them at all times. But the downside is when you cannot get their attention because they are staring at the cell phone and texting while you are trying to talk with them.

Cell phones can potentially increase dangers in police work as well. Recently, I was at work as a duty officer when we had an incident in which a distraught man was locked in a bathroom threatening suicide with a steak knife. Our Tactical Support Unit was managing the situation. After they had established communication and were negotiating with the man, they realized his girlfriend was down the hall texting with him while he was speaking on the phone with the police crisis negotiators. She could have been telling him the officers are about to breach the door, putting her boyfriend and officers in danger.

Many people equip their homes and vehicles with audio and video devices that can capture their interactions with anyone, including police. Hidden cameras can also be a severe threat to officer safety if they warn armed suspects of police activities. These technologies need to be a critical consideration for officers in every aspect of police work – they could cost or save lives. In March 2012 it came to light that during maintenance of the video cameras in a new WPS facility, one of the cameras had been inadvertently left on. It recorded 2,400 hours of video before being discovered. This creates a major problem as every person who was arrested and brought into the station during those 2,400 hours may now be entitled to disclosure of the video (McIntyre 2012). The effect is that officers must now operate on the assumption that they are being recorded at all times because technology has the potential to be everywhere.

INCREASED ACCESS TO INFORMATION

In an age in which more books and articles are published every year than in all of recorded history before the mid twentieth century, government no longer has a monopoly on power through the control of information (Brooks 2002). Public servants must be responsive to a globally connected world, in which the Internet has reduced the monopoly on the power of knowledge that government officials used to have over individual citizens. The average person can now do a quick Internet search and be privy to the same level of information, or more, that only government officials could access in the past. In recent years, I completed my master's degree in public administration with only a few trips to the library. Most of the journals, books, and other sources are now available electronically through the Internet. In contrast, when doing my undergraduate courses in the 1980s I spent hundreds of hours searching library shelves for books and scouring academic journals, newspapers, and microfiched articles.

Modern governments are also experiencing a challenge in meeting increasing public demands for information, much of which is now required to be disclosed under access to information legislation. Lawful access to information requests place growing logistical and administrative demands on all government agencies. In a sense these demands have hardened information-protection policies within government agencies and non-government organizations (NGOs), creating barriers that never used to exist. For example, information from hospitals, social service agencies, land titles offices, phone companies, banks, credit card companies, and Internet service providers is very useful and often critical for legitimate police investigative purposes. Historically, investigators developed contacts in all of these varied agencies and information was shared for lawful purposes. Successful detectives would have numerous contacts so that information could be obtained from almost anywhere. Now, information in all of these agencies is more closely guarded because many employees fear, with good reason, that they will be taken to task for unauthorized disclosure.

In some cases, lawfully withholding information from the police jeopardizes public safety. Some agencies are good about providing information, once they are assured it is required for public safety purposes; others are less cooperative. I recall a case in which I spent the better part of a day negotiating with a major Internet-based social networking company's head office in the United States, trying to get them to release information to us from a high-risk runaway's account so that we could find her and bring her to safety.

On another occasion, I threatened to arrest the manager of a Winnipeg office of a major international Internet provider for obstructing a police officer when they refused to remove child pornography that had been posted on their server and to provide evidence that they held. I had a lawfully issued search warrant but they refused to assist, stating that the information was on a server that was in the United States, even though it was the same company. We had to apply for a Mutual Legal Assistance Treaty (MLAT) warrant through a Canadian liaison in Washington. It was a prohibitively lengthy and complex bureaucratic process, but it was the only tool available to us to force the company to provide the evidence that we needed to make a case, arrest the suspect, and put restrictions on him that would protect children in Winnipeg. I suspect that two decades ago a phone call from a police officer would have garnered the cooperation and evidence we needed. In this case, it took more than three full days of writing the warrant and administrative phone calls and processing for a detective to get the same result.

Access to information has also resulted in the loss of anonymity and increased accountability for civil servants. Governments no longer manage in vacuums; they are influenced by outside interest groups, other agencies, and even individual citizens (Savoie 2004). Many scholars have described how the growing complexity and size of government as well as increasing transparency have changed the focus of accountability, meaning that civil servants are now more accountable for the execution of their duties (Franks 2006; 2004). It is no longer acceptable to rely on the chain of command as an excuse for decisions. The public expectation is that police officers and police managers are knowledgeable and will challenge wrongful orders and policies, while still being accountable for good stewardship over public resources.

Increased accountability creates challenges particularly in emergency services where split second decisions, taking orders without hesitation, and swift actions are sometimes required in tactical life-and-death situations. Occasionally, police members are required to fulfill a tactical task without full knowledge of all the aspects of an operation, leaving little time to question orders. At other times, officers are expected to have full knowledge and understand the reasons for the actions they take. They must be able to articulate in court why they made an arrest, searched a person, kicked in a door, seized items, or any number of other police actions. This is a major change from twenty years ago when acting on orders was the main rationale required of an officer. The dynamics in the chain of command have also changed and managers are placed in positions where they are negotiating more and ordering less. They are also sometimes responsible for supervising officers who are undertaking highly technical tasks that the managers do not fully understand and senior commanders may occasionally be challenged by trying to retain responsibility for highly technical tasks being performed by the people they oversee.

NEW SCIENCE AND ITS IMPACTS

A new and popular genre of television shows over the past decade has developed based on the seemingly insatiable public interest in police sciences. These highly dramatized and fictional police series have created real problems for police officers when members of the public, lawyers, juries, and even judges on occasion have confused what they have seen on television with the actual state of science and what the police are capable of. This is commonly known as the "CSI effect"(Bergslien 2006; Harris 2011; Toobin 2007). Suffice it to say that these television shows are fictional and are so far removed from reality that most police officers joke about them. Real police officers can only wish that they could enter a person's name into a computer and gain immediate access to multiple databases that generate reports on everything there is to be known about a suspect or that DNA could be analyzed in matter of minutes.

The proverbial "flatfoot" or "gumshoe" detectives of by-gone eras were known for their tenacity in knocking on doors and talking to informants without rest until they got the small but critical piece of information that cracked a case. The modern gumshoe must still do all of that, as well as possess technological savvy and the tenacity to sit for hours, days, and weeks scouring records and databases and writing lengthy and complex search warrants in order to find information that will identify a suspect or gather evidence to solve a case.

Those of us who have been involved in policing over the past twenty years have experienced the shift from paper records to electronic databases. Ten or fifteen years ago, when a suspect admitted to a series of break-ins, in the WPS we would go to the "yellows," the copy of the quadruplicate paper police reports that was kept on file in every police station. The original white copy went to the Bureau of Police Records and the pink went with the arrest report if an arrest was made. The fourth, blue, copy went to the court, with part of it sent to the identification unit to tell them that the person was due to come in for fingerprinting. I actually miss those paper days, as there was practically an art form involved in learning how to separate the pieces and where to send them all.

When someone admitted to us that they had committed a series of offences we would read through the reports to find the right ones. Now, this is an electronic search and often we need to call on data management experts to assist in finding and recovering information. Electronic databases are efficient in gathering massive amounts of data but the information is often inaccessible to investigators. In many circumstances, the information that is required to solve cases exists, but it is buried in databases and can only be accessed and extracted by experts.

Increased regulation to protect privacy has often worked against the effectiveness of legitimate police investigations. As the coordinator of the WPS Missing Persons Unit, I saw many cases where existing information could have located missing persons but the information was inaccessible to investigators. Such cases are often urgent when there is evidence that a person has been abducted, is contemplating suicide, has come to harm, or in some cases had just skipped out in an effort to escape debt and start a new life.

In many cases, we had great support from organizations that provide information to support investigations. In others, we could not gain critical information without a warrant. Missing persons cases expose a gap in the law as you cannot obtain a warrant to search for records without providing grounds to believe that a crime has been committed and that the search warrant will gather evidence of such a crime. Suspecting that the missing person has been victimized, abducted, or murdered is not sufficient for a warrant to be issued unless we have grounds to believe, not just to suspect, that a crime has been committed. The fact that a person is missing does not in itself give us grounds for a search warrant to find them; we must be seeking evidence of a specific crime. So, we rely on the goodwill of organizations to support our efforts in the name of the public good.

Health records are one area that is particularly guarded. I have long believed that most, if not all, people seek some form of medical attention sooner or later. If police agencies had complete access to health records and could coordinate their interagency efforts, they could potentially solve a portion of the hundreds of missing person cases across Canada. Quebec, Ontario, and British Columbia in particular have hundreds of unidentified human remains that could potentially be linked to missing person cases across Canada. For instance, unidentified remains in Vancouver could be those of a missing person from Winnipeg. If this person had sought health care in British Columbia, it might be possible to solve the case. A National DNA data bank might accomplish the same results, but much more slowly and only with respect to human remains, not in cases where the missing person is still alive. Access to health records could provide closure for families of missing loved ones and could potentially allow police to find patterns that would identify serial murder victims and suspects. Health information, however, is very personal and is not likely to be opened for public use.

How search warrants are processed is another example of dramatic changes that have occurred over the past twenty years. In my first years on the job I recall working with senior officers who had experience in vice and drug work. On occasion we received intelligence from informants and sources who provided grounds for search warrants. We would meet with a magistrate to report what we knew and swear as to the validity of the information. The magistrate would then assist us in typing the grounds for the warrant in the box on the information section of the affidavit form. The information would be approximately one paragraph long, sized to fit into the box on the form. Over the years, the courts have placed more and more requirements on the police, to the point that search warrants are now a highly technical and complex process. The box on the form that used to contain the entire body of information now usually contains only the words "See attached appendix."

I received special training in order to become designated by the attorney general as an affiant, with authority to apply for warrants to intercept private communications under the Privacy Act. As such, I was trained and had experience in obtaining numerous types of warrants and authorizations. The average straightforward Information to Obtain (ITO) is ten to twenty pages long. In the past, we simply stated words to the effect that I am a police officer and

I believe there are illegal (drugs, weapons, stolen property, etc.) at such and such a place and this is why I believe they are there. Now we must present much more information. Affidavits today basically contain a prima facie case that includes enough information to take a person to trial.

Our search warrants for child pornography and computer equipment for the ICE Unit were fifty to eighty pages long and included full legal definitions of all forms of computer equipment, the current case law defining child pornography, the history of this type of investigation, information on how we planned to conduct this particular investigation, the grounds on which it was believed that the evidence would be at a certain location, and full details of the entire investigation. Larger affidavits like Privacy Act applications can be hundreds of pages long and include full details of how the investigations will be conducted, the rationale for sealing the order from disclosure in order to protect informants or ongoing investigations, and the requirement for rewrites and updates as the investigation unfolds.

Writing search warrants used to be a basic skill that every detective needed to learn. Within a couple of months into your first detective assignment, you would be mentored through writing one and then your competence and confidence would grow from there. Over the past fifteen years writing search warrant ITOs has become a highly specialized skill. The requirements are so stringent that specialized training courses are required, and certain officers with an aptitude for writing ITOs tend to become "the affiant" for whichever unit they are in.

In contrast to twenty years ago, preparing search warrants now takes the police off the road for long periods of time and ties up substantial resources. For instance, the WPS regularly have large numbers of officers tied up "holding" a residence suspected to contain illegal drugs, weapons, or stolen property while a team of officers are in a police station writing an ITO for a search warrant that they hope will not be turned down by a magistrate. The officers writing the ITO worry about the wording of a search warrant and its possible rejection while large numbers of police officers are guarding a scene or waiting for hours to execute the warrant. This stress escalates for high-risk warrants as numerous specialty units and resources are required; these could include a senior officer acting as incident commander, tactical units, negotiators, dog units, locksmiths, command post operators, detectives, general patrol units, and others.

I have been in that position dozens of times, having numerous officers securing a residence and specialty teams waiting in the station, making tactical plans to execute the warrant, while I am at the courthouse trying to get it approved. There is relief when the warrant is issued, and the victory call to the office, "OK, good to go, see you in twenty." Then you start hoping that the information was good, and that you got the warrant before the drugs, weapons, or stolen property disappeared and that you will not be embarrassed if the search comes up empty.

There have been cases where the drugs, weapons, or stolen property are gone by the time the warrant is executed. But that is not nearly as embarrassing as searching the wrong house, which has happened (thankfully not to me). Looking at the execution of warrants also provides insight into the kind of balance and discipline that police officers must have in the execution of their duties. They may be executing a search warrant for weapons in a gang house, but there may also be completely uninvolved innocent people at that address. We commonly call uninvolved people "found-ins." The police have to tackle the task tactically to ensure the safety of the suspects and officers while simultaneously treating all people as innocent and protecting everyone's rights, while also recognizing that anyone can be a threat. Once the door is breached the police may find that the inhabitants have weapons, are extremely tough and violent and just waiting for an opportunity to stab or shoot an officer or destroy evidence – or they may be completely innocent. It is not like the movies, where the good guys and the bad guys are usually clearly identified.

The difference between great success and embarrassment – or worse – often comes down to police officers' skills and judgment in another fundamental aspect of policing: informant handling. Some of the worst scandals that have ruined officers' careers have occurred due to the necessary evil of confidential informants. The officer who was the WPS outlaw motorcycle gang coordinator for many years used to say "You don't get information about crime by hanging around a church." Some of the most effective proactive cops have been successful because they can think like criminals, speak their language, and relate to them. The problems start when they begin to act like them as well, usually in attempts to take down bigger criminals. The profession has lost officers to the other side but there are also far more cases in which officers became casualties as a result of their passion for fighting crime, getting themselves in trouble by taking short-cuts or risks in order to catch criminals.

There are police officers out there at all hours of each day, in back alleys and bars, meeting with people they would rather not talk to, even befriending them, in order to gather information that will help them take action against criminals. After my years in the Anti-Crime Tactical Unit, I was relieved to get cleaned up and shave off the beard and put a uniform back on. It is amazing how differently people treat you when you are clean-shaven and wearing a suit and tie as opposed to wearing casual or tattered clothes and sporting a rough-looking full beard and long hair.

Most people probably do not realize that judges, magistrates, and lawyers also make sacrifices in order to perform their jobs. On many occasions, I have been in a magistrate's home in the middle of the night, swearing out ITOs for search warrants. On one occasion where a young child had been killed I swore the ITO for a general warrant to search the house in which the child was killed to a judge who had come into the courthouse in the middle of the night to sign the search warrant.

In rural Manitoba, the magistrate or justice of the peace is often an upstanding citizen such as a schoolteacher or a local businessperson. In Thompson, Manitoba, where I had gone with the ICE unit, we had to ask the magistrate to come from home to the local RCMP detachment for me to swear a search warrant for child pornography. I was surprised to learn that magistrates are paid a pittance for performing this civic duty, something in the neighbourhood of $20 for being called out in the middle of the night to sign a warrant. They accept the responsibility of authorizing a warrant as part of their civic duty, while also accepting the risk of being challenged or publicly embarrassed in court because of a warrant they have authorized. Having a respected citizen act as magistrate, a system that has not changed for decades, is clearly a direct descendant of Canada's early settlement and the establishment of European-style law and order.

The police also call Crown prosecutors at all hours of the day and night for consultation on charges, warrants, and legal issues. On one occasion in 2009, I was called in from home on a Sunday regarding a case in which a child had been abducted from Winnipeg; the airport police were warned and the abductor and child were stopped in Britain en route to Russia. I had to ask a director of public prosecutions to come into a police station from home on a Sunday to sign international interdiction agreements in order to bring both the abductor and child back to Canada. This was a tense situation because the British authorities in London were threatening to release the abductor and the child if we did not get the orders drawn up and signed by the proper authorities and faxed to the RCMP liaison in Ottawa and to the authorities in Britain within a few hours. We knew that if the abductor was released she would disappear with the child and never be seen again. We found a director, sent all the paperwork, and had the abductor and child back within a day. This is one example of the partnership between the police and prosecuting attorneys, as well as of the effects of globalization on policing.

Prosecutors should be given due credit for the tireless dedication and public service that they bring to the justice system. They are generally overworked, often earn less than their colleagues in private practice, and are honourable in their concern for victims and their commitment to teamwork with the police. It is clearly a tough job and I believe that many prosecutors could have a much easier career in other aspects of the practice of law. It seems to me that many of them continue to work as prosecutors out of their passion for seeking justice. That being said, at least prosecutors have job security and benefits. Many defence lawyers have extremely difficult jobs, always on-call and dealing with clients who are accused of criminal acts, often in a crisis situation. I have met many honourable defence lawyers who have described criminal law as a tough career choice compared to other specialty areas within the legal profession.

Science and police investigative techniques have changed significantly. Most notably, computer science and the capacity to record DNA have altered the legal landscape by expanding our capacity to gather and analyze information and to link people positively with crime scenes. We now have analytical tools with significant capacity but lack the human resources to use them to their full potential; twenty years ago we had staff resources that exceeded the capacity of technological tools.

Many uses can be envisioned for new technologies. The greatest challenge, however, is not in capturing or gathering information but in figuring out what to do with the information once it is captured. This takes management, analysis, interpretation of data, and then planning what to do with the information; in other words it takes human resources. As with all aspects of policing, it comes down to deciding how we can get the best results with limited resources and competing priorities. Do we take detectives off the road to gather and analyze crime data? Some organizations have dedicated a great many resources to analysis while others preferring to use traditional hands-on policing tactics. There are potential research opportunities in the use and effectiveness of analysis and the related outcomes of analytical resource allocation in policing.

Traditionally, and today, fingerprint analysis has been considered the only infallible form of positive human identification, although other methods, such as retinal scanning and DNA analysis, are being used more often. Fingerprints have been accepted as unique to each human and therefore of use in criminal investigations for at least a hundred years (Dror 2006). A positive match can place a person at a crime scene where their print was left and later lifted by an identification specialist.

The weakness in the identification process is the expert who makes the identification. Some research has suggested that the context in which prints are identified can influence expert opinions, thus rendering them fallible. Research has also found that experts can occasionally succumb to pressure to make an identification (Dror 2006; Lack 2006; Randerson 2007). Canadian identification specialists are held to such a high standard that one wrong identification gets them transferred immediately out of the identification field, even if they had worked in it for many years and had extensive training.

DNA analysis is another area where the science has created more opportunities than existing resources can handle. While DNA comparisons are often thought to produce positive results, they actually only propose probabilities that need expert interpretation. Lab fees are expensive, the reports can take many months to return, and DNA experts have to be included on witness lists for trials, which often requires travel expenses. Therefore, DNA analysis is not used for less serious crimes. For example, there are many cases where blood is left at a scene but it is not analyzed because DNA analytical resources are not available due to the expense and the overburdened state of the laboratory system.

The RCMP manages the national DNA laboratory for all Canadian police agencies. The increased use of DNA across the country has resulted in a backlog, which has led to lengthy wait times and heavy restrictions on what samples the laboratory will analyze. Use of the RCMP laboratory has become so restricted that police forces are often using private laboratories, which are faster – taking perhaps six weeks instead of six months – but more expensive.

The RCMP is protective of their monopoly on the DNA analysis system in Canada and will not compare results from private laboratories with samples that are on file in their databases. Therefore, some thought needs to go into the decision to use a private laboratory. If you are interested in comparing two or more samples that are in your possession, then a private laboratory can do it. If you have one sample and want to compare it to samples obtained from dangerous offenders across Canada, for instance, then you need to run the new sample through the RCMP as well, no matter how long it takes. The worry is that the wrong people could be suspected of crimes during the course of an investigation that could have been concluded if the laboratory result had been obtained sooner. Also, more people could be victimized by an offender while we are waiting months for lab results that will provide us with the grounds we need to make an arrest. While it is on every police officer's wish list, quick DNA analysis is not yet on the horizon (Speier 2011).

While the streets have become more violent and dangerous, technology has improved officer safety. When I started two decades ago, we had mobile data terminals (MDTs) in the cruiser cars, which had a five-inch square screen like a small computer into which we could type basic information. This was advanced technology compared to what the previous generation had, which was simply buttons that indicated your status as dispatched, en route, arrived, or cleared. We could also type in basic information to update a police report. We used to clear a call on a "code one" or "code two." Code two meant no report was required. For example, in the case of a neighbour dispute over a fence, we could type in "Appropriate advice given, NFPAR" (no further police action required). This information would be available to police units that might be dispatched to the same address again in the future. Code one meant a typed report would be completed later in the station. Now cruiser cars have mounted laptops with full functionality to interface with all of the police systems that can be accessed from police offices. These include internal, local, national, and international databases that can answer queries within minutes on criminal records, driver's licence status, vehicle insurance, and even international warrants. Twenty years ago the only information we had at a scene was whatever we could garner through a phone call or on the radio. Often, we would call our clerks who were connected to the Canadian Police Information Centre (CPIC), and they could tell us if a person was wanted or not and if they had a criminal record. Other than that, we were on our own for information. The challenge now is for officers to remain aware of their surroundings and not to become so absorbed in the computer and cellphone equipment that they become vulnerable to the dangers of wearing a uniform out on the street.

Cruiser cars now also have GPS, so that dispatchers and duty officers can see the locations of responding units. In 2011, the WPS added a helicopter. Video from the helicopter streams into the duty office or to other locations so that commanders on the ground can make tactical decisions while watching real-time videos from the air.

Technology cuts both ways; it is working for the police and also deeply affecting our work. Technology has advanced to the point that high-quality miniature video and audio recording devices are readily available to the public. Canadians now carry smartphones that have higher quality recording equipment than was available to police surveillance operations twenty years ago. Officers involved in police actions in the community may see a recording of themselves on YouTube before they get back to the police station to start writing the incident report. Officers are always aware that gang members, gang-houses, and cars are often wired for audio and/or video recordings that could eventually show up in court, in the media, or on the Internet. Compared to twenty years ago, this is an entirely different reality for police officers.

Technology has also collapsed jurisdictions and expanded local police mandates. As this book was being revised for publication the WPS and sister agencies across Canada were exploring various ways to increase interactions with the public by using social media. Social networking sites such as Facebook and Twitter have significant potential for improving community interface and investigations. At the First Nations Police Chiefs conference in Winnipeg in May 2012, Sergeant Jackie George of the Nishnawbe-Aski Police Service described how her organization was connecting with remote communities in Northern Ontario thorough social networking sites. She told a story about a time when she flew to a small, remote community. While there, a community basketball game in which she had been invited to participate was repeatedly postponed. When she finally asked why people were not showing up at the school for the game, she was told that the Internet was down, so there was no way to call everyone to the game. The interesting thing, said Sergeant George, was that the community was so small that someone could have gone door to door and talked to everyone. The community had become so reliant on the Internet that the simple solution of talking to each other hadn't even been considered. She described how people are Tweeting and Facebooking around the clock and reported that in many cases her police agency deliberately does not respond immediately to information on social networking sites because they need to discourage people from using such sites rather than emergency dispatch systems to request police response to urgent situations.

The Internet has incredible untapped potential to improve communication. Social networks that expand upon the already massive information-sharing value of the Internet need to be utilized more by police agencies. Criminals certainly are using them. The next section briefly outlines some of the impacts and implications of globalization and the Internet.

GLOBALIZATION, BORDERLESS CRIME, AND TERRORISM

Terrorism, Internet-based child exploitation, international fraud, and a wide range of other borderless crimes are a new feature of law enforcement in the twenty-first century. Municipal police forces can no longer effectively handle all of the crime that occurs within their jurisdictions in isolation from the larger global community. Police can no longer afford to think that criminals acting outside their agency's jurisdiction do not affect them. This was illustrated on a national level in June 2006 when seventeen Canadian citizens were arrested in Toronto as part of a global terrorist conspiracy spanning many countries. Police thwarted their plan to bomb Canadian targets using three times the quantity of explosives used in the massive bombing of the Oklahoma federal building in 1995 (Bell and Kelley 2006). The only way for modern law enforcement to effectively combat borderless crime is to join forces.

The Internet has connected people globally; predators and criminals now have a way into many Canadian homes and offices through Internet access points. Web-based child exploitation, trafficking in drugs, weapons, and human beings, fraud, and terrorism have become truly global crimes, with no jurisdictional boundaries. Computer hackers engage in corporate espionage and fraud, using what we in policing sometimes refer to as "war marks" to indicate places where unprotected wireless Internet ports can be accessed in businesses and homes. They note the locations where they can return for free Internet access or to conduct their hacking activities.

Effective investigation in these areas requires new techniques, greater communication, and innovative inter-agency strategies. Police services are no longer responsible only for what happens within their boundaries. They have to rely on help from outside agencies to detect and investigate crime that is occurring in their own back yards and they have a corresponding duty to protect others at a distance. Police officers twenty years ago operated in much more localized environments, with true jurisdictions. Now an officer in one country may come across information that can solve crimes or prevent victimization in other countries, anywhere in the world.

Manitoba's internationally recognized Integrated Child Exploitation (ICE) Unit was an example of effective inter-agency police teamwork. Our unit, which was the first of its kind, became the model for ICE units that were later developed across Canada. However, initiatives like this are often context-specific. In the first few years, and with the people involved during that time, it was highly successful. Within five years of being founded, however, that changed; the unit was disbanded, for a variety of reasons, largely tied to issues related to different organizational cultures.

At the outset, the ICE unit was able to overcome the typical organizational problems with integration that have caused the demise of many previous joint task forces. The project was recognized nationally as a success not only because of the innovative techniques that were developed and implemented by the unit members but for overcoming traditional organizational culture differences and forming a truly integrated team. In fact, it was such a significant accomplishment that our unit was awarded the RCMP Commissioner's Ensign Award, which is given to police units that contribute innovative techniques to Canadian policing. This success was a result of the open-minded and flexible support of senior leadership in the WPS, RCMP, and Brandon Police Service. More significantly, the members involved all had the selfless, non-territorial attitude that made the initial team a success. This attitude affected all the members of the team, to the point that a psychologist, engaged to work with the ICE Unit and regularly debrief its members in order to reduce the impact of the deeply disturbing materials we were working with, was impressed that he could not tell the municipal police officers from the RCMP officers.

Overcoming the tensions inherent in multi-jurisdictional task forces was difficult. While I was part of the ICE Unit, I recall speaking with a senior WPS sergeant who had been in numerous previous joint police agency task forces, mainly to do with organized crime. To my astonishment, he outlined exactly the frustrations that we were going through in the ICE Unit. The issues all involved the challenges of integrating two or more organization cultures that in some ways did not mix well. For instance, WPS members had a much easier time getting authorization to take action as our entire chain of command was close by. The RCMP, on the other hand, often had to seek approval through a more involved process, sometimes all the way back to Ottawa. This situation could cause frustration as the municipal members might want to act, whether it be making an arrest, talking to the media, starting a new initiative, using new technology, or suggesting a new direction for the unit, and could be held up by the RCMP side. At the same time, the federal RCMP members could become frustrated by the municipal members impetuousness.

The ICE unit illustrates the global nature of many aspects of modern policing. For example, there is a small police unit in Wiesbaden, Germany, that actively investigates Internet child pornography. On one occasion they sent a package to Winnipeg with DVDs containing transactions involving trading images of child pornography over the Internet that an undercover officer had engaged in with an unknown person. I volunteered to do the follow-up investigation.

The package from Germany contained pornographic images that had been sent to the unknown person through the Internet in exchange for hard-core child pornography. The Internet Service Provider (ISP) for the person who had sent the child pornography to Germany was traced to the Manitoba Telecom Services. I obtained a search warrant for the subscriber information, which turned out to be located in Winnipeg, and then obtained a search warrant for the subscriber's house. The resulting seizure was among the largest made in Canada to that time, with several hundred thousand images of child sexual abuse confiscated. The suspect had gathered collections of child pornography and meticulously organized them into groups of compact discs. He had also gathered information about a number of Winnipeg women he was stalking. He had images of the women, fantasies he had written about them, and maps to their homes. In this case communication through the Internet by a police officer in an office in Germany resulted in women and children being protected from a sexual predator in Winnipeg.

Today it is not uncommon for investigations to span the globe and involve simultaneous cooperation between numerous countries and agencies. Criminals, however, operate without the constraints of laws, treaties, jurisdictions, political boundaries, bureaucracies, or operating budgets. Major issues such as the investigation of terrorism and global crime have therefore, become a concern for every local law enforcement agency, as well as their national counterparts. No agency can tackle issues that affect their jurisdiction from outside their borders without cooperation with others.

Events in England shed light on the reality of terrorist threat levels in Canada. Former British Prime Minister Tony Blair's Intelligence and Security Committee Report into the London terrorist attacks in 2005 outlined how four Islamic extremist suicide bombers simultaneously killed themselves on three crowded subways and a double decker bus, killing fifty-two innocent people and injuring hundreds more. The inquiry's findings reinforced conventional wisdom in the field of counter-terrorism, that terrorism is a global threat and is not restricted to one set of borders (Murphy 2006). The British home secretary at the time, Dr John Reid, said the inquiry revealed a need for better international cooperation against borderless groups that pose global threats, as well as greater community-level preparedness to support victims of terrorism (Reid 2006). This points to the need for not only better cooperation between all levels of government within Canada in emergency preparedness but for international cooperation in identifying and thwarting terrorist threats.

Contrary to what many may wish to believe, Canada is not immune to terrorist threats. In a presentation on his work investigating the London subway bombings to senior emergency services managers in Winnipeg in 2005, Andrew Clancy of New Scotland Yard's Counter-Terrorist Intelligence Section stated that the threat of suicide bombings by extremists is expected to carry on for another forty years. He stressed the fact that this is an international phenomenon and that Winnipeg·and all of Canada are at risk as much as any other places in the world.

Dame Eliza Manningham Buller, director-general of the British Security Service MI5, said publicly that in 2006 the British Government was tracking 1,600 terrorists and investigating thirty different plots to kill people and damage the economy (Freeze 2006). Martin Rudner, a counter-terrorism expert at Carleton University in Ottawa, responded that the threat of terrorism is recognized as existing in Canada as well. The Canadian Security Intelligence Service (CSIS) is known to have been tracking 274 terrorism suspects in 2005 (ibid.). In 2003, over 10,000 Tamil terrorist suspects were believed to be living in Canada. Some have become involved in street crime, for instance joining gangs in Toronto, while others are believed to be living peacefully, but could be called into active service at any time by their former organizations (Pugliese 2003).

Sir Peter St John, an international expert on terrorism and counter-insurgency, discussed these emerging global threats in Winnipeg in November 2006 and 2010, reporting on them to local and federal police members, and numerous other agencies involved in national and local security and disaster response. He focused on the Internet as a tool that increases the international networking capacity of terrorists, increasing their ability to communicate and plan with counterparts throughout the world. At the same conferences, Thomas Marks, chief counter-terrorism officer, military intelligence, United States Armed Forces, reported that Canada's increased military commitments in Afghanistan and other parts of the Middle East have raised its international profile as a target for terrorist threats at home and abroad.

After the 2006 arrest of seventeen terrorist suspects in Toronto, RCMP Assistant Commissioner Mike McDonell noted that the group posed a real threat and had "the capacity and intent to carry out these attacks" (Bell and Kelly 2006). This clearly illustrates that terrorism is a concern for Canadian police agencies. While the CSIS, the RCMP counter-terrorism groups, military, and international partners in the intelligence field will gather information and investigate suspected terrorists, it is frontline police officers who are most likely to encounter them in the field. Increased training and awareness in this area will be needed, as well as improved integration between frontline policing and mandated specialist agencies and intelligence networks. In addition, there needs to be better cooperation on the technological front as police forensic computer technicians are also likely to encounter terrorist activity in their criminal investigations.

Even before the 9/11 terrorist attacks in New York City, Frittelli (2005) had provided an overview of issues surrounding terrorist threats related to air, land, and marine travel and cargo transport systems in the United States, drawing attention to the issue of security as a weakness within these systems. Retired Justice of the Supreme Court of Canada Frank Iacobucci has described how terrorism paradigms have changed. Historically, terrorism was conducted for narrow political objectives, attempting to force a government to respond to specific issues. For example, in Northern Ireland the Irish Republican Army attempted to persuade the British government to take specific actions. The new Islam-based terrorism does not have such a narrow political focus but instead threatens "the entire democratic world" (Iacobucci 2010, 189).

The possibility of terrorism must become part of our community vulnerability assessments and emergency plans. In recent decades researchers have reported an increase in both natural and human-induced disasters around the world (Cornall 2005). The initial front-line response to a disaster, such as a major explosion, is essentially the same regardless of the cause. However, there is much room for improvement in this area. Emergency services must focus on improving coordination to ensure multi-agency emergency preparedness, mitigation, response, and recovery from disasters. The more prepared we are to manage catastrophes, whether they are human-induced or a result of a force of nature, the better off we will be. In their book *Risk Issues and Crisis Management: A Casebook of Best Practice*, Regester and Larkin (2005) aptly pointed out that Noah started building the Ark before the rain came.

Technological advances have changed police tactics and accountability. They have also changed the demands on officers who must be able to use or at least understand new technology and tools as they emerge. New generations of officers are well equipped in this respect, as the majority of young adults have been raised on a steady diet of computer gaming and Internet-based social networking. They are better equipped for the modern technological sea of change that has baffled many baby boomers who started their careers with manual typewriters, pencils and erasers, and telephones that had to be plugged into a wall jack. The next chapter explores how police demographics have changed, and the related impacts on policing.

5

Demographics: How the Police Have Changed

THE NEW INTERGENERATIONAL WORKPLACE

The Great Depression of the 1930s was followed by a population explosion. After the Second World War, economic conditions improved, Canadians married younger, and birth rates increased proportionately. Annual birth rates in Canada rose from 253,000 in 1940 to 479,000 in 1960. Within twenty-five years, the baby boom had produced about one and a half million births more than the norm in previous decades. By 1965, people began marrying later, birth control methods improved, more women entered the workforce, and the birthrate dropped (Krotki and Henropin 2006).

The "baby boomers" were born between 1946 and 1965. By 2031, most of them will have retired from the workforce. This population bulge has major implications for workforce continuity. By 2016, the median age of Canadian citizens will be forty, whereas in 1994 it was thirty-four (Krotki and Henropin 2006). In 2011, 46 percent of Canada's workforce was sixty-five or above (Rose 2006). Many Canadian corporations are losing about half of their managers to retirement in this decade. Organizations are losing significant corporate knowledge and experience. In 2012, the Bank of Canada warned that by 2031 one in four Canadians will be over age sixty-five and it has been suggested that failure to make adjustments to deal with Canada's aging population may result in a lower standard of living in Canada (Pona 2012).

Corporate memory retention is particularly important in policing, a profession that is continually changing as social issues change. For example, if projects have failed in the past or led to problems in court, experienced people can correct the course of action before mistakes are repeated. The technology I mentioned earlier is a good example of lessons learned. You can spend all of the money in the world on crime analysis and database tools, but if you do not have sufficient human resources to enter the data and then make use of it, the technology will simply collect dust. Pitfalls like this are hard to predict unless experienced people are around to identify them.

Public administrators also cite the intergenerational issues resulting from generations X, Y, and baby boomers co-existing in the workplace as one of the greatest challenges to management in the twenty-first century (Weitzel 2004). Executive-level leadership is at a tipping point of change (Gladwell 2002). The large group of retiring police officers is being pushed from below by a critical mass of officers who have less experience and different worldviews.

While it is important to emphasize that people are individuals, there are some common characteristics that can assist us in understanding the differences between generational groups. The bulk of replacements for the mass exodus of baby boomers will be from Generation X, born between 1966 and 1980. Ondeck (2002) describes the cultural characteristics of Generation X as being generally intolerant of bureaucracy, cynical and not very serious about themselves, creative and valuable in the workplace, with a need to focus on soft skills. Generation Y people, born from about 1980 on, are currently in their early thirties and beginning to establish themselves in leadership positions in the work force (Kusch 2006). Those in Generation Y are influenced by an increased awareness of technology and of the uncertainty caused by international terrorism, street violence, and borderless crime. They also have greater technical understanding than their predecessors – Ondeck describes this group as masters of technical skills. They watched their parents and friends go though the uncertainty associated with corporate downsizing of the 1980s and 1990s and have a different sense of loyalty to their employers. According to Ondeck, Generation Y people are inexperienced and need supervision and structure, but are generally good employees who prefer working in environments that are comfortable and non-bureaucratic (Ondeck 2002). This group is affecting the makeup of the workforce and changing organizational cultures.

New Generation X and Y police officers are contextual learners who need to understand the reasons for policy and practice. They routinely question the validity of the duties they are assigned. This new breed of police officer does not respond well to the rigid, auto-cratic, "just follow orders" management style of the stereotyped, tough, post–Second World War veteran desk sergeants. They, for the most part, were white men with only a high school education or less and who had worked within a social and organizational milieu that was less complex than it is today. I say "tough" because back then the organizational culture was different. Young officers feared their ser-geants and respected their rank. Now, ranks are still significant but the nature of our communication is different. Effective police super-visors today must be sensitive to changing demographics and diver-sity within their organizations and be ready to manage accordingly.

Young police officers are interested in their benefits and what their union is doing in collective bargaining. When I started in 1989, I was more interested in learning the job and building a career and was satisfied with a smaller beginning salary. I ate, lived, and breathed policing, and could not get enough of it. More recently, it is not unusual to hear new officers planning their retirements in their first few years, a phenomenon that surprises many senior officers. In my first year on the job, I referred to everyone by his or her rank. I recall my sergeant saying, "Bob, when you are finished probation [which was one year long at that time] you can call me by my name." The work environment seems much less formal now. The respect for rank is still there, but decisions and orders are much more open to interpretation and debate than they were twenty years ago.

Intergenerational issues are a major concern in modern manage-ment. The majority of senior supervisors in 2012 are baby boomers who often express frustration with the apparent lack of commitment in the new generation. They cannot understand why so many younger people are reluctant to work overtime. On the other hand, younger people tend to value work-life balance and cannot understand why the older generation would stay in one job for life. Generation X and Generation Y individuals cannot understand why older people would quit a job rather than learn how to use computers (Ondeck 2002). In policing as in all sectors, modern leaders need to find common ground for effective communication between the generations.

The police occupation has become a portable, transferable skill set. Two decades ago, many Canadian police agencies protected their training investments through informal agreements to not hire trained officers away from each other. It was rare for police officers to move between agencies. Loss of the investment of over $100,000 required to train an officer is particularly hard on organizations such as the WPS, where wages and benefits are paid from the first day of recruit class (Winnipeg Police Service 2006). This is a smaller problem on the east and west coasts of Canada, where prospective officers are required to pay for and complete a degree or diploma in law enforcement at a regional post-secondary institution before they are considered for employment by police agencies. Agencies now compete with each other for good applicants, and it is not uncommon for graduating recruits to receive job offers from other police agencies. In the past, this was unheard of. Some Canadian police forces, such as Calgary, have actively recruited in the United Kingdom.

Experienced officers are highly valued. Some agencies are even offering wage parity and guaranteed assignments and rank as incentives to officers who are willing to relocate. This can potentially affect training practices, as services must now carefully consider their investment in officer training and the potential liability if new officers were to suddenly leave. Smart police services have built redundancy into critical roles, so that someone is mentored and prepared to step into every role and no member is indispensable. This is achieved through a focus on mentoring and transfer policies that prevent people from staying too long in specialty assignments as well as ensuring they can return to uniform duties and share their skills and knowledge.

BRAIN DRAIN AND SUCCESSION PLANNING

Canadian corporations, including police services, are experiencing significant loss of corporate knowledge and experience as a result of mass retirements. Recruiting qualified replacement officers has become a real challenge. In the WPS, for example, a recruit class of twenty-four per year was typical up to the late 1990s. In 1989, 4,000 initial applications were screened to fill twenty-four seats in a recruit class. The Police Service has received fewer qualified applicants in successive years. In 2004, forty-seven recruits were selected from 957 applicants (Winnipeg Police Service 2005). By 2005, the organization began running classes with empty seats because of a shortage of qualified applicants. This continual decline in the number of applicants has precipitated debates over whether recruiting standards have been, or should be, lowered in order to fill training classes and to meet organizational requirements.

In 2012, WPS standards are still seen as high but filling recruit classes is increasingly difficult. Members in other Canadian police organizations have expressed concerns that standards may have been compromised by the challenges of hiring qualified recruits. Perceived changes in standards have several impacts. Frontline officers can have reservations and doubts about new officers with whom they will be working and on whom they must rely in life-and-death situations if they are suspected of being substandard. An even more significant concern is the sensitive work and risks that officers share. The inference that new officers are substandard or were hired under a compromised standard could give newly hired officers the feeling that they need to prove themselves – a feeling that could last an entire career.

Police organizations in particular have liabilities that are directly linked to the performance of each individual officer. One decision by a single officer in the field can cause years of litigation and create case law that puts constraints upon police agencies and officers across Canada.

One example of a case that changed constraints on policing is *Regina vs. Feeney* (Supreme Court of Canada 1997). An officer arrested a person in his home for an offence that had occurred earlier. The courts later ruled that the officer required a warrant to enter the person's residence in order to make the arrest. The officer had not done anything that was considered wrong at the time of his action, but this one incident resulted in changes to tactics and policy for police agencies nationally. After the *Feeney* decision, officers across Canada were required to seek entry warrants when they planned to arrest persons in their homes, which has had a major effect on policing because of the time and work involved. For example, twenty years ago officers responding to an assault complaint that gave them grounds to arrest someone would simply arrest the suspect. If the arrested person met conditions of the Bail Reform Act, they would be fingerprinted or given an appointment to get their fingerprints taken at a later time and given an appearance notice or a promise to appear at court and then released. In busy times, officers could do this process quickly and get back on the street. The reports would be required weeks later, before court. In the case of serious charges or reverse onus, where the accused must convince the magistrate that they will show up in court if they are released, the report would have to be done immediately, as the information would be required for bail court. Reverse onus occurs in situations such as when the accused lives in a different jurisdiction. In my years of uniform patrol duty, it was not uncommon to make three or four separate arrests on any given workday with people released on appearance notices or promises to appear.

After *Feeney*, police involved in the same scenario were required to take a report from a victim, return to the station for several hours to investigate and articulate in an affidavit their grounds for believing that the suspect is in a certain residence and why they need to enter the residence to arrest him, and complete an arrest warrant application. Officers then need to attend the courthouse to swear an ITO and have an arrest warrant issued. Only then can they start seeking to arrest the suspect. If a serious offence where public safety or loss of evidence is at risk is involved, officers have to have colleagues guard the house where the suspect is until they can obtain the required *Feeney* warrant for entry and execution of the arrest warrant. It would be interesting to analyze how many officer-hours this one court decision has consumed across Canada. Officers who are newer to the police service do not know that there is a different way to handle such situations, but veteran officers are often frustrated because they remember earlier times when police resources were not tied up in these complex administrative processes.

As a result of "brain drain" resulting from mass retirements, succession planning, training, and successful recruitment have become crucial aspects of effective police management. Problems associated with sharp demographic changes are exacerbated in policing, in comparison with other professions, because of the accelerated retirement plans in the police. Canadian police officers generally retire after twenty-five to thirty years of service (Seagrave 1997). Some agencies, such as the WPS, have an optional reduced pension, which enables retirement after twenty years. In 2011, over 20 percent of the over 1,300 sworn police officers comprising the WPS were eligible to retire. Replacement and succession planning will continue to be a challenge in coming years.

The WPS is typical of police agencies across Canada. For decades leading up to 2000, the WPS hired and trained one recruit class, consisting of twenty-four officers, every year. From 2000 onward, the WPS has fielded one or two classes of forty-eight recruits every year. This is up to four times the number of officers that were traditionally required to maintain the per capita complement, not counting occasional increases. The problem is even more pronounced in

centres such as Calgary, which had an economic boom in the early
1980s and hired hundreds of officers, meaning they will have a large
number of people reaching retirement at the same time. Human
resource challenges are one of the most pressing issues for governments today.

In speaking with my colleagues in Dallas, Texas, I learned that in
Texas they are aggressively attacking this mass retirement problem
through incentives to stay on the job. In Dallas, any officer who is
eligible to retire can draw their pension and stay on the job. The
rationale is that they save the costs of training new replacement officers and, therefore, it is cost effective for the police service to pay the
pension as well as full wages to officers. My counterpart, a sergeant
with thirty years of experience, would "drop" (as they call it) and
start receiving his pension while remaining in his usual job. The
police agencies prosper by retaining an experienced officer who
might otherwise retire. This is the type of aggressive retention planning that Canadian agencies may soon need to explore. The RCMP
in Manitoba have started hiring back retired officers for duties such
as highway patrol for six months a year during peak seasons. The
WPS has also started hiring back retired members to conduct recruit
background investigations.

Scholars have argued that downsizing, restructuring, labour issues,
and changing composition and demands are the four factors that
affect public service capacity (Ingraham, Peters, and Moynihan
2000). Agencies require the capacity to recruit, hire, and retain the
right people. Yet leaders often fail to see the importance of human
resource management (Frechette et al. 2007). John McFerran, chief
operating officer of People First Human Resources Services, describes
most corporations as failing at succession planning. He writes that
nearly half of American corporations with revenues exceeding
$500 million have no substantial succession plans, despite being
aware of the impending mass exodus of baby boomers. McFerran
also emphasizes the need for leadership development, which requires
long-term mentoring and extensive work experience (McFerran
2006). Police agencies must identify the key roles that need to be
filled and actively develop officers who can take on these responsibilities before those now handling them retire. Decreasing seniority
will soon create a scenario where executive leaders will be selected
from a less experienced pool of candidates (Ehrich and Hansford

1999). Organizations also miss valuable opportunities when they fail to conduct exit interviews with retiring members.

Leadership potential should be continuously assessed and developed early in a police officer's career, not after they have been successful in their first competition for promotion, which in the wps generally occurs after at least ten years of service. Development should include support and encouragement for officers capable of and motivated to seek advanced formal education. Human resource departments need to coordinate leadership development training, mentorship, and challenging assignments in order to push people out of their comfort zones and give them the experience they need to develop as leaders.

Many police agencies have a human resource strategy of replacement rather than succession planning. These strategies are often entrenched in collective bargaining agreements and are therefore difficult to change. When positions need to be filled, a competition is held and the most qualified candidates are selected to fill the vacancies. If a person is selected to fill a position only once it has been vacated, there is little if any opportunity for mentoring or advance training for the job. By identifying key positions that will need to be filled several years in advance and identifying the competencies associated with those positions, administrators could select officers with the potential to excel at these jobs and could work toward their development.

Operational planning can also mitigate the liabilities and impacts of reduced experience by, for instance, assigning senior members to work with younger ones. The ongoing debate within police circles on whether to have two or one officer patrol units sheds light on the issue. It is an emotional debate for many officers who feel that their safety may be jeopardized if their agency adopts a one-officer car policy.

The wps is envied by many Canadian law enforcement officers for our policies of minimum street strength and continued use of two-officer patrol units. Minimum street strength means that there are a minimum number of officers on duty at any given time. Many jurisdictions have gone to one-officer units, in part because they create higher visibility among the public as there are twice as many police units on the road (Blake and Coupe 2001; Kessler 1985). Minimum street strength was entrenched in the wps Collective

Agreement after an incident two decades ago, in which an officer refused to go out on patrol, claiming that working conditions were unsafe due to insufficient backup. The resulting labour arbitration ensured that each shift starts with a minimum number of two-officer units and that, if necessary, the agency must call-in sufficient members from home, on overtime, in order to field the required number of field units going on duty. Police officers are in fact called in routinely in order to comply with minimum strengths outlined in the collective agreement.

Many officers attribute Winnipeg's low number of line-of-duty deaths to the use of two-officer units. This is an anecdotal observation, however, and warrants further research. At a minimum, two-officer units during the highest risk overnight hours contribute to reduced risk for officers (Frontier Centre for Public Policy 2001). Research in the United Kingdom has found that in some cases two-officer units can respond more quickly to calls. Jurisdictions that are utilizing one-officer units have found that when two officers are needed, one of the one-officer units inevitably responds from farther away, causing delays (Blake and Coupe 2001). Kessler (1985) found the same situation in similar research in the United States. Del Carmen and Guevara (2003) examined attitudes among officers in fifty different American states, half of which use two-officer teams, while the other half use one-officer units. They found that, overall, officers felt their performance would be the same whether they were working alone or in teams of two. The majority agreed, however, that dangers might be reduced during high-risk overnight hours by having two officers in each car.

One perspective on the debate over two-officer units, which does not seem to be covered in the literature, is the higher risk caused by a sense of duty. Use of one-officer units necessitates policies for officer safety that require officers to wait for backup on high-risk calls. Imagine the inner conflict that an officer experiences if she or he has to remain in the patrol car and await backup while someone is being stabbed, raped, or robbed. The reality is that officers would not wait for backup in many of these cases; most would risk injury rather than wait when someone is being victimized. As a street supervisor I experience this on a daily basis as I work alone and am often required, by policy, to wait for backup before attending high-risk calls. In a case where a child is being assaulted or a vulnerable person is being injured, I do not always wait for backup, though I am directed by policy and reminded by the dispatchers to do so.

An even greater risk is posed by the low-priority service calls that we attend – the ones where complacency can create danger. Seemingly innocuous calls can turn out to be high-risk, like a parking complaint that turns out to be a fight between groups of violent people, or a call for domestic advice that turns out to be a violent domestic fight. There are also dangerous police haters who set traps, hoping to lure a lone officer to deal with an innocuous complaint in order to attack. In 2012 it seemed that almost every day we had to circulate bulletins about police haters who had threatened to attack the police.

Traffic stops are among the most dangerous police activities. For example, in April 2012 a lone Toronto police officer pulled over a car and was viciously stabbed in the neck (Ha 2012). In major centres, officers can call for backup when they find themselves in trouble, and it will be there fairly quickly. The danger is much higher for officers working in rural settings where backup can be hours away. As a result, many departments are resisting going to the perceived higher efficiency of the one-officer unit model (Calgary Herald 2007).

Conventional wisdom in policing holds that many risks can be reduced through effective training. The next chapter discusses training and development for police officers, and how it has changed over the past two decades.

6

Training and Education in Policing

POLICE TRAINING

Police officers from frontline to senior management will find it challenging to remain effective in the modern environment if they do not stay abreast of continually evolving technology, trends, and issues. Good training early in a career sets officers on a path for success in a challenging and dynamic profession. In a paper entitled "Critical Issues In Police Training," Haberfeld (2002), reviewing police recruit training across the United States and Canada, reports that citizen expectations are often unrealistically high. It is important to distinguish between the high expectations people have of officers entrusted with immense power and authority in the interest of public safety and the capabilities of actual individuals and systems. It is one thing to expect officers to be disciplined, highly trained, and ethical. It is quite another to expect the impossible. An example that comes to mind is the question that has come up in court over lethal force issues. Lawyers and even judges have asked questions such as, "Why didn't you shoot him (or her) in the hand, rather than in the centre of the body?" Such an action is nearly impossible for human beings operating in adrenaline-charged situations. Such questioning often occurs even in light of an extensive and growing body of research that has confirmed the physiological reactions officers experience, which are beyond their control during high-stress incidents (Kitaeff 2011; Lindemann 1944; Mantell 1994; Maslach and Jackson 1979; Maslach 1982; Mitchell 1983; Mitchell and Everly 1993; Russell and Beigel 1990; Waters, Irons, and Finkle 1982; Waters and Ussery 2007). These include tunnel vision, where officers focus on one key

element of a situation, such as the gun in the assailan
Auditory exclusion reduces the officer's ability to hear a la
trum of sounds that occur during an event. And time can
slow down so that a period of several seconds can feel to a͟
like minutes or longer (Kitaeff 2011). I have experienced all of these
effects at different times and to various degrees.

One experience that stands out in my memory is the time I was in
an unmarked surveillance car in middle of winter, with snow piled up
on the curbs. A truck tractor pulling a flatbed of steel was also travelling in the same direction I was and took a wide turn across my path.
I was in his mirror blind spot and the driver did not see me. It was icy
and I could not get traction to stop before the flatbed ran me up the
snow-bank – directly into a telephone pole. The flatbed with its load
of steel ran right over my car. The steel toolboxes ripped into my car
before the rear wheels of the truck trailer finally ran over my car. As
the windows popped out and the car was flattened from the back
bumper all the way to the front, I managed to jump out of the passenger side. Luckily the door opened for me or I could not have gotten
out. In the end, the car was so flattened and torn up that you could
not even tell what kind of vehicle it was. The only thing that remained
was the hood ornament from the car; I kept it on my desk for years.

An event that took seconds, felt like minutes. I can recall minute
details about some aspects of that event, while the rest is a blur.
Having been through a lot of high-speed pursuits, I became condi-
tioned to accidents so that I did not get too excited, but even in an
acclimatized state of mind, I experienced the same physiological
responses that often occur in high-stress events. If I had been asked
later about certain specifics that I was unaware of due to physiological
effects during that event, I could have appeared incompetent to
anyone who lacked knowledge of the psychological and physiological effects of stress.

In recent years, the policing profession has become more skilled
and adept at providing such explanations and making use of experts
who can educate people on the fine line between competence and
unrealistic expectations that fail to take into account human fallibil-
ity and capability. We need experts to explain to juries, courts, and
inquiries why an officer involved in an extremely stressful incident
involving lethal force sometimes legitimately cannot recall certain
details. It is not a question of being evasive but the result of a natural
psychological process.

Increased knowledge of police psychology has led police unions and lawyers in many jurisdictions to advise officers who are involved in high-stress incidents to wait for several days before providing their account of an event. This is very difficult for officers, who do not want to slow down investigations of serious incidents. However, it is now recognized that police officers will provide a different, more accurate account of events if they have had a few days to process the occurrence (Beehr et al. 2010).

In my experience, the public expects high levels of professionalism from police officers. The experience and technical expertise that can be developed and applied in policing is immense. Every new assignment is like an entirely new career, with basic policing and leadership skills developing in parallel to the specific demands of each new challenge. Effectiveness in an environment with continuously changing demands requires that modern police officers at all levels be lifelong learners. They need to keep abreast of a wide range of evolving technology and science, case law, justice and social issues, labour law, current affairs, best practices in investigative strategies, cultural and gender sensitivity, and management and leadership trends (Schulenberg and Warren 2009). In addition to policing-specific challenges, modern executives in all areas have similar concerns. A 2011 Institute of Public Administration Canada survey found that Canadian leaders, deputy ministers, and chief administrative officers all share concerns about managing crises, deficits, and working with stakeholders. Ninety percent of those surveyed also highlighted that these growing challenges all hamper long-term planning (David-Evans 2012). All of these demands require ongoing training and education. A growing body of research highlights the need for more training for officers across the broad spectrum of tasks they are called upon to do (Herz 2001; Quinet, Nunn and Kincaid 2003; Vermette, Pinals and Appelbaum 2005).

Research on police training across North America in 1993 found that the most highly trained police recruits receive about 800 hours of instruction, whereas barbers receive 4,000 hours, lawyers 9,000 hours, and doctors 11,000 hours (Edwards 1993). In 2013, twenty years after the Edwards study, police recruits in Winnipeg receive 1,552 hours training in total. This 1,552 hours is comprised of 104 eight-hour days in the academy (832 hours), followed by four months of field training (640 hours), followed by 80 hours additional training in the academy. The field training period is arguably not entirely spent on training as the recruits most often become part of the regular minimum strength compliment, taking calls to clear the queue, rather than having their field training officers select specific types of calls for training purposes. While in field training a recruit should have the opportunity to handle a variety of incidents such as sudden deaths, suicides, medical assists, break and enters, thefts, assaults, assists to other agencies, traffic enforcement and accident investigation, impaired driving, and so on. Sometimes they are so busy being sent to the next emergency that they do not get a chance to take calls for training purposes. I do not have exact numbers from across Canada, but I believe that recruit training is similar in most jurisdictions.

Marta Burczycka, a Statistics Canada analyst who surveyed Canadian police officers, states that police consistently note that their jobs are increasingly complex (Macleod 2011). Research on police training has found that generalist training is provided in recruit classes and then specialist in-service training from a variety of different sources is sought later for specialty assignments (Charles and Copay 2003; Conti and Nolan 2005; Cuttler and Muchinsky 2006; Haarr 2001; Lonsway, Welch, and Fitzgerald 2001; Morrison 2006).

Specialty assignments have also increased in number as a result of the growing demands and complexities of modern policing and there are numerous courses for detectives entering increasingly specialized fields such as sex crimes, child abuse, Internet-based crime investigation, and a long list of others. Management training is also being offered more frequently than it was two decades ago.

In the WPS, officers may receive their first promotion, from constable to patrol sergeant, after eleven to sixteen years of service. They are then sent on a five-day course that covers liability, policy, and administrative issues. Most leadership development before or after this is a matter of personal initiative. In recent years, a five-day workplace leadership course has been added. Initially the course was offered only to mid-level sergeants, but it is now available to all frontline patrol sergeants.

The rank progression in the WPS is constable, patrol sergeant (street supervisor), sergeant (in charge of a platoon of up to twenty-five patrol officers or an investigative unit), staff sergeant (in charge or second in charge of a division) inspector (in charge of a division), superintendent (in charge of a branch of the service), deputy chief (in charge of either support services or operations), and chief. The level of responsibility assigned to the various ranks has evolved differently across police agencies. In some services, a staff sergeant will run an investigative unit or a platoon while in others a sergeant will fulfill the same role. This has become a matter of contention at collective bargaining. For instance, in the WPS a sergeant carries the responsibility for running a unit without the higher pay that a staff sergeant receives for carrying the same responsibilities in Calgary.

In recent decades there has also been a tendency towards using fewer high-ranking officers. Twenty years ago, in Winnipeg, a district office with between one hundred and two hundred constables was overseen by a superintendent, an inspector, two staff sergeants, and a sergeant in charge of each of the six platoons. Now the same districts are managed by an inspector and one staff sergeant, with a sergeant for each platoon.

Progression through the ranks, from constable to sergeant to inspector, etc., is similar in police agencies across Canada. In Winnipeg the promotion plan forms part of the CBA and is based on a formula awarding points for seniority, exam scores, and an interview. Recently a 360° feedback process was added wherein people familiar with the officer applying for promotion are asked to submit confidential written reports about him or her. In the WPS, sergeants are promoted after between sixteen and twenty years of service and receive another three to five-day policy training course. The next promotion to staff sergeant generally occurs at twenty years of service or more. At this point, many members are also starting to consider retirement, because their pension is mature after twenty-five years of service.

Progression through the ranks is fairly standard across Canadian police services. The three-week senior police administrator course at the Canadian Police College and continuing education provided for executives at the Police Executive Centre of the Canadian Police College allow for some continuing development, but opportunities to attend are limited. The FBI National Academy in the United States runs an international course for senior police executives, but very few are privileged enough to attend. For example, the WPS sends one member every few years.

Decreasing seniority and increasing demands require carefully planned leadership development. In previous decades, when police agencies were less diverse and demands were fewer, decisions were less debated at both the policy and the investigative levels. As discussed earlier, earlier wrongful criminal convictions are now often attributed to tunnel vision and groupthink on the part of investigators and command staff (Criminal Law Quarterly 2007; Findley and Scott 2006).

Groupthink is a word that was coined in regard to the decision made by President John F. Kennedy's management team to invade Cuba with a small armed force. The resulting "Bay of Pigs" invasion was later recognized as a poor decision that came about because key people failed to challenge decisions. Kennedy was surrounded by "yes men," all of whom agreed on the invasion without raising the negative consequences of the decision. Incidents like the Bay of Pigs and ongoing social psychological research have revealed that effective decision-making groups need to incorporate strategies for avoiding groupthink and tunnel vision (Janis 1971). These strategies can include assigning a "devil's advocate" or dissenting voice to point out the negative aspects of any decision or involving people from diverse backgrounds in decision-making groups. Increasing diversity in police forces helps reduce the likelihood of groupthink by bringing different perspectives into the discussion. However, it also presents the new challenge of integrating people from diverse backgrounds into cohesive teams. Effective police leaders possess the skills to guide diverse groups in reaching consensus, while making difficult decisions.

In the investigative context, investigators' biases can be affected by tunnel vision, which leads them to become focused on one suspect over others, gathering evidence that supports one theory and discounting evidence that weakens it. Groupthink can result in poor decisions that play into tunnel vision. It does not take a lot of imagination to realize that there can be immense pressure to close high-profile cases, such as serial rapes, gang shootings or other heinous crimes, which can make tunnel vision seem more reasonable in an attempt to appease police executives and the public.

There are important distinctions to be made between education and training. Education is intellectual development, usually through university programs that are more or less directly related to a person's work. Training, on the other hand, provides job-related skills development. Education may not be directly job-related but benefits the employer by producing more objective, mentally agile, and capable employees. Higher education can develop a police officers' mental acuity and awareness, providing the cognitive skills essential for thinking critically and avoiding the pitfalls of tunnel vision and groupthink, while respecting and taking advantage of diversity (Hellriegel et al. 1998). Many police officers routinely invest their time and personal finances in their own training and education. I have trained and worked with officers from all over North America, particularly from across Canada, and can say with confidence that this attitude of dedication to professional development is a thread that runs through the culture of policing everywhere. Police work is a calling for most officers; they want to develop personally in order to succeed in their chosen profession.

In every police service, there are also officers who prefer to work in general patrol and on the frontline for their entire careers. They tend to continuously improve in that role and often become excellent mentors and field trainers. There are others who take opportunities to diversify and work in specialty units. Each specialty assignment can be like an entirely new career. I recall my first promotion, from constable to patrol sergeant. One day I was sitting in jeans in an RCMP building as a member of the ICE Unit, analyzing the child pornography evidence we had seized in one of our knockovers (a search carried out on the basis of a warrant). Then I received my promotion to patrol sergeant and two days later I was back in uniform as street supervisor, second in charge of a platoon of twenty general patrol officers in Winnipeg's North End. On my first two nights, I participated in and supervised three high-speed pursuits. The challenge of changing roles and demands, often on the spur of a moment, is another common policing experience.

In my case, I heeded the advice of one of my first sergeants, who encouraged me to take every opportunity to diversify and work in various units throughout the Police Service. I have transferred back and forth every few years from uniform operations to a wide variety of specialty units. This has given me the opportunity to be involved at the start of many interesting, cutting-edge initiatives. Each of these roles required specialized training.

For instance, when I was working in the Child Abuse Unit I was asked to fulfill a newly established role as sex crimes analyst. I took distance education courses and undertook self-directed study on criminal profiling as well as taking several analytical courses on how to use resources such as crime mapping, geographic profiling, and criminal intelligence analysis. As this was a newly created position,

I was authorized to travel to Ottawa for three different two-week courses at the Canadian Police College: Major Case Management Team Commander, Tactical Intelligence Analysis, and the Major Case Investigation course. Those courses were truly beneficial, in particular because I was sequestered for two weeks each time with officers from across Canada and around the world. Networking and learning how things are done in other jurisdictions helps formulate standards in practice, and the sharing of ideas is incredibly valuable.

People would be surprised to learn how hard officers work at training. For example, in the Team Commander course we were assigned to syndicate groups and asked to create a complete plan for a task force to deal with a major gang problem. That meant creating a seventy-page business case that covered everything from short and long term strategies and objectives, resources, buildings, cars, phones, security, insurance, interagency memos of understanding, accountability measures, and so forth for the operation of a multiagency task force. The syndicates worked until about 11:00 p.m. every night creating our proposals and doing assignments after listening to lectures all day. Then, on the last day, commanders were brought in from various agencies in Canada to sit on a panel and we presented our business plans to them. Most Canadian Police College courses involve long hours of after classroom work, but officers generally embrace them as valuable learning and networking opportunities.

In my Sex Crimes Analyst assignment, one of my mandates was to oversee long-term missing person investigations. I quickly recognized the liability that these cases posed for the wps and, more importantly, that the families and loved ones of people who have been missing for long periods of time deserved to see the police working hard to solve these investigations and achieve closure. I could see the similarities between our pending long-term missing person cases and the serial murder cases of Robert Pickton and the "Highway of Tears," the stretch of road that runs through Northern British Columbia and Alberta along which numerous Aboriginal women had gone missing and where some murder victims had been found over the past decade (Canadian Press 2011a). As a result, I focused on these issues and eventually obtained executive support for increasing the Missing Persons Unit by several investigators. Missing persons issues are complex and intense and when they became a priority, my work became focused on them and many other initiatives that I was involved in as the sex crimes analyst ended. This is the nature of policing, as with all public sector services; limited resources must be divided between constantly changing and competing demands and priorities.

There is an ongoing debate about assignment lengths in policing. For example, the WPS made a large investment in training me to become an analyst and within two years I was assigned an entirely different role, supervising the Missing Persons Unit. Members working in highly specialized areas often need extensive and ongoing training. The value of their growing expertise must be balanced against the need for officers experienced in specialty assignments to be moved back into frontline uniform operations where new generations of officers need mentoring and leadership from these experienced members. Transferring highly trained officers from specialty units back into general patrol also creates opportunities for other members to learn new specialties and gain new experience. It is an expensive process, but the benefits can be high.

Transfers are also required to allow members to recharge after they have spent years working in highly demanding and specialized assignments. The intensity of work within specialty units can differ between agencies. I saw a clear example of organizational culture differences around such units in my assignment to the ICE Unit. The RCMP members seemed to be less concerned about how long they would be assigned to the unit, so they could settle in and really take their time to develop expertise and make professional contacts with similar interests in other agencies (and across the country). WPS members hit the ground running, knowing they have two years, three at the most, in that assignment. They often work at a burn-out pace attempting to close big cases, get specialized training, contribute to positive changes, and make an impression in that area before being transferred out.

The RCMP were a great partner in the ICE unit as they were better connected nationally. Their involvement in rural contract policing as well as national mandates was a significant asset and also resulted in unique challenges. They had contacts and resources nationally, even internationally, which often helped in investigations that involved numerous agencies around the world. The challenges came when things we wanted to do locally were hampered by their more bureaucratic national chain of command. In some case senior officers in

Ottawa held up decisions on local operations, or policy came down from Ottawa that did not necessarily fit well in every location across Canada. This could frustrate both RCMP and municipal officers working in a joint task force.

I have always had the highest respect for RCMP officers and the personal sacrifices they make when they (and their families) are required to transfer to remote postings in communities across Canada. The standing joke that municipal police officers share with our RCMP counterparts is that if they get into trouble with their superiors, city police officers may be transferred to another district but RCMP officers may be transferred to a remote rural outpost. This explains a lot about some of the organizational culture differences between federal and municipal policing. The RCMP organizational culture is often more regimented in the chain of command than municipal policing. Municipal officers seem to work more autonomously and when they do need authorizations from their chain of command, they often have a more direct route to getting it because all their bosses are close by. City police are also unionized, while RCMP officers are not, although they have been working for years to organize (Pablo 2012). This can give municipal police officers more security and a voice in their careers as they have union support when they have complaints about forced overtime, shift adjustments, transfers, promotions, allegations of breach of conduct, or a range of other work-related issues.

In order to remain effective against increasingly sophisticated criminal elements and to meet the greater demands of modern-day policing, police officers at all levels require more specialized training and ongoing education than their predecessors. We must train and learn continuously in order to meet the increasing and ever-changing demands of the justice system, as well as those of stakeholders and the community at large. We also need to work on standards across agencies and on inter-agency cooperation.

WORKING TOGETHER

A word search of the review of the FBI's handling of intelligence and information related to the 9/11 terrorist attacks in the United States produces eighty-four instances of the word "training," which illustrates the necessity for improved capacity through collaboration in law enforcement (United States Department of Justice 2005b). Officers need continual skills development and training with colleagues in partner agencies in order to be able to communicate and work together effectively. Collaboration, information-sharing, and joint planning takes effort and a willingness to learn and respect others' needs. Law enforcement agencies also need to improve their internal capacities for gathering, analyzing, and sharing information, and responding in a coordinated way to events.

Cooperation is especially critical in disasters, which are, by definition, beyond the scope of normal emergency procedures and exceed the resources and capabilities of any single organization (Brunacini 1985; Carlson 1983; Kramer and Bahme 1992; Kuban 1993). Contemporary emergency preparedness training and government programing for disasters has focused largely on attempting to improve interagency cooperation and training to overcome the traditional inefficiencies of operating as stand-alone agencies. Experience in fighting wild fires in California over the past decade has shown officials at all three levels of government in Canada and the United States that greater interagency cooperation is the only effective way to manage such large scale events (Fricker, Jacobson, and Davis 2002). They have learned that without a common language and structure for command it is difficult for multiple agencies to work together effectively. Consequently, the "incident command system" that evolved through experience with California wildfires has been widely adopted and is being taught to emergency responders across North America. This system is a basic framework that ensures multiple agencies work well together during major events (Carlson 1983). Under it, the first responder takes command. Each individual reports to only one supervisor and a common terminology has been developed so that communication is facilitated. A strategy based on clear objectives is outlined and adopted and resources are itemized and tracked until the end of the emergency.

Recognition of the need for one standardized command structure that crosses jurisdictional boundaries is necessary to overcome ineffective past approaches to agency cooperation (Boyd and Sullivan 2000). The incident command system teaches officials that interagency disaster response efforts should focus on community recovery, even during the initial response and mitigation phases of a disaster event. Awareness of these dynamics also highlights the need for greater multiagency planning (Auf der Heide 1989; Dynes 1970; Lindell and Prater 2005; Murphy 2006).

These same principles apply even more to law enforcement support services – without support staff the intelligence gathering and analysis elements that frontline officers can provide would be ineffective. Improved collaboration and cooperation necessitates increased training for skills development and the establishment of standards that get everyone working on the same page. To promote this, police training has become centralized in institutions such as the Canadian Police College and the Canadian Emergency Management College in Ottawa, where police officers and other emergency management officials from across Canada train together. The disaster management example illustrates the need for coordination of emergency services. More complex social issues, such as gang violence, drug abuse, and human exploitation, also call for better collaboration amongst all the stateholders, as well as in law enforcement.

Surveys of 1,000 law enforcement agencies identified a need for much better preparedness and interagency coordination (Fricker, Jacobson, and Davis 2002). In his paper, "Weapons of Mass Destruction: The First Responder," Paulin (2003) confirms the need for better training of first responders in dealing with acts of terrorism.

Emergency responders have a common predisposition to rush in and help people, regardless of the dangers. The old saying among police officers and firefighters across Canada is, "We run towards danger when others are running away." This places emergency responders at risk, particularly in the case of terrorist acts. Firefighters jokingly refer to police officers as "blue canaries" – if firefighters arrive at a scene and the red stripe along the officer's pant leg is parallel to the ground (because the officer is unconscious), there may be dangerous gas in the area. When the Sarin gas attacks occurred on a Japanese subway in 1995, most of those injured were in the second wave of responders. There is a clear need for ongoing chemical, biological, radioactive, nuclear, radiological, explosive (CBRNE) and counter-terrorism training for emergency services personnel (Beton et al. 2005). If officers in Japan had been trained to recognize the warning signs they might not have continued to rush in and been injured by the chemicals involved.

Regular inter-agency coordination and joint exercises are needed to ensure open communication and effective resource sharing. Traditional methods have been effective in the past, but they are inadequate to deal with the evolving threat of terrorism (Boyd and Sullivan 2000). Global borderless crimes, such as terrorism, require new attitudes and increased multiagency information and resource sharing. The Law Commission of Canada publication "In Search of Security: The Future of Policing in Canada" suggests that contemporary policing should involve networks of mutually supportive public and private agencies (Law Commission of Canada 2006).

These new multiagency relationships are blurring traditional jurisdictions and mandates and call for a focus on improved standards in policing to ensure that agencies can work together effectively. A 2006 report by the CACP called for the development and adoption of a national policing strategy, outlined by police leaders and based upon a system of national standards of police service delivery, that would recognize the need for increased interagency cooperation and resource sharing.

Administrators occasionally face the challenge of having to argue for the resources to prepare for events that may never happen. It is truly a catch-22 for public officials who must balance the probability of events against the costs. No official wants to admit to citizens that a cost-benefit analysis was used in deciding what resources are dedicated to public safety but such decisions must be made on a regular basis (Kettl 2007). Police administrators do the best they can with resources available but in hindsight, after an incident, they can always be criticized for not having had the prophetic vision to be prepared for the unexpected.

As a member of the WPS disaster management team, I have seen this challenge repeatedly. For example, we learned from Britain's experience during events like the London subway bombings and New York City's experiences in the 9/11 attacks that cell phone towers quickly become overloaded and stop service. Cell phone companies do not invest the large amounts of money that would be required to build capacity that exceeds routine usage. Should we spend money on satellite phones that we may never need, just in case of a major event? The money to do that would need to be taken away from other competing priorities for the very small discretionary budget that a police service has left after wages and equipment are paid for. If we spend thousands of dollars on satellite phones that we may never use, it may mean that officers are denied resou investigative tools or that new safety gear used daily by cannot be purchased. On the other hand, satellite phone potentially save lives during a disaster. The discretionary budget is generally about five percent of the total budget, and how to spend it causes the debate and concern on a daily basis in the policing world.

Risk management will not happen on its own. Regester and Larkin (2005) emphasize that companies should develop and train people for crisis management. Analytical resources and advanced planning need attention from within and between the many agencies that are involved in law enforcement and emergency management. Sorting out these challenging issues requires critical thinking and deep analysis of problems that have become increasingly complex over the past twenty years. Higher education can help police officers develop critical thinking skills to approach such issues.

ADVANCED EDUCATION AND POLICING

The police profession is increasingly demanding and may soon require educational levels beyond the traditional grade 12 requirement for hiring (Schultz 2004). Post-secondary and advanced education has certainly become a potential key to success in policing careers; however, its value is hotly debated within the policing community. In his book *Character and Cops*, Delattre (1989) wrote that it is difficult to determine if police officer success is a result of advanced education or of pure ambition and talent. This resonates for me today, as each senior police executive values advanced education differently.

One study examined eighty-four officers in a large American police department over a ten-year period, with a focus on the relationship between college education and job performance. It studied the relationships between college education and promotions, disciplinary ratings, and supervisory ratings. The research found no clear relationship between job performance and college degrees at lower levels. It did find positive relationships between college education, executive salaries, and management performance measures such as interpersonal ability (Truxillo, Bennett, and Collins 1998), indicating that there is a correlation between career achievement and higher education, albeit not necessarily a causal relationship.

Research has tried to explain whether advanced education creates better leaders; the results have been inconclusive because one cannot tell if the ambition to achieve higher education is separate from or related to the desire for career advancement (Truxillo, Bennett, and Collins 1998). Those with more education may have mastered study skills in the course of their education that give them an advantage in promotion processes. The experience of preparing for and writing tests, as well as the intellectual agility and communication skills that a person develops in the course of their education, may also be an asset in promotion processes. Attributes gained through education, which may give candidates an advantage in a promotion process, are in fact many of the very skills that are sought in effective leaders (ibid.).

Frontline officers often complain that promotion processes recognize people who are focused more on promotion than job performance. For example, some officers are reluctant to praise a colleague's actions and initiatives if they believe they were performed only for recognition and promotion. It is basically impossible to discover the true motivation behind an officer's actions. The truth is that officers, just like most public servants, want to contribute and make their organizations better. If they also hope for recognition through promotion, or are willing to take on the greater responsibilities of higher ranks, as long as their work is good the true motives do not really matter. What does matter is that the most qualified and competent people should achieve higher ranks.

In her article "Recruiting Police Officers and Education Standards: College versus High School Applicants," Taiping Ho examined formal education in police work and encountered the same problems; education correlated with success but did not predict it (Ho 2004). Research by Polk and Armstrong reveals that higher education results in a higher likelihood of receiving prime assignments and administrative and supervisory positions. They argue that it is to an agency's advantage to support officers in getting additional education, regardless of the perceived applicability of their program of study to the officer's specific assignments, and recommends that advanced education be supported through flexible shifts and incentives (Polk and Armstrong 2001).

Research on the relationship between higher education and increased or reduced discipline problems has also been inconclusive (Truxillo, Bennett, and Collins 1998). Character may be more significant in deterring corruption than education. Police agencies understand this concept, screening primarily for character and values when hiring. Honesty is arguably the most important trait in the policing profession. Police officers are occasionally charged and fired for offences involving deceit because if an officer cannot control the urge to lie or steal, how can they be trusted in peoples' homes and businesses, and with citizens' most intimate secrets and property? In court appearances, once an officer loses credibility, he or she is basically up against an insurmountable professional barrier for the rest of their career; a police officer's word is everything.

Education does not necessarily improve professionalism. Many exceptional officers do not have degrees and many average officers do (Polk and Armstrong 2001). While higher education does not ensure possession of higher ethics, its value as an indication of intellectual abilities is irrefutable. Some research has found that college-educated officers tend to have better communication skills, particularly with the public, higher professionalism, improved discretion in decision-making, and receive fewer complaints (Carter and Radelet 1999) That is not to diminish any of the accomplishments of those who have worked their way to the top without advanced formal education. Character and values are more significant in policing than the added skills that advanced education develops.

In an article entitled "Tertiary Education, Commitment, and Turnover in Police Work," Jones, Jones, and Prenzler (2005) examined the effect of higher education on turnover in police services. They found that some managers have an unsubstantiated belief that seeking higher education is a form of disloyalty. They examined the common misconception that people with higher education will quit for other opportunities and therefore their training is a poor investment for organizations. In my experience the opposite is the case. Most officers I have spoken with are seeking higher education to enhance their ability to contribute to policing. There are some who take up training for post-policing careers, but generally (again in my experience) they are thinking about what they will do after retirement, not about leaving policing early. Research contradicts the view that education, possession of a degree, or education seeking indicates a clear intention to leave an organization (Jones, Jones, and Prenzler 2005).

In the United States, it has been estimated that between 1960 and 1988 the percentage of police officers with no college education fell from 80 to 34 percent (ibid.). Canadian numbers would be relatively similar. A WPS recruit class of fifty in 2011 had seven members who had completed one year or more of university, fifteen who had completed university degrees, fifteen who had completed substantial work towards or completed diploma programs, and twelve who had no post-secondary education beyond high school.

Increased educational levels may reflect changes in the general population rather than police organizational hiring policies. Most police agencies in Canada maintain the requirement of a high school diploma as a hiring prerequisite. If they required a university degree instead of high school completion, agencies would have even more difficulty recruiting from target communities such as Canadian Aboriginal peoples.

The growing combination of maturing Generation X and Y employees and early retirement options creates potential for more turnover and less stability in the modern workforce. As previously mentioned, the younger generations have been found to be less committed to completing an entire career in one organization or profession; they are more likely than previous generations to change occupations. It is too early to say how this will affect the policing profession. However, the risk of the loss of corporate knowledge is a phenomenon that did not exist twenty years ago.

Advanced education creates opportunities and therefore may be correlated with increased early retirements. This is highly speculative, however, as the previously noted research has found that officers seeking advanced education are not retiring early. Very few officers have taken early retirement within the w P s, despite concerns, when the twenty-year reduced-pension option was first negotiated, that a large number of early retirements might occur.

Other research has revealed correlations between higher education levels and reported higher job satisfaction, more perceived opportunities for special assignments, and greater stability and longevity (Lynskey 2001). Polk and Armstrong's (2001) study demonstrated conclusively that police officers with higher education, regardless of their personalities, are usually promoted more quickly and reach higher rank levels. They point out that this research is encouraging for those who believe officers should be more highly educated. It does not, however, indicate what type of education officers should possess. Puryear (2003), in his interviews with successful military leaders, found that they consistently valued the importance of lifelong learning, not necessarily university degrees.

Lifelong learning does not have to take place in a classroom. It can occur daily through an individual's commitment to staying informed. Self-directed learning combined with departmental training can be effective lifelong learning. Self-directed learning, however, will take most people only so far in learning to think critically before then they need teachers. The problem with self-directed study is that one does not know what is missing (Lowenthal 1981).

Most of the successful military leaders interviewed by Puryear (2003) started with undergraduate degrees that provided them with a solid educational foundation on which to build their self-directed studies later in life. University courses and programs teach people how to see the various facets of an issue and help them develop vital critical thinking skills while learning how to learn. The most significant aspect of education is that it teaches you how much you do not know; it teaches you how to think critically and challenge assumptions.

Graduate-level studies may be becoming the high end of industry standards in Canadian police management; however, police executives possessing graduate degrees are still the exception rather than the rule. In their paper "Overlapping the Actual with the Academic: The Education-Training Continuum," a group of professors from Roger Williams University described how university resources could be better utilized in training and development for police officers. They suggest that universities often have resources that are underutilized by government agencies like the police (Pesare et al. 2003) and that police agencies and universities could cooperate in leadership development and professional education. Some agencies are working in the right direction, in their development of future leaders. The Rotman School of Management in Toronto, for instance, runs a graduate level business administration (MBA) program tailored to police executive development (Rotman School of Management 2002).

In his paper "Law Enforcement Executive Education: Towards a Paradigm for the Twenty-first Century," Weiss (2001) notes that potential leaders in many countries attend police college or a similar institution prior to entering the profession. In India, for example, potential police leaders must enter a highly competitive program and achieve a degree before being hired. They enter the force as supervisors and are developed as leaders from the start. This is similar to the system utilized in the Canadian and American militaries, where most applicants are hired with degrees and placed immediately into the leadership development stream as officers.

Canadian law enforcement agencies take a different approach: officers all start as constables, developing technical skills for the first years as generalists and then as detectives, depending on the direction their careers take. As previously mentioned, some officers spend their career in uniform while others move between specialty units. Others take administrative assignments and some of them spend most of their careers in non-operational units such as training, human resources, records management, and policy development divisions. Officers generally start to develop leadership skills later in their careers.

Weiss (2001) notes that American police agencies generally do not require advanced education as a condition of promotion and therefore face challenges in leadership development unless they can start grooming officers early in their careers. I have observed a similar dynamic in Canada. We are, however, moving in the right direction. Two decades ago, there was a period wherein full seniority points in the WPS promotion plan for first level patrol sergeant were awarded for up to eighteen years of service rather than twelve years as it is now. This meant that twenty years ago, many members were promoted after eighteen to twenty years, receiving their first promotion as they were starting to plan for retirement. This system left no room for new leaders to develop.

Police organizations, like all public service sectors, are generally failing to identify mid-level and executive members for long-term development to fulfill future roles. The current culture across Canadian police agencies more often involves members developing themselves for advancement, and less often involves succession planning by senior executives. One may argue that this dynamic motivates people to continually seek self-improvement. The other side of the argument, however, is that those with the capacity to excel do not know how to improve, or whether or not they are part of the agency's succession plan. Greater success could be achieved if members with potential were told what programs or skills development they should strive for, rather than fumbling along trying to figure it out for themselves.

The policing culture still embraces the idea that every officer is a constable first, and executive positions are basically just different assignments with different responsibilities. A chief of police is "a patrolman promoted" (Eisenberg 2005). The WPS chief of police used to be called chief constable, a title still retained by the chief constable of the Vancouver Police Department.

Higher demands on Canada's police officers clearly necessitate an increased focus on professional development and expanded training budgets. If the Canadian military can spend millions of dollars training a single fighter pilot, surely the value of developing key executive-level police leaders, who are guarding Canada's domestic safety, is worth a $30,000 investment for graduate-level education (Office of the Auditor General of Canada 2007). Education levels of police in Canada are falling far behind the military, where the value of advanced education was recognized decades ago. Now, a junior officer in the Canadian Department of National Defence must have a university degree, upon hiring, in order to receive a commission. Senior military officers must complete the equivalent of a master's degree to continue into senior ranks.

In policing, the same evolution is starting to occur, albeit twenty years later than the military. For example, the City of Winnipeg now reimburses up to $2,000 per year for officers pursuing graduate programs on their own time. There are increasing numbers of police officers with advanced education, which is a catalyst for a culture shift and, in some cases, for a rift between those who choose to enhance their careers with advanced education and those who do not. There is an ongoing debate about whether pursuing an advanced degree is worth the effort. I have always maintained that the prospect of career advancement alone was not enough to motivate me to persevere with the rigours of completing my graduate degrees, part-time, while raising four kids and continuing a demanding policing career. In order to overcome the challenges of graduate-level studies one needs to be motivated from within and truly value lifelong learning. However, among the 1,500 people employed by the WPS, only a handful, maybe five or six, have completed graduate degrees.

Characteristics of military leaders are germane to any analysis of police leadership. Both professions are oriented around objectives that are based in representing the values of the greater society. Dangerous assignments, the need for teamwork, and changing technology represent similar challenges in policing and the military. Trott (2006) wrote that both military and police officers operate in uncertainty, crisis, and danger, coupled with having to bear the responsibility for the well-being of others. Success in both military and police leadership roles depend upon "timely, rational, and innovative thought processes."

The common message expressed by the military leaders interviewed by Puryear (2003) is the importance of selflessness, the ability to make decisions, and the willingness to challenge existing systems. In a word, strong leaders possess character. Leaders with character will succeed if they have sufficient experience, mentorship, education, and motivation.

In 1996 the Los Angeles Police Department started sending officers to West Point, a prestigious American military academy, and subsequently implemented a successful leadership program wherein officers attend class once a week for fifteen weeks. Prior to this program, the Los Angeles department relied on trial and error, on-the-job training, a few gifted role models, or the initiative of a few individual officers to seek advanced leadership education. The more structured process has reportedly allowed the Department to identify and develop leaders in a more systematic way (Dinse and Sheehan 1998).

The police profession involves continuous decision-making, guided by values and ethics that, ideally, mirror the values of society at large (Hohl, Bradford, and Stanko 2010). Police decisions reflect the values of the community, tempered and constrained by the limits of the law and competing limited resources. The discipline of police work is in doing what is right without losing footing on slippery ethical slopes. Consider whether you would breach a person's legal rights to save a young child or an elderly person from a lifetime of victimization. Would the police (or anyone) be justified in torturing a person to prevent a terrorist act that could kill thousands of innocent people? This is an extreme example, but police officers are routinely required to make difficult decisions that protect the rights of victims and suspects alike. A willingness to do the right things for the right reasons and to enforce society's values is a quality that lies at the core of strong police leadership.

One of the first things a new police officer learns is that people lie. They minimize, they defer responsibility, they sometimes unconsciously mislead, and occasionally they outright deceive. In some circumstances, people also admit to things they did not do (Drizin and Leo 2004; Gudjonsson 2003; Kassin 1997; Kassin and Gudjonsson 2004; Lassiter 2004; Leo and Ofshie 1998). Recent research in the United States has revealed that in 15 to 20 percent of cases where people have been exonerated of crimes for which they were convicted through DNA evidence, they had confessed to the crimes (Garrett 2008; Kassin 2010; Scheck, Neufeld, and Dwyer 2000). These false confessions occur for a variety of reasons and it is best police practice not to rely entirely on confessions if possible.

A common assumption exists in the debate about physical coercion: many people believe the truth can be tortured out of people. A fact of human psychology is that the more coercive the force applied, the less likely it is that what the interrogator extracts will be the truth. People will often lie, say anything, to get out of a situation, particularly if it is coercive or painful. This aspect of human nature is the cause of many of the previously mentioned false confessions. People tell investigators what they believe the investigators want to hear, for a variety of reasons. If a suspect is tired, hungry, scared, or uncomfortable, they may say anything, including confessing to serious crimes, without caring until later about the consequences. This is why the Canadian Charter of Rights and Freedoms and as well as other laws protect people's rights.

In policing we seek the truth, but the truth is always somewhere in the middle between almost any two stories. It is not a realistic scenario to expect that an officer would be put in a position where it would be possible to save lives by torturing someone because in almost all cases an investigator cannot be sure that the person could provide such information, or that they would tell the truth. For this reason alone physical coercion is not justified. (Of course, this debate depends on how torture is defined. For the purpose of this discussion, I am defining torture as extreme physical abuse.) The truthfulness of confessions and self-incriminating admissions should, in best practice, be corroborated by other proof such as witnesses, circumstances, and physical evidence.

It is worth mentioning again that there are fundamental differences between public service and the private sector, where the primary goal is often profit. The public sector is responsible for the most difficult services in society. It takes on the toughest jobs – like policing and child welfare. A corporation can delay dividend cheques to its shareholders or even declare bankruptcy if it fails to show a profit. A police force does not have the option of quitting, declaring bankruptcy, or even withholding services when times are tough. The public service, including police agencies, is comprised of people who choose to serve their communities in demanding roles. In many cases talented public servants could potentially be plying their skills for greater financial rewards in the private sector. Public sector jobs do tend to have greater security and benefits, particularly at the lower levels and mid-level management. At executive levels many public sector jobs become much like the private sector, with contracts.

While many private sector jobs require sacrifice and may involve extreme danger, policing, other emergency services, and the military involve the potential for extreme risk, such as deciding to run into a burning building or being murdered because of the role you have undertaken. You cannot put a dollar value on risking or sacrificing your life to protect the community or an individual.

It takes character and special skills to lead people in these high-risk environments. Skolnick (1966) described the subculture of policing as evolving around three key elements: "danger, authority and efficiency." The unique organizational culture of police work relies on mentoring as a significant part of training (Colwell et al. 2006; Qureshi and Farrell 2006). The following section highlights mentoring and experience as vital aspects of police training that have been affected by shifts in demographics and demands over the past two decades.

EXPERIENCE AND MENTORING

Experience is a significant component of police skills and leadership development. Polk and Armstrong (2001) found experience to be a more significant indicator of corporate success than education. In *The Leadership Machine*, Eichinger, Lombardo, and Ulrich (2004) describe experience as the best teacher, observing that individuals do not arrive at organizations equipped to handle all situations, no matter how talented they are. They need to learn and develop through experience. In his national bestseller *The Truth About Managing People*, Robbins points out that experience is not valuable in itself unless it is experience that develops a person's skills. The same one-year of experience repeated twenty times would not increase its developmental value. Experience is controlled to a large extent by employers. Employers who recognize this can make good use of experience to develop leadership and management skills. For instance, in succession planning, organizations need to consider the learning opportunities offered and the sum value of a person's experiences. Senior administrators should consider the opportunities developing leaders have had, what they have learned from those opportunities, and, perhaps most importantly, what they accomplished with the opportunities they were given (Robbins 2003).

Another important aspect of policing is mentoring. Changing demographics within police services have caused a deterioration of important mentorship processes. In their paper "Cultural and Organizational Learning," Cook and Yanow describe how corporate culture, idiosyncrasies, and skills are all taught and learned through mentoring (in Shafritz, Ott, and Jang 2005). All Canadian police agencies start new recruits with several months of formal mentoring or field training. However, for many officers, recruit training is the last substantial mentoring experience they will have in their career. While officers at all ranks have a duty to mentor those subordinate to them in the chain of command, the effectiveness of the mentorship process depends upon whether you are fortunate enough to work around people who go out of their way to develop others. Eisenberg (2005, 1) points out that senior executives who are "patrolman promoted" (working their way up through the ranks) often find themselves making major decisions with skills that are limited by their experiences and the mentoring they have received.

Mentorship can serve a wide range of purposes. For example, in the nursing profession the mentor/mentored relationship is designed to teach technical skills, whereas an MBA mentoring program may be oriented more toward introducing students to new management roles. In policing, mentoring is invaluable for skill development. An effective mentor can impart the essential nuances of police work; foremost among these are the effective communication and decision-making skills that cannot be developed in a clinical classroom environment. You cannot learn the fine art of interview and interrogation without long hours of hands-on work with experienced people to help guide you. For example, in my years of detective work, I honed and developed interrogation skills through training, practice, and, most importantly, through mentoring by seasoned officers.

Earlier I mentioned the rash of arsons that occurred in Winnipeg in 2000. Bruce Leonard Moreau was ultimately arrested for setting fire to many Winnipeg landmarks, including several churches, a miniature passenger train in Assiniboine Park, numerous businesses, and the devastating Osborne Village fire that levelled several businesses (CBC News 2000). Several of the businesses and churches were occupied when the fires were started; there was a real potential for a disaster and death in these crimes. Investigators were unable to get a confession from Moreau when he was initially arrested – in fact he threatened officers and refused to speak with them. Moreau was then detained in the Winnipeg Remand Centre pending a psychiatric assessment. Without a confession, there was not enough evidence to convict Moreau in court.

My regular partner and I in the Arson Strike Force planned our interview strategy for over a month while we waited for the psychiatric assessment to be completed. Moreau was finally found fit to stand trial. When we took him out of the Remand Centre for the interview, we spent a long time talking with him about his background and beliefs, likes and dislikes. We bought him a fast food meal that he liked and eased him into the interview. Through our approach and the trust we gained, we obtained a confession from Moreau for over forty major arsons that had kept Winnipeggers in fear for several months. I attended Moreau's sentencing and he shook my hand as he was being taken to Stony Mountain Penitentiary to serve his prison term.

My partner and I, and our team, could never have learned in a classroom all the nuances of communication that make possible this type of confession or case management. My belief is that the compassion we showed this man resulted in his trusting us enough to admit his crimes. The ability to develop that kind of trust, to negotiate with him over a period of hours and get him to admit his crimes, even when he knew an admission would mean he was going to prison, was the result of the mentoring my partner and I had in our careers, coupled with personal experience and training.

The mentoring process, when properly used, can be a highly effective tool for leadership development (Ehrich and Hansford 1999). Given the strong and unique culture of police organizations, mentoring is a tool that should be incorporated into police leadership development. While the value of mentoring is universally understood, Canadian police agencies tend not to have formalized mentoring programs for members once they are beyond the frontline constable rank. There are only limited mentoring opportunities for frontline, mid-level, or executive police leaders.

The unfortunate reality is that municipal police forces will never have the resources required to send potential leaders away for months of in-house training, as funds for this would have to come out of the relatively small discretionary budgets that were mentioned earlier. Police organizations can, however, do more in the area of leadership development through mentoring, with little added cost. Effective training, with almost no interruption to the regular flow of work, can be done by utilizing an in-service training model. The LAPD model mentioned earlier is a good example of this. That report came out of the independent commission on the Rodney King incident in Los Angeles and stated that police managers are leaders as well as managers and need formal leadership training (Dinse and Sheehan 1998).

Cultural and workplace diversity is a growing priority in policing, in particular in Canada, which is a multicultural nation and a major destination for immigrants. Aboriginal issues are also especially important in Canada, where First Nations and Metis people make up a large portion of the potential workforce. The following chapter is dedicated to Aboriginal issues in relation to law enforcement.

7

Aboriginal Peoples and Justice

ABORIGINALS IN CONFLICT WITH THE LAW

About 1,325,000 First Nations, Metis, and Inuit peoples make up four percent of Canada's current total population (Statistics Canada 2008; Richardson and Blanchet-Cohen 2000). Aboriginal populations have increased rapidly over the past twenty years and have higher birthrates than other ethnic groups. In 2001, Aboriginal unemployment was 311 percent higher than among the non-Aboriginal population in Canada (Hallet Thornton and Stewart 2006). According to Human Resources and Skills Development, Canada (2012), in 2006 unemployment among Aboriginal people was 6.3 percent higher than the national average. While these statistics are encouraging, more research may be warranted to ensure the validity of this report. Twenty-eight years of law enforcement experience has taught me that many homeless and indigent people live under the radar of government systems that seek to account for them.

Severe challenges in many, if not most, Aboriginal communities have been attributed in large part to assimilation policies. Many have characterized Canada's attempts to assimilate Aboriginal peoples into a settler society as cultural genocide (Higgins, 2008). Loss of land and reduced access to traditionally available natural resources are also among the challenges that the Aboriginal communities have faced in dealing with the imposed European-based society. The residential school system resulted in many people becoming disconnected from their families, communities, and indigenous culture. Income is significantly lower among Aboriginal people than in the non-Aboriginal population (Colin and Jensen 2009) and in 2006 Aboriginal people were four times more likely than non-Aboriginal Canadians to live in a substandard residence (Statistics Canada 2008).

The Indian Act of 1876 formalized the relationship between European settlers and indigenous peoples (Younging 2009). Aggressive assimilation policies implemented through mandatory, church-run, government-funded residential schools were the beginning of widespread social problems that persist to this day (Hallett, Thornton, and Stewart 2006). The residential school system ran from approximately 1892 to 1969 (Barlow 2003) – the last of Canada's 130 residential schools was closed in 1996 (CBC News 2008) – and sought to replace traditional Aboriginal languages and cultures with European ones (Galley 2009). The program was well received by some in the Aboriginal community but the many abuses that occurred have now overshadowed any good work that the people administering the programs may have intended (CBC News 2011; Chrisjohn and Wasacase 2009; Truth and Reconciliation Commission of Canada 2011). In 2008, the national government formally apologized for the residential school system, which has left deep scars in Canadian indigenous communities (Menzies 2009).

Paradoxically, residential schools and mass adoption policies compounded the effects of racial segregation while attempting to assimilate Aboriginal peoples into settler society (CBC News 2011; Chrisjohn and Wasacase 2009). With the benefit of hindsight, we now know that Canadian assimilation policies isolated indigenous Canadians from settler society, creating a disparity that is exacerbated by growing urban ghettos that are being largely inhabited by Aboriginal peoples.

History has demonstrated that British-inspired resettlement programs, including the South African township model (Noor 2011), as well as similar programs on Canadian Indian reserves, had high human costs for those forced into them and we are just now beginning to understand the effects of intergenerational trauma caused by displacement and cultural genocide. Indian reserves, in part because of such programs, ultimately became rural ghettos with such poor living conditions that Canada is now being chastised internationally for failing to improve them (Goar 2006; Welch and Rabson 2011). The federal government has invested large amounts of money into Canada's Aboriginal communities, yet many Canadian Aboriginal peoples still live in Third World conditions within a country with high overall living standards (Welch and Rabson 2011; Puxley 2011). Aboriginal peoples continue to migrate in increasing numbers from poor rural reserves into the equally poor urban cores of many Canadian cities (Norris et al. 2000; Norris, Kerr, and Nault 1995).

Structural violence in the form of socio-economic stratification was not invented in Canada. The rich get richer is a systemic fact of twentieth-century capitalist economic development in many countries throughout the world. In 2011 the Conference Board of Canada (2011) reported that between 1993 and 2008 the income of the wealthiest Canadians increased while that of the poorest and middle income earners decreased. Economic class differences continue, in part, because those in power tend to leverage their positions in order to retain and increase their wealth. It is no surprise that the same patterns have played out in Canada. Welfare systems, for example, while providing people with the means for basic living standards, can tend to perpetuate dependency. In many cases people choose to live on welfare or find they cannot get off of it. The answer to this conundrum may be to invest more in supporting people to complete post-secondary education and obtain better jobs. In my policing career I have seen and met many able bodied people on welfare (and in prison for that matter) who are capable and interested in working and contributing if they were given a chance.

Structural conditions that create market competition also result in oppression, because certain parties always gain advantage over others (Cheldelin, Druckman, and Fast 2003). This competition over resources continues to occur in all colonized countries, and explains why indigenous peoples in Canada have been disadvantaged. If there were no competing interests the treaties would have been settled long ago. The challenge for Canada is to find solutions that meet everyone's needs.

Canada, like other industrialized countries, has made gradual progress in righting the historical wrongs that were created by the colonization of indigenous peoples (Held 1996). However we still have a long way to go.

Structural transformation can be negotiated between parties or gained by force through revolution (Cheldelin, Druckman, and Fast 2003). Kiera Ladner of the University of Manitoba is a leading Canadian scholar of Aboriginal politics. In a presentation entitled "Understanding Aboriginal Governance within the Context of Aboriginal and Treaty Rights," given in March 2012 at the

Manitoba Legislature, Ladner stated that if the provinces do not address the economic disparity between mainstream Canada and the Aboriginal communities through settlement of the seven treaties in the next twenty years, "it will not be pretty, Oka was nothing," referring to the protracted siege by the Mohawk tribe near the Quebec town of Oka in the summer of 1990 (Ladner and Simpson 2010).

However, collaborative approaches are better for everyone than zero-sum games in which one party must lose in order for the other to win (Jeong 1995). Such approaches seem most likely to succeed when people are empowered to take responsibility for their own fate. Self-reliance requires mutually beneficial arrangements and starts at the grass roots. Supporting Aboriginal peoples to build resilience, self-government, and the means to deal with social problems in their communities seems like the appropriate vision for righting our historical wrongs.

Investing money without effective strategies is not a viable solution to modern-day socio-economic disparity. Byrne et al. (2009), in their analysis of the effects of money infused into the economy of Northern Ireland, found that there was a need for more effective planning and control over how funds are distributed; they note that proper strategies can help ensure that investments are effective. Similarly in Canada, the federal government has invested large amounts of money in Canada's Aboriginal communities, yet many Aboriginal peoples still live in poverty (Puxley 2011; Welch and Rabson 2011).

Many Canadian Aboriginal people are caught between widespread mismanagement and squabbling within Aboriginal governance structures and federal government programs that are paternalistic and ineffective. In 2012, more than one third of Manitoba's twenty-three bands were co-managed by elected band councils and federally appointed third party managers. In 2010, $300 million in federal funds were co-managed on twenty-one reserves by government-contracted accountants (Welch and Rabson 2011). Former Auditor General Sheila Fraser argued that these arrangements are ineffective and are more about saving government money than improving conditions on reserves (ibid.). Government efforts to empower Aboriginal communities in order to reduce substance abuse, gang involvement, suicide, and violence among their youth need to see that investments of money come with the resources to build leadership and community resilience, foster self-respect, and empower self-governance.

The 2008 government apology acknowledged that there were still unsettled treaty rights related to the redistribution of wealth, but little has occurred since then to correct this acknowledged injustice. There has been some recent political movement in Canada in the direction of support for Aboriginal self-governance (Galloway 2011). However, increasing the autonomy of Aboriginal groups raises questions about the benefits of developing multiple nation states within one country's borders (Chrisjohn and Wasacase 2009).

Among Aboriginal adults aged forty to forty-nine who have completed high school, less than half have some post-secondary education and only four percent have completed a post-secondary degree (Indian and Northern Affairs Canada 2006). Students living on reserves in Canada currently receive anywhere from $2,000 to $7,000 less in provincial funding per child than students in mainstream society (Smith 2012). Throughout the 1990s, awareness of Aboriginal issues increased dramatically in Canada and a wide range of programs and initiatives were undertaken in efforts to improve rates of Aboriginal completion of post-secondary education. Eric Howe has argued that increased funding for education that allows Aboriginals to eventually obtain better jobs is a sound investment as Canadians would recoup the money through the higher taxes that Aboriginal peoples would pay (ibid.).

McCracken and Michell explore modern challenges facing Aboriginal peoples and find that they simultaneously face the barriers of low-income as well as the effects of colonization and racism. The authors explain the important connection between the education system and the labour force it should be developing and argue that ineffective education systems result in workforce shortfalls (McCracken and Michell 2006).

Educational challenges faced by Aboriginal people also affect the number of qualified individuals available for all professions, including justice and law enforcement. At the root of Canada's challenges in integrating Aboriginal peoples into the workforce is, at least in part, the relatively poor performance of some education systems in attracting and retaining this part of our society.

Efforts have been made to improve accessibility of education in geographically remote areas. In northern Manitoba, for instance, Internet-based distance education courses have been established through institutions such as the University College of the North (University College of the North 2006). While these programs are moving in the right direction, they seem to have limited success at engaging people in professional development for roles such as policing. In one positive initiative, in October 2012, the University of Winnipeg appointed Wab Kinew as their first director of indigenous inclusion. In the university's news release on his appointment, Kinew stated "In one generation in my family we've gone from the residential school era where education was a tool of oppression, to the modern era where it is a tool of self-empowerment" (University of Winnipeg 2012).

It seems clear that for Canada's Aboriginal peoples, as is the case for all Canadians, education is the key to long-term improved access to professional opportunities, reduced criminal involvement, and healthier, happier lives. However, education is hard to achieve when you have poor living conditions. Assembly of First Nations Chief Shawn Atleo has argued that, on top of the need for improved education funding, Aboriginal communities across Canada have numerous other urgent needs (Smith 2012). Pamela Palmater of the Centre for Indigenous Governance at Ryerson University in Toronto, has pointed out that the failed 2005 Kelowna Accord, which allocated $5 billion in new money to Aboriginal needs, addressed the multiple calamities that Aboriginal peoples now face in housing, clean water, and education (ibid.). More than one hundred reserves in Canada do not have safe drinking water. In 2011, the Canadian government reported that 71 percent of First Nations communities' water systems are health risks for the 20,000 people using them; this stark acknowledgement resulted in enactment of the Safe Drinking Water for First Nations Act in 2012 (Smith 2012).

Government has a moral and economic imperative to help improve living conditions for Canada's indigenous peoples. Improved social justice through higher living standards may have a positive effect on post-secondary education completion and work attainment, helping to reach equality with the rest of Canadian society in these areas. Improved social justice and living standards may also reduce the need for social services, health, corrections, and justice resources.

Bert Lauwers, deputy coroner for the Province of Ontario, participated in a study on the Pikangikum First Nation, a geographically large, isolated, Ontario reserve with about 2,500 residents. Between March of 2008 and May of 2009, nine Pikangikum youth between the ages of ten and seventeen committed suicide. In a presentation to the First Nations Managers and Practitioners Conference in Montreal in April 2012, Dr Lauwers said that he and his team found that the residents of this reserve live in Third World conditions with no running water, outhouses that sometimes infect drinking water, minimal electricity provided only through diesel generators, and extreme substance abuse rates among several generations of residents. The study of the suicide epidemic revealed that six of the suicides occurred directly following a week in which four non-suicide related deaths had occurred on the reserve. The youth on the reserve lacked the resilience to deal emotionally with deaths in their families, as a result of their poor prospects in life. Dr Lauwers reported that these nine suicides were part of what may be the highest suicide rate in the world. Suicide rates among Aboriginals are six times higher than the rate for non-Aboriginals (Shah 1990; York 1990; Statistics Canada 2001; Chandler et al. 2003). Poor living conditions, substance abuse problems, and suicides are conditions seen on many reserves and among Aboriginal populations across Canada. In June of 2012 the Aboriginal community in Manitoba mourned the suicides of five youths that took place over a period of six weeks (Paul 2012).

Many Aboriginal reserves are under-resourced in terms of services such as policing. At the Aboriginal Policing conference, Ontario Provincial Police (OPP) Commissioner Lewis said poor conditions and lack of resources are endemic in reserves across Canada and that problem needs to be corrected. Lewis said that, for instance, Pikangikum has seven police officers in a stand-alone agency. The OPP did a workload analysis and determined that if they took over policing in that community, they would deploy a detachment of thirty officers.

Disproportionate numbers of Aboriginal people are in conflict with the law (Griffin 2001). Sheldon (2001) describes the American justice system as perpetuating existing hierarchies of class, gender, and race. This may also be true of Canada, where Aboriginal peoples are grossly overrepresented in the prison system and are by far, relative to their population size, the most substantial targets and/or consumers of justice system services. The 2012 annual report of Howard Sapers, Canada's correctional investigator, states that "over the last ten years, while the overall non-Aboriginal inmate population has modestly increased by 2.4 percent, the Aboriginal inmate population has increased significantly by 37.3 percent. Approximately 4 percent of the Canadian population is Aboriginal, while 21.4 percent of the federal incarcerated population is Aboriginal" (Correctional Investigator of Canada 2012, 35).

Many inmates have been diagnosed with Fetal Alcohol Spectrum Disorder (FASD) (Sanders and Welch 2011), a birth defect caused by maternal consumption of high levels of alcohol during pregnancy and related to the high concentration of substance abuse problems in Aboriginal communities.

The unique cultural issues facing Aboriginal communities have caused community groups and formal bodies, such as the Aboriginal Justice Inquiry (AJI) of Manitoba (Hamilton and Sinclair 1991), the Commission on Systemic Racism in the Ontario Criminal Justice System (1995), the Royal Commission on Aboriginal Peoples (1996), and many others, to call for reforms in education and justice systems affecting Aboriginal peoples. Many inquiry recommendations seek to correct the trans-generational effects of colonization that have resulted in high criminal involvement (Comack et al. 2009; Canada, Indian and Northern Affairs 1996; Hallet, Thornton, and Stewart 2006).

Volkan (1997) describes intergenerational traumas and the challenges that governments face in attempting to address structural inequalities and social problems that have persisted for multiple generations. He found that traumas are often transferred from generation to generation. This explains a great deal about the challenges currently faced by Canada's growing Aboriginal community. The vicarious trauma that many Aboriginal youth feel as they see their parents reeling from the impacts of the residential schools and the government seizure and adoption of Aboriginal babies in Canada in the 1960s, coupled with the far too common personal trauma of being abused or neglected at home, has contributed to endemic substance abuse, high suicide rates, and increasing criminal involvement (Comack et al. 2009). Understanding this context will help begin to change the public discourse as the foundation of sustainable long-term solutions to problems like gang violence. Retaining a focus on criminalization of Aboriginal people is not a solution that will create true change.

Aboriginal peoples are a disproportionately large percentage of those in low-rent tenements or homeless in Winnipeg's urban core. While 13 to 15 percent of Manitobans self-identify as Aboriginal, the number of Aboriginals among those using frontline emergency services in the low socioeconomic areas of the city exceeds 60 percent (Hallett, Thornton, and Stewart 2006). Similar numbers end up in jail. Increasing poverty and unemployment in recent decades coincides with higher criminal involvement among Aboriginal peoples. Any initiative that reduces Aboriginal contact with the justice system will substantially reduce government spending and help the community at large. Increased Aboriginal participation in administration of all aspects of the justice system, from frontline policing, prosecutions, and sentencing to the prisons and social work would help make inroads in reducing Aboriginal over-representation.

The opening of Manitoba's Peguis First Nation Provincial Circuit Court in October 2008 was a good start at addressing Aboriginal justice issues (Manitoba Government 2008). However the justice system only manages the symptoms of deeper problems. The provinces and territories need to adopt more comprehensive approaches to improving indigenous education and workforce integration.

The trajectory of violence among Canada's growing population of Aboriginal youth is a problem for all of society. The responsibility for correcting these problems rests with everyone, not just government and the police. All Canadians stand to lose if the deep-seated problems faced by Canada's Aboriginal youth are not addressed through leadership and collaboration. The next section examines Canada's Aboriginal youth gang and street violence problem in detail, and offers some potential paths to its solution.

CANADA'S ABORIGINAL YOUTH GANGS

Over the past two decades many parts of Canada have experienced increased street-level violence. Aboriginal youth gangs form a substantial part of this growing social crisis and in many parts of Canada are committing suicide and engaging in acts of extreme violence at levels far higher than those of any other Canadian ethnic group. This tragic social trend has been characterized as an epidemic of violence that will double in intensity over the next decade if it is not interrupted (Totten 2009).

Youth gang involvement in Canada is estimated to have increased from 7,000 confirmed gang members in 2002 to as many as 14,000 in 2008 (Huber 2008). Twenty-two percent of Canada's gang members are Aboriginal, with two thirds of them concentrated in the prairie provinces (Astwood Strategy Corporation 2004; Criminal Intelligence Service Saskatchewan 2005; Correctional Service Canada 2001; Totten 2008).

Youth gangs are generally comprised of twelve- to thirty-year-old males organized in gangs with distinct names, dress, tattoos, and rituals for the purpose of profit and violence (Gordon 2000; Totten 2000, 2008). Gangs have fluid memberships and loose structures that are usually protected from infiltration by outside groups and law enforcement through the use of violent entry and exit rituals (Totten 2009). The violent rights of passage protect the gangs from infiltration by undercover police officers. For this reason, many organized criminal gangs have historically preferred to recruit individuals who can be confirmed as having served prison time. The structure and organization of these criminally oriented groups vary but their members often share common values that include gaining status through acts of violence and obtaining money through criminal means (Mellor et al. 2005; Totten 2008).

The gang activity and street violence problem has evolved alongside the increasing socio-economic disparity between Aboriginal communities and mainstream Canadian society. The phenomenon of street violence is exacerbated by the continuous migration of Aboriginal peoples from rural reserves into the economically depressed urban cores of many Canadian cities (Richardson and Blanchet-Cohen 2000). Disproportionately high levels of street gang participation among Aboriginal youth is attributable, according to Totten (2009, 3), to factors including "racism, colonization, marginalization and dispossession; the loss of land, traditional culture, spirituality and values; and the breakdown of community kinship systems and Aboriginal law." While the exact predisposing formula for gang involvement is difficult to define, it is clear that poverty places Aboriginal youth at risk. A large portion of such youth live in impoverished, overcrowded housing (Bittle et al. 2002; Dooley et al. 2005).

As well, many young Aboriginal people on reserves have experienced varying degrees of brain damage as a result of inhaling gasoline as well as a higher than average incidence of FASD. Young Aboriginal people are exposed early in life to high levels of violence, either directly as victims or indirectly as witnesses, especially on reserves, where homicide rates are eleven times higher than elsewhere in Canada (Canada, House of Commons Standing Committee on Aboriginal Affairs 1990; Royal Commission on Aboriginal Peoples 1996). Aboriginal women and children are particularly vulnerable to exploitation (DeRiviere 2005).

For many Aboriginal people, low post-secondary education completion rates are a key barrier to social justice and opportunities to achieve higher socio-economic status (Royal Commission on Aboriginal Peoples 1996; Statistics Canada 2001). Aboriginal young people also have a higher-than-average incidence of contact with and placement in child welfare and mental health institutions (Grekul and LaBoucane-Benson 2006; Trevethan et al. 2002; Blackstock and Trocme 2004).

Despite this bleak social picture, most Aboriginal youth do not become gang-involved. However, the incidence of their street gang involvement is higher than for other Canadian ethnic groups and seems to be increasing (Totten 2009). Much of today's youth gang violence problems can be attributed to poor social structures and economic conditions. We are all products (or victims) of the circumstances of the walk of life into which we are born.

Understanding the phenomenon in its historical and modern contexts helps in developing potential paths toward solutions for the disturbing trend of gang involvement, street violence, and criminalization of Canada's Aboriginal youth. Indifference worsens current injustices and perpetuates socioeconomic disparity and related gang and violence problems. Any solutions will include much-needed shifts in the public discourse to acknowledge the root causes of the problem and create an impetus for social change. Collaborative approaches that empower service agencies and the community at large could help interrupt patterns of gang involvement and violence among Aboriginal youth. Working together in collaborative, victim-centred networks (recognizing that gang-involved youth are victims) is critical for realizing truly effective and sustainable solutions to these serious, complex, and growing social problems. The path forward should include culturally sensitive support for empowerment of Aboriginal peoples. Those that choose the traditional path should be supported in retaining and regaining their cultures. People within Aboriginal communities who want to help children break free from the influence of drugs, despair, and gangs should be encouraged and supported. However, this does not mean that all responsibility for gang problems should be placed on Aboriginal peoples.

An ancient African proverb says "it takes a village to raise a child." In today's globalized world, technology and awareness have broadened the concept of the village far beyond the geographic boundaries that have historically defined it. Greater contemporary awareness of social justice issues has increased the responsibility of all citizens to contribute to solutions and ensure equality. The traditional village has become the whole of society. Governments and societies at large share responsibility for the living conditions of all of its citizens. Many Canadians now feel, as they should, a duty to ensure that every citizen has a minimum standard of living. It is tragic that a country with the high standard of living that Canada enjoys tolerates a large number of its citizens living in extreme poverty. The social injustices created by colonization and racism need to be rectified if national harmony is to be achieved between Aboriginal people and mainstream society in the future.

There is also a growing need to reduce the economic costs of Canada's medical, child welfare, social welfare, and justice systems, which have been largely ineffective in responding to the needs of Aboriginal populations (Donohue 2007). The economic argument alone compels improved engagement, prevention, and social justice for the descendants of displaced indigenous peoples. Without this, Canadian society will continue on its trajectory of increasing social injustice and will be forced to live with the symptoms of these profound ills: poor post-secondary education completion rates and job attainment, socio-economic disparity, and gang involvement and street crime for many Aboriginal youth (Comack et al. 2009). The primary justification for change, however, is the recognition that people all have equal value and should all have access to education, jobs, financial success, and all the other elements of a just society (Held 2004). Donald Kettl of the University of Pennsylvania School of Public Policy spoke about globalization at the Institute of Public Administration, Canada (IPAC) national conference in Quebec City in August 2008, emphasizing that today's problems are so complex and globalized that no single agency or government can do anything important alone. Canada's Aboriginal youth gang violence problems cannot be addressed by any single agency or system. Institutions and communities need to work together. However, working together requires trust and interdependence. Canadian Aboriginal residential school survivors and their descendants have a persisting distrust of government. Today's increasing gang violence problems can be linked at least in part to this legacy of distrust (Comack et al. 2009). Many Aboriginal people distrust their own Aboriginal leaders as well as mainstream government agencies and leaders. Many also distrust the police.

The RCMP are not the only policing agency that was involved in the residential school system. However, they were the most visible agency for most of those involved. Many Aboriginal people saw the RCMP as assisting Indian Agents in enforcing the Indian Act and the Family Allowance Act, the pass system that controlled Aboriginal peoples' movements on and off reserves, as well as government bans that prohibited Aboriginal peoples from consuming liquor, holding dances, and gathering to conduct the traditional ceremonies that are important to their culture and heritage (LeBeuf 2011). In 2004, RCMP Commissioner Zaccardelli officially apologized for the RCMP's involvement in the "Indian Residential School Legacy" (RCMP 2004).

Aboriginal peoples' relationships with the police are crucial to the issue of street gangs and violence. If gang affiliated youth and their extended families and friends do not trust the police, the government, and the non-government agencies that work with the police, then there is little hope of effective police intervention in the cycle of violence. Trust is earned; people need to feel that they are on a level playing field, that justice is fair, and that they have control over their choice to obey the laws and support the system. If people feel that they can be arbitrarily detained, searched, and arrested, or that the laws are enforced differentially, they will not see why they should accept the laws. Why would people cooperate with a civil authority that does not appear to represent their interests? Lack of trust creates barriers to collaboration between Aboriginal community leaders and service agencies that could work together to intervene with youth that are at risk of violent gang involvement. The same lack of trust compounds problems with gang-involved youth who see confrontation with the law and incarceration as a badge of accomplishment and a requirement for gang eligibility (Comack et al. 2009).

Kaariainen (2007) found that the perception of government corruption is directly correlated with decreased public trust in the police in sixteen different European countries. These findings are relevant to Canada's Aboriginal youth street gang epidemic as government and the police in both rural and urban settings are likely to be seen as contributing to the problems in the Aboriginal community. The Canadian government has invested large amounts of money, often without improving the quality of life for many Aboriginal people. Many Aboriginal peoples have lived for decades with largely ineffective government support as well as in-fighting between Aboriginal leaders and ineffective governance structures (Welch and Rabson 2011). The effectiveness of Canada's emerging governance structures may depend largely on Aboriginal peoples and mainstream governments being perceived as more effective and learning to trust each other.

Jackson and Bradford (2010) found that trust is improved when the police are perceived as being competent and fair. Other research has confirmed that in order to trust the justice system and its agents, Aboriginal people, and all citizens, must feel that the system protects all parties' interests equally (Hohl, Bradford, and Stanko 2010; Tyler 2005; Waddington 2010). These findings generalize from the police to other government agencies as well; perceived unfairness creates distrust.

Westmarland explored the relationship between police and communities in England to determine whether trust is improved by community-based approaches that engage the public. Her research found that citizens generally want more input into police priorities and decisions. The police, on the other hand, are cautious about people's motives and are uncomfortable with sharing information and decision-making authority unless they are sure the citizens involved are competent and able to make valuable and informed contributions (Westmarland 2010). A question arises over who should assess competence to work with the police, and how is that to be determined? This study sheds interesting light on the two-way nature of trust. The police, as well as the public, need to earn trust in a two-way relationship in order to work effectively together. These findings also apply to all government agencies. A focus for all government agencies involved in gang prevention and diversion strategies should be to earn trust through competence and fairness.

Achieving and maintaining trust requires a difficult balance as government agencies can lose trust through attempts to manipulate who they work with, while simultaneously losing credibility and effectiveness by attempting to work with people who are not considered representatives of the community at large. The previously mentioned fractures within and between Aboriginal groups are a case in point. Members of several prominent Aboriginal families from Manitoba have told me that there is so much corruption on some reserves that when one member of a family gets elected to council, many people that do not belong to the extended family of the elected individual leave the reserve. Sometimes people leave because they know that the newly elected chief is likely to favour their own extended family in terms of funding and job appointments. When a new band chief is elected, an entire extended family will return to the reserve while many members of another extended family will move out (confidential informants).

If government agencies are seen to be working with the wrong people on issues like gang prevention, others may not trust what they do. Therefore, government resources should be directed into assisting marginalized communities to make the best use of bridge-building opportunities by developing the skills of community members who could represent people competently, fairly, and in a victim-oriented, non-political manner. Skill and sensitivity development must also take place in mainstream society and within police agencies in order for non-Aboriginal and Aboriginal peoples to work together effectively. This sensitivity should be a key focus in the changing public discourse that this book encourages.

Goldsmith (2005) studied police trust in developing and post-authoritarian countries and asserts that without public trust in police, "policing by consent" is difficult or impossible and public safety suffers. Goldsmith's findings resonate with Peel's second principle, that the police depend upon public approval, and his seventh principle, that the police are the people and the people are the police (Peel 1829).

The same research found that non-governmental organizations (NGOs) play an important part in trust-building and service delivery. Individual citizens are often intimidated or ill-equipped to raise issues or complaints about the police or to advocate for their own or others' rights. NGOs can monitor and challenge police and government policies and activities, educate the police, government, and the public, and improve communication that is crucial in trust-building (Goldsmith 2005). NGOs, therefore, become an extension of the community, sharing in the responsibility to contribute to the achievement of social justice.

What does not work to reduce gang involvement, according to Totten, are the gang suppression strategies that have won out over prevention-oriented approaches in many places across Canada. Totten has pointed out that these "get tough" approaches and other ineffective strategies include child welfare models that group troubled teens together. Gang-suppression programs that focus on flooding gang afflicted areas with police resources and prosecuting gang members do not address the root causes of the problem (Totten 2009).

At the First Nations Police Chiefs' Conference in Winnipeg in May 2012, Manitoba's minister of justice, Andrew Swan, said "We can't just arrest our way out of problems." Manitoba RCMP Assistant Commissioner Bill Robinson stressed at the same conference that "we need community-based policing," highlighting the need for community partnerships.

While the need for more preventive approaches is undeniable, there will always be a need for the police to respond and protect citizens in the here-and-now. When a person has just shot someone and is walking down the street with a loaded sawed-off shotgun is not the time to analyze why they didn't finish high school. While this description may sound simplistic, it is the reality that police officers face daily. When a lifetime of bad choices has led a person to a point where they have just killed another person over something trivial, they are already far beyond the point where a little counselling could turn their life around. The blunt instrument of the justice system must be there to make the streets safe from people who have succumbed to forces that create violence. In the long run, however, it is clear that society's goal should be to intervene early to prevent people from making those first bad choices. We also have to consider the most effective use of the justice systems that exist, ensuring that they are focused on correcting social problems and not just creating perceptions that problems have been corrected because punishment has been administered.

Jailing people is effective in some cases and ineffective in others (Aos, Miller, and Drake 2006). In fact, studies across Canada and the United States have concluded that charging and jailing gang members tends to increase their gang-related activity (Benda and Tollet 1999; Nafekh 2002; Nafekh and Stys 2004; Olson, Dooley, and Kane 2004). Placing gang members together only increases their opportunity to bond with the values of those groups (Esbensen and Osgoode 1999; Esbensen et al. 2001; Klein 1995; National Institute of Justice 1998; United States Surgeon General 2001).

Supporting Totten's assertion that "get-tough" approaches are ineffective, Comack et al. researched Winnipeg street gangs and found that prison sentences are seen less as deterrents to crime and more as badges of honour that perpetuate violence (Comack et al. 2010; Totten 2009). One gang member summed up the problem of recidivism and the effectiveness of imprisonment succinctly, stating, "They put us in a society [prison] where violence is prevalent and tell us not to be violent" (Comack et al. 2010, 3). Gang members also talked about the lack of structure in young peoples' lives, describing eight- to ten- year-olds unsupervised in Winnipeg's core neighbourhoods and, not surprisingly, being adopted by street gangs (Comack et al. 2010). (Drawing again on twenty-eight years of law enforcement experience, I am uncomfortable with the term "adopting," as it infers a caring and nurturing intent. I would characterize the gangs more as loosely structured social groups comprised of many wayward souls, some of whom care in various ways about each other, some of whom seek to exploit, use, and damage each other, and many who are indifferent about the well-being of either themselves or their peers.)

What does work, based on the National Working Group on Crime Prevention (2007), are "community-wide, cross sectoral strategies" that address the "multiple factors related to gang violence" (Totten 2009, 146). Effective programs focus on prevention, rather than after-the-fact reaction. The most effective programs, according to Totten (2009) focus on the highest needs of children, starting with newborns to six year-olds, public health–oriented support for families, comprehensive FASD prevention programs, and education. Totten also emphasizes the need to build community capacity through collaboration, a theme I have stressed throughout this book.

Over two decades of frontline policing has reinforced my understanding of the importance of family and community, and the fact that many youth find in gangs the support, identity, and structure that they are seeking, but not finding, elsewhere. Children need love, interaction, structure, and support (Waldfogel 2006). If they do not have this at home, why would children not take to the street and seek camaraderie among their peers?

Maslow's hierarchy of needs is highly applicable here (Maslow 1954). Maslow showed that people of all ages must have their needs for safety, food, and shelter met before they can think about their needs for fulfillment, education, or, ultimately, self-actualization

(Maslow 1954). Many street involved youth are not getting the attention and structure they need at home, setting them up for failure in school and making them vulnerable to exploitation or recruitment into street gangs. However, seeking to fulfill needs for affiliation, identity, and a sense of belonging through gang activity is dangerous because gang activity inevitably places young people in harm's way. These young people are not always making conscious decisions to place themselves in danger. They are making bad choices that inevitably end in ways that they either did not anticipate or failed to care about. The inability to connect one's decisions and actions with the probable results of one's actions is a symptom of FASD, which affects many gang-affiliated Aboriginal youth (Sanders and Welch 2011).

Research has attributed increasing gang involvement to the ever-growing drug trades (Huber 2008). Some American studies have found that increased police crackdowns on the drug trade paradoxically increases violence between gangs (Blackwell 2010; Bolan 2009). Between 1989 and 2006, fifteen different studies in British Columbia found that money spent on policing and increased drug arrests correlated to increased inter-gang violence (Blackwell 2010).

Dr Evan Wood, a professor of medicine at the University of British Columbia, has argued that "when you destabilize the market by taking key players out, violence will ensue" (Blackwell 2010, 1). He argues for legalization of some street drugs to reduce the competition over them, similar to the way that alcohol was historically criminalized and then later legalized. Taking an opposite position, veteran Toronto police member and president of the Ontario Police Association Larry Molyneaux has argued that enforcement is effective against the drug trade. He stated, "When you start to take down and arrest people who are involved in the drug war, I see the opposite," he said. "What in fact you do is, you diminish crime because these people have been taken out of their element" (ibid.).

Working with youth through preventive policing and intervention rather than purely reactive enforcement (charge and jail) before they become gang-involved makes sense. From a policing perspective, it seems that chasing gangs and reacting to existing problems often does very little to address the root causes and fix the core causes of problems such as gang violence.

Research on the economic benefits of crime prevention is still surprisingly limited (Aldhous 2007). Aos et al. (2001) examined over four hundred crime-reduction programs in Canada and the United States over the twenty-five-year period preceding 2001 and found that investments in juvenile interventions resulted in a 2,000 percent saving in justice dollars over the long run. Imagine saving the cost of police processing, prosecutions, legal aid, courts, probations, sentencing, and a host of other costs associated with the justice system, not to mention the human costs of gang violence. Aos et al. found that some programs are a good investment for tax dollars and others are not.

Linda DeRiviere (2005) conducted research on sex-trade workers in and around Winnipeg, examining the financial impact of life in the sex-trade on the justice, medical, and social welfare systems. She found strong evidence that money spent on prevention is a far better investment than traditional reactive strategies that do not address the root problems associated with criminal activity. Prothrow-Stith and Spivak (2004), two doctors who led a social reform campaign to reduce street violence in Boston, report that one shooting victim can cost the community over $1 million.

This economic research perspective resonates as an effective tool for understanding the effects of gang behaviour and designing strategies to reduce it. It provides a strong financial argument for intervention. There is much room for research on the costs of gang violence, which include but are not limited to the anguish felt by both the victims and the perpetrators of violence, the financial costs to the justice system and all of its components, health care costs, business and property values in gang violence affected neighbourhoods, and less tangible costs such as general fear and despair among the citizenry. The fundamental problem in prevention-oriented approaches is that they require extensive resources upfront and may not show measurable success for many years (Prothrow-Stith and Spivak 2004). It is challenging for politicians, who tend to work in four-year election cycles, to justify expenditures on programs that will not yield positive results until long after they have left office, even if those preventive programs are the most effective approaches to address the problems.

This leads back to the discussion about the importance of the public discourse. Aboriginal people make up a relatively small proportion of Canada's total population, which may partially explain why their conditions have been slow to improve. There is chronic indifference among a large portion of mainstream Canadian society to the suffering of marginalized Aboriginal peoples who are living in poor conditions on many reserves and in low socio-economic urban core neighbourhoods. The discourse in Canada leaves much unsaid about unsettled treaty claims, which are viewed by many non-Aboriginal Canadians as not their personal problem but rather as government's responsibility. Many Canadians' only exposures to Aboriginal peoples are the homeless that they see in the streets, who are often suffering from substance abuse and mental illness. Armed stand-offs, land occupations, and protests have occasionally heightened public attention; however, they have not motivated a political or societal will for major structural changes. The threat of increasing street violence has the potential to motivate change. However, as Aos (2001) pointed out, large investments of money and resources do not necessarily fix problems.

Prothrow-Stith and Spivak describe how the community of Boston pulled together to reduce youth violence dramatically in the 1990s. They emphasize that the only way this success was achieved was through cooperation between multiple programs over a long period of time and by tapping the talents, skills, and understanding that exist in the community. They argue that, "often the prescriptive approach dampens the motivation and energy of a community effort" (Prothrow-Stith and Spivak 2004, 4). With this insight, the path seems clear for approaches to reduce gang violence in Canada; we need fewer prescriptions by government agencies and more listening to the affected people.

Acknowledgement, trust, empowerment, and community-based restorative justice approaches may be the key to disrupting Canada's trajectory of youth-gang affiliation and street violence. Following the release of Canada's Truth and Reconciliation Commission (TRC) interim report in February 2012, Commissioner Justice Murray Sinclair stated the TRC panel members were struck by the lack of understanding and awareness among Canadians of Aboriginal peoples and the history of residential schools (Theodore 2012). However, indifference and a lack of awareness is now giving way to growing interest and concern within mainstream contemporary Canadian society as gang activity and street violence continues to intensify. Any hope of disrupting the cycle of violence for many of today's Aboriginal youth requires acknowledgement and understanding of the intergenerational effects and social injustice of marginalization that resulted from Canada's colonization.

Numerous agencies and disciplines, government services and N G O s, and all citizens, including Aboriginal peoples, must work together, focusing on the highest needs of young children, if Canada's Aboriginal youth gang and street violence reality is to be overcome. In many cases, doing this will require a major paradigm shift to acknowledge where systems have failed and to be willing to change. It also requires mutual trust by all parties so that they can work towards a common purpose: a safer community with social justice and equal opportunities for all. The course of the current phenomenon of gang-related street violence may be changed through a shift in the public discourse from general indifference to advocacy for the principle that ascribes equal value to every life, even for gang-involved teens, who have less free choice over entering gang life than many people realize. Ultimately, solutions to Canada's gang problems lie in changing the social structures that currently limit opportunities. When education completion and employment rates are improved, gang violence should be proportionately reduced.

Enforcement, in the meantime is still necessary for public safety, and the police are on the frontline. Until the root causes of violence are addressed, the police must take action, for everyone's safety. Substantial responsibility also lies with the courts and correctional systems. The next section takes a brief look at traditional restorative justice as an alternative to European-based crime and punishment justice models.

RESTORATIVE JUSTICE

Restorative justice is based on the principle that both offenders and victims live in the community and both, as well as the community at large, need to be involved in resolving conflicts. If justice systems are to respect Aboriginal beliefs, the focus should be on restoring harmony in the community and not as much on adjudication between adversaries (Huber 1995; Umbreit 1995). Traditional restorative justice models may therefore be effective for Aboriginal communities (Hamilton and Sinclair 1991), holding the potential to reduce prison populations, expand accountability of offenders, and reduce reliance on policing and corrections systems through deeper community involvement (Griffin 2001).

Linden, Clairmont, and Murphy (2001) outline the ways in which criminal justice issues can be specific to one community and culture, pointing to the need for different processes for different cultural groups. Participatory approaches are important to ensure that the people who are most affected have a voice and a leadership role in the process. Griffin (2001) describes how restorative justice processes can empower the community by involving many people. Roach (2000), on the other hand, explores a wide range of issues around restorative justice and finds that, while it has potential to improve community involvement, it also runs the risk of becoming ineffective if it is not done properly.

The challenge will be in finding the resources to implement restorative justice models, which require more work and resources upfront in order to affect long-term impacts and reduce recidivism. Previous attempts to implement restorative justice programs have been hindered by a lack of support. For example, a program for community justice forums was initiated by the RCMP in 1996, based on a successful Australian model (Canada, Department of Justice 2012b). Training was offered across Canada and numerous police officers volunteered (myself included) and were trained as facilitators. The idea was to bring offenders and their supporters to a meeting with victims and their supporters in order to negotiate resolutions that work for all parties. In cases that met criteria agreed to by Crown attorneys, offenders could be diverted from the normal court system if they agreed to participate in a community justice forum. This process was extremely effective. Offenders avoided criminal records (for minor first offences) and many of them experienced true remorse when they met their victims face-to-face. Victims also felt a sense of true justice, something that often seems to be lost in the impersonal, formal, mainstream criminal court system.

The primary challenge for community justice forums was logistics. The process takes significant coordination, time, and resources. For example, although I was trained, I never had the opportunity to conduct a forum because my position in uniform operations meant I lacked the time to gather fifteen or more people together for a meeting. Frontline policing operations cannot afford to have units off the air for a full day or more attempting to coordinate meetings. The most time that frontline operations could allow uniform officers is the time required for the initial investigation and then attendance at a meeting/forum arranged by others. A deep analysis might well reveal that increased use of community justice forums reduces recidivism and overall long-term costs, justifying its implementation as a preventive measure. However, the same challenges of finding resources for preventive measures described earlier apply here.

To my knowledge, everyone in the system acknowledged that the program was a successful example of restorative justice and a model that could be very effective. Unfortunately, the program was left mainly to the police to administer and is not used much in busy urban centres like Winnipeg due to high demands on officers' time.

Traditions of restorative justice that respect First Nations' traditions may be the key to reducing this particular community's overrepresentation in the justice system. In January 2011, Canada's federal government announced a $2.1 billion expansion of prison facilities to create 2,700 new prison beds at a cost of $800,000 per bed to build and $100,000 per year to house each inmate (Evans 2011). That is a massive increase compared to the cost per year in 2000. A proportionally higher rate of recidivism among Aboriginal inmates increases their consumption of justice dollars. These intractable problems call for top priorities in crime prevention. In Manitoba, federal funding should be aimed at Aboriginal offenders, particularly through preventive programs that will improve education and interrupt the gang activity, substance abuse, and criminalization that contributes to recidivism.

Locating the Canadian headquarters of the TRC in Manitoba is fitting, as the residential school system and the government seizure of Aboriginal children in the 1960s significantly affected Aboriginal peoples in this region of Canada. Rightly, the commission is taking steps to make itself accessible to isolated communities and is considering ways to meet with inmates in prisons in an effort to take statements from the largest number of victims possible (Truth and Reconciliation Commission 2011).

This nation-wide reconciliation effort should contribute greatly to healing the wounds of Canada's colonial past. Visiting the TRC offices in June 2011, I was impressed with the high level of respect and consideration involved as this body attempts to draw out the truth. For instance, tissues are provided to victims while their statements are taken and are treated afterwards as sacred, because they contain the tears of victims.

Experts in trust and peace-building have observed that truth is often more important than justice to victims of oppression (Borer 2006). In June 2011, I travelled to South Africa to study post-conflict trust-building, looking for lessons learned from the post-apartheid experience and the ways the police rebuilt trust with the community. I had the opportunity to meet Dr Piet Meiring, who sat with Desmond Tutu as one of the first truth and reconciliation commissioners. He advised me that people who testified at South Africa's Truth and Reconciliation Commission were often more interested in having their victimization publicly acknowledged than in seeking compensation. Applying this closer to home, the University of Manitoba's recent apology for its role in training teachers who worked in the residential schools was met with accolades from the Aboriginal community across Canada (Martin 2011).

Hopefully, Canada's truth and reconciliation process will transform Aboriginal peoples' historical mistrust of government into a greater willingness to play a part in solutions – including their participation in the justice professions.

ABORIGINALS IN POLICING

Inquiries following defining events like the death of Dudley George during his 1995 protest at Ipperwash Provincial Park in Ontario and the AJI following the 1988 death of J.J. Harper in Winnipeg have made many similar recommendations for reforming Canada's justice system and encouraging more Aboriginal participation in policing. The AJI specifically recommended strategies for increased consultation with the Aboriginal communities in education, justice, law enforcement, the courts, and the prison system. Manitoba law enforcement agencies were directed to improve Aboriginal recruitment in order to better reflect the cultural composition of the community at large (Hamilton and Sinclair 1991). This was important in 1991 and is even more crucial today, particularly given the mass police retirements described earlier and the increasing intensity of Aboriginal issues across Canada in 2013. Manitoba police agencies have increased their Aboriginal membership over the past fifteen years; however, they have not come close to meeting the numbers that were recommended by the AJI (Hamilton and Sinclair 1991). Aboriginals are still underrepresented in policing across Canada – Statistics Canada reported that the number of Aboriginal police officers in Canada has risen from three percent in 1996 to four percent in 2006 (Li 2008; Police Sector Council 2006). These numbers are challenging to assess, however, as many people do not self declare that they are of Aboriginal descent. While the number of Aboriginal police officers may seem to approach the percentage of Aboriginal people in the population at large, it comes nowhere close to the high proportion of Aboriginal people that police officers in most areas deal with as clients in their daily work.

The make-up of police agencies is expected to reflect the cultural and ethnic demographics of the communities they serve (Hamilton and Sinclair 1991; Peel 1829). Truly representing the community and its diversity resonates with Peel's seventh principle: the police are the people and the people are the police (Peel 1829). In Manitoba, police agencies face significant challenges in recruiting a representative percentage of the province's Aboriginal community. The previously described challenges and demands on policing also apply to Aboriginal officers and are complicated by the barriers associated with ethnic diversity. Numerous Aboriginal recruitment and development programs have met with limited success. What has emerged are disconnects between development and recruitment programs and the agencies seeking recruits; attempts to bridge this gap have been disappointing.

There is often a lack of coordination between post-secondary institutions and the professional organizations for which they are developing candidates. Very few new police hires come from existing development programs (University College of the North 2006). The urgent need for educated professionals and the persistent under-representation of qualified Aboriginal peoples in justice fields highlight the need for partnerships and initiatives between post-secondary institutions and justice organizations. Increased coordination between police agencies and educational institutions, may potentially reduce the barriers to good candidates entering law enforcement careers.

Some existing programs are designed to provide post-secondary education for people entering law enforcement. Many, such as the law enforcement program at the University College of the North (UCN), are designed with built-in support for Aboriginal students (University College of the North 2006). The problem is that not many participants of that program are entering law enforcement careers.

Aboriginal peoples face the same challenges as everyone else in their policing careers, in addition to being members of a minority group (Dei, Karumanchery and Karumanchery-Luik 2007). Therefore, they need ongoing support beyond just getting hired. The challenge for the provincial post-secondary education system and professions such as law enforcement is to support qualified candidates within the Aboriginal community not only in entering the profession but also in providing the education and skills required for success in future leadership positions. The true challenges of policing start later in one's career, when an officer assumes a leadership role. This post-hiring, mid-career support is generally lacking and is an area where there is much room for improvement, I suspect, across Canada.

Another challenge to Aboriginal peoples in policing is the stress that they often feel performing the role. Inspector Len Busch, director of the Professional Development Centre for Aboriginal Policing, Canadian Police College, spoke at the First Nations Managers and Practitioners Conference in Montreal in April 2012. He described the cultural dissonance that Aboriginal police officers often experience, on top of the normal pressures of the profession, when they deal with Aboriginal peoples and are seen, or see themselves, as doing the bidding of government bureaucracies that have been oppressive or unresponsive to Aboriginal needs.

The RCMP has historically had policies of attempting to post people where their jobs will not require them to deal directly with their own family members. However, this still happens on occasion. Stress is still bound to occur for officers who want to serve Aboriginal peoples and feel constrained by policy, time, and limited resources to do more. Superintendent Susanne Decock, commander of the OPP Aboriginal Policing Bureau, at the First Nations Managers and Practitioners Conference in Montreal in April 2012, advised that even very experienced, non-Aboriginal officers often feel traumatized after doing short assignments in impoverished places like Pikangikum. The stress for Aboriginal officers must be even more intense. Sensitivity to social justice and cultural diversity issues in modern times is promoting a growing recognition of the importance of resources and the need to focus on officer wellness. Diversity and racism are explored more deeply in the following chapter.

8

Race, Gender, and Changing Attitudes

ABORIGINAL-POLICE RELATIONS

Incidents at various times and locations across Canada have created conflict between Aboriginal communities and the police. Unsettled land claims and treaty agreements have been the source of repeated tension and have often resulted in the police being put in the difficult position of attempting to maintain order while upholding the lawful rights of all parties to disputes. The confrontation at Burnt Church, Nova Scotia, over fishing rights and the 1999 Supreme Court decision to uphold convictions against Donald Marshall for fishing eels out of season, fishing without a licence, and fishing with an illegal net are examples of court battles that have resulted in protests and have exacerbated tensions. The Aboriginal view was that Marshall's conviction contradicted the Mi'Kmaq Treaty of 1760, signed between the British and the Aboriginal communities (Fitzgerald 2002). The Canadian government's slowness in resolving treaty claims has been a continual source of conflict, and tension in Aboriginal communities seems to be continually rising.

The prolonged siege by the Mohawk tribe near the Quebec town of Oka in 1990 heightened tensions for all parties involved (Ladner and Simpson 2010). That conflict left many physical and emotional scars on the Aboriginal community and the police officers who were involved. The death of Dudley George during his 1995 protest at Ipperwash Provincial Park in Ontario was another conflict that scarred both the police and the protestors. In a presentation for the First Nations Managers and Practitioners Conference in Montreal in 2012, OPP Commissioner Chris Lewis described how, after the

Ipperwash incident, officers felt they had not been supported by management after their duties had put them in a difficult position. As a result of the Ipperwash Inquiry, the Provincial Aboriginal Liaison Team was established in 2007 in an attempt to improve police-Aboriginal relations. At the First Nations Managers and Practitioners Conference in Montreal in April 2012, Susanne Decock, commander of the OPP Aboriginal Policing Bureau, noted that the program has been very effective in mitigating conflicts.

In *Conflict in Caledonia: Aboriginal Land Rights and the Rule of Law*, DeVries (2011) describes the 2006 occupation of a housing development in Caledonia, Ontario, by Aboriginal peoples claiming ownership of the land. The book examines growing tension between the Aboriginal community, police, local residents, developers, and the courts. This conflict has been so protracted that the OPP set up a permanent detachment there in order to manage the conflict. In April of 2012, following a rally to protest what was alleged to be a two-tiered justice system in the OPP, three members of Six Nations bands were arrested on charges including assault with a weapon, possession of a dangerous weapon, assaulting police officers, and assault with intent to resist arrest and obstruct police (Hamilton Spectator 2012).

There have also been cases where police officers have acted in a biased manner, and not merely because they were stuck in a difficult position between two sides of an argument over legal rights. One of the most blatant events, and one that caused almost irreparable damage to Aboriginal trust in Canadian policing, was the so-called "starlight tours" case in Saskatchewan. In November 1990, two police officers were convicted of forcible confinement and sentenced to eight months in prison for taking an Aboriginal man to the outskirts of town and leaving him in the cold to walk back to town (Henry and Henry 2006). Three Aboriginal men were found frozen to death in the same area. One man survived being dropped off, after a "starlight tour" and filed a formal complaint, launching an RCMP investigation of the Saskatoon Police Service (Green 2006). The subsequent inquiry found that the initial investigation of Neil Stonechild's death (one of the victims) was severely lacking (Reber and Renaud 2005; Wright 2004). The commissioner of the inquiry, Honourable Justice David Wright, framed the problems within the Saskatoon Police Service as "administrative" rather than race-based (Lugosi 2011; Green 2006; Wright 2004).

Backhouse (1999, 13) has described how Canadians, generally view ourselves as "raceless" and the criminal justice system tends to perpetuate that perception of racelessness. Others have written about Canada's pride in multiculturalism and respecting diversity (Thobani 2007). As a result, Canadians tend to be reluctant to recognize even blatant problems such as what happened to Neil Stonechild and the other victims in the "starlight tours" era.

The previously noted events highlight aspects of conflict between police agencies and Aboriginal peoples of Canada. In order to highlight some of those dynamics in a deeper way, I look at several cases involving the Aboriginal Justice Inquiry (AJI) in Manitoba, as I have personal knowledge, insights, and impressions that I can share.

The 1987 trial of two men for the 1971 murder of Helen Betty Osborne in The Pas, Manitoba, revealed racism in the small town of The Pas, in rural northern Manitoba, and created a conspiracy of silence that allowed the suspected murderers to remain at large for many years; it later raised concerns about the handling of the investigation by the RCMP, fostering a lingering distrust of police agencies and officers in our province by many people in the Aboriginal community (Chartrand et al. 2001).

In another tragic set of circumstances, in 1988 a middle-aged Aboriginal leader named J.J. Harper, from Wasagamack, Manitoba, was shot and killed by a WPS officer as he resisted being spot-checked in the area of a reported stolen vehicle. Tragically, Harper's daughter Zoey hanged herself in protest over the ensuing investigation (Bumstead 1999). The incident increased Aboriginal-police tensions; the resulting Manitoba AJI later found that "Aboriginal-police relations in Manitoba were in a very poor state" (Hamilton and Sinclair 1991).

In November 1989, the evening before he was to testify at the AJI, WPS Inspector Ken Dowson, who was in charge of the investigation into Harper's shooting, killed himself with his service revolver and left a suicide note that was critical of the AJI for persecution of police officers and the WPS. Numerous other police officers were called to testify at the AJI and suffered severe stress, most notably Constable Robert Cross, the officer who fired the fatal shot. He suffered from post-traumatic stress and died young, in 1999, of a heart-related ailment (Hamilton and Sinclair 1991).

A single incident, the shooting death of J.J. Harper, was the tipping point for a public examination of the Manitoba justice system. Police officers were questioned publicly over issues such as whether racial jokes ever occurred in the workplace and how investigations are handled. On the recommendation of the AJI, numerous policies were changed and every WPS officer later received cultural diversity training (Hamilton and Sinclair 1991).

The AJI was a defining event for the WPS, resulting in many changes and a great deal of organizational learning. Ongoing cultural sensitivity training and mechanisms for better communication with the Aboriginal community were established. Aboriginal liaison officers and advisory groups were established and eventually the police organizational culture changed, so that racist views, like sexist views, are now rarely expressed openly in the workplace.

In my experience, there has been a significant change in organizational culture as it pertains to racial and gender bias and sensitivity to diversity in the WPS and the Canadian policing profession in general. This is due, in large part, to increased awareness as well as to labour laws that prohibit discrimination. The change is also due, in no small part, to the increased use of technology, as officers know that they may be recorded at any time and have their indiscretions aired on YouTube, social networking sites, or the evening news.

My first policing assignment after recruit class was in Winnipeg's North End, where large portions of Winnipeg's Aboriginal population live. This was in 1990, directly after the AJI, when racial tensions were at their most intense. More recently, up until 2010, I served for several years as the WPS Missing Persons Unit coordinator, interfacing with the Aboriginal community over the issues associated with missing and murdered women. These deaths became a rallying point for Aboriginal leaders over the perceived lack of action by the justice community. Amnesty International (2004) claims that many violent crimes have gone unsolved over the past three decades because Canadian police agencies have failed to identify or prioritize cases, or put appropriate resources in place.

During this period, I often answered for the WPS regarding this pressing social issue and my work in missing persons brought me into a close working relationship with all levels of several Aboriginal communities. I found that many Aboriginal people of all ages do not trust the police and many have had bad experiences with law enforcement.

The negative effects of colonization experienced by the Aboriginal population are exacerbated by feelings that vulnerable Aboriginal women and children are being preyed upon and sexually exploited, and that police and the government have not done enough to address and take appropriate action to correct the situation (Canadian Press 2011a; Highway of Tears 2011; Joyce 2003; Nay 2008; Skelton 2005; Stittle 2007). As Bernadette Smith said in a report by the Native Women's Association of Canada, entitled "Voices of Our Sisters in Spirit: A Report to Families and Communities" (2009, 68), "We consider ourselves an advanced and compassionate society, yet we treat so many of our fellow citizens as invisible because of their culture, colour, sex, age, lifestyle and other attributes." Police officers have pointed out this passage as being helpful because it calls for compassion in society and a public discourse about protecting the vulnerable.

On the other hand, police officers are often frustrated by the love-hate relationship that many "clients" have with them. Private praise is often given simultaneously with public criticism. Public allegations may advance an agenda but harm police-community relationships. Police officers generally become accustomed to being berated in broad allegations against "the police." What a lot of people do not realize is the sacrifices that police officers make, to varying degrees, in their work. It is an expression of prejudice when someone makes allegations against all police officers, as if they are all the same. Policing is a profession with a strong organizational culture that is much like a family; officers identify strongly with the culture and therefore feel insulted when the profession is belittled. A police officer who has made great sacrifices in her or his work may find that comments against policing in general are a test of her/his dedication and commitment.

The narrative in both the police and the community includes themes of frustration over lack of communication, and the need for more involvement and cooperation on both sides. Police officers suffer the frustration of not being able to resolve cases, working long hours, and forming emotional commitments to victims and their families. Families and friends of victims and missing persons also suffer frustration because there are no actions they can take that would make them feel that they are contributing to finding perpetrators or missing loved ones. Victims are usually not aware of the internal struggles of professional police officers who are stuck between the constraints of bureaucracy, the limitations of investigative resources, technology and laws, and the needs of the victims and families they are trying to serve.

The community often perceives the results of frustration within the police ranks as a lack of transparency and willingness to share. In many cases, officers are seen as not providing information when they are actually reluctant to raise the hopes of victims' families with false expectations, or to dampen them with negativity. The community is often left with a long wait while the system attempts to provide justice, which sometimes never comes.

What the public face of policing does not display is the struggle that officers often have to remain sensitive while surviving the stress of the work. In many ways deliberately maintaining sensitivity is masochistic: when the psychological body armour is removed, police are exposed to the pain and suffering of the victims they are trying to serve. It is a fine balance that many people in the community have admired and appreciated, while others have been less understanding.

Both sides want improved cooperation and acknowledgement of problems. The police want to clarify realistic expectations of what they can do and improve cooperation with the community. The Aboriginal community wants empowerment that equates to improved cooperation with the police.

Lederach (1996) writes about conflict transformation, emphasizing the need for citizen empowerment to participate more in solving societies' problems. His suggestions provide a useful paradigm for transforming police-community tension into positive collaboration. The situation within Aboriginal communities and the agencies of justice needs to evolve to engage police officers, victims, and the community, to give them a voice and create a common discourse with shared interests so that they can work together to reduce crime and improve quality of life. Moving both parties from their opposing positions to more interest-based goals may reduce the tension and allow for better collaboration (Fisher, Ury, and Patton 1991).

Public trust, as mentioned previously, is critical to police effectiveness (Goldsmith 2005). The police need to gain the consent and support of Aboriginal communities in order to serve them. Strategies should involve improving communication and understanding for realistic expectations and improved cooperation in order to best empower Aboriginal communities as well as the ability of the WPS members to serve them.

Sustained dialogue addresses all of these issues. Lowry and Littlejohn (2003) describe reconciliation through sustained dialogue as taking place through (1) being able to explore differences and common ground, (2) identifying common religious values, (3) developing a common way of thinking and talking about differences, and (4) expressing a shared sense of urgency to rebuild community. All have elements have applications for police agencies in establishing and maintaining rapport with the community.

The goal of sustained dialogue is to keep the conversation going and shift the focus from winning to mutual understanding and shared goals (Littlejohn and Domenchi 2001; Lowry and Littlejohn 2003; Rorty 1979). Careful attention needs to be paid to simple communication barriers. For instance, Lowry and Littlejohn found that physical issues such as seating arrangements at meetings could have dramatic effects on communication. Police officers have a heightened awareness over the past twenty years of the importance of issues such as spatial arrangements and body language during meetings, interviews, and interrogations. Sitting in a better chair, or a higher chair, or one with wheels, while the other party is on a fixed, stationary chair can make subtle differences in the dynamics of a conversation and dramatically affect the outcome of a negotiation (Lowry and Littlejohn 2003). Skilled interviewers are alert to these subtle dynamics. Similarly, showing respect to Aboriginal leaders by observing their status and customs can dramatically affect the outcome of a discussion.

Establishing a productive context for effective dialogue, for instance between the police and community groups, can be accomplished by asking the right questions. These include questions involving (1) identity; Who are we?, (2) principles; What do we stand for? (3) intention; Where are we going?, and (4) assumptions; What do we presume? (Ferdig 2001).

Action plans should also include some form of performance measurement. Reflective practice, described later in this book, can ensure that action plans and strategies are continually assessed and adapted for full effectiveness (Schön and Argyris 1978). Nemeroff (2008) stresses that this method of continuous improvement and learning applies to community groups as well. Both the police and community groups should reflect on how they are interacting and make any adjustments needed in order to maintain optimum cooperation. This may take professional mediation, in order to educate people on either side about the dynamics at play and how to work together most effectively.

The key goal of sustained dialogue, according to Nemeroff, is to transform the following five elements of relationships: (1) identity,

(2) interests, (3) power, (4) perceptions and stereotypes, and (5) patterns of interaction (Nemeroff 2008; Saunders 2003). Police officers could benefit from more education in mediation principles and their dynamics, ultimately improving effectiveness.

Researchers have emphasized the importance of getting the right people to the table for dialogue (Saunders 2003; Zartman 2008). Saunders describes the importance of involving people from diverse groups in the process, not just high-level negotiators. He also points out that there can be conflict within identity groups, not just between them and others (Saunders 2003). This dynamic is highly relevant to work with Canadian Aboriginal groups. It is a significant mistake to think of Aboriginal people as one large homogenous group. There are large differences between groups and even deep conflicts between different families within the same communities. Careful consideration should also be given to which police officers are involved in any conciliation process. People with authority to affect change should be involved but it is also important to involve frontline officers who will continue to work with the community.

Sustained dialogue should therefore be established between key police officials, frontline staff, and representatives from the Aboriginal community. Careful consideration should be given to the individuals involved as well as the process followed in the work. This lesson was learned following the Ipperwash inquiry in 1997 and led the OPP to create their Provincial Liaison Team, comprised of officers with heightened sensitivity, awareness of Aboriginal issues, and negotiation skills that help resolve issues. The provincial liaison team becomes involved in any incident involving Aboriginal communities that may become political or contentious. At the First Nations Managers and Practitioners conference (Montreal 2012), Deputy Director General Marcel Savard of Quebec's provincial police agency, the Sûreté du Québec (SQ), noted that Quebec also has provincial liaison teams, similar to Ontario's, as it has proven to be an effective model.

Dialogue should focus on continued trust-building, mutual understanding, and achieving shared goals, moving people on both sides from their historical adversarial positions into a focus on common interests. When new strategies are developed to adjust existing systems, sound change-management principles can ensure that changes are effective. Reflective practice can then ensure that the innovations are continually assessed and practices adjusted as needed. Through reflective practice the police-community team can become a learning entity that continually improves.

Fair, equitable, and unbiased execution of police authority is a theme that recurs throughout this book. The perceived use of racial profiling is one particular issue that has been the subject of much ongoing discourse about police conduct. The next section explores the issue of police profiling and stereotyping.

RACIAL PROFILING, RACISM, AND POLICE WORK

Much of the debate about racism is based on assumptions about police officer intent. Has racism occurred in policing? Absolutely. Are most police officers well-intentioned and attempting to do the most professional job they can? Of course. Nobody enters a profession intending to do a poor job. However, there are some who need to improve the way they perform their jobs and the way they are perceived by visible minorities; there are also many opportunities for improving systems and processes as well as police and public education about the realities and challenges of policing. This book seeks to partially fill that gap.

Satzewich and Shaffir (2009, 200) define racial profiling as "heightened scrutiny based solely or in part on race, ethnicity, Aboriginality, place of origin ancestry, or religion, or on stereotypes associated with any of these factors" (200). Examination of 1.7 million police "contact cards" filled out by Toronto Police between 2003 and 2008 reportedly revealed that blacks were three times more likely than Caucasians to be stopped by the police (*Toronto Star* 2010). But what does this finding actually mean?

The 1995 Commission on Systemic Racism in the Ontario criminal justice System found that 43 percent of black male Toronto citizens reported being stopped by police in the previous two years compared to 25 percent of Caucasian male residents and 19 percent of Chinese male residents. The commission found that "perceptions that the police discriminate against black and other racialized people are widespread." The commission survey found 74 percent of black, 54 percent of Chinese, and 47 percent of white metropolitan Toronto residents believe police treat black people differently than white people (Ontario, 1995 executive summary, ix). The same surveys found widespread perceptions that judges discriminate based on race as well.

A 2000 survey of Toronto high school students revealed that black students who were not involved in criminal activities were still four times more likely to report being stopped by the police and six times more likely to report being searched than white students (Wortley and Tanner 2005). In 2003, thirty-six black Toronto police officers indicated they had been stopped and questioned by other police officers on the basis of their skin colour and not for justified reasons (Tanovich 2006). Many research projects have found that minority groups perceive a racial bias against visible minorities within justice systems (Solomon and Palmer 2004; Wortley and Tanner 2003).

Does that mean the police are racist? Or does it mean there is a higher level of visible criminal activity within some groups in the black community as a result of systemic structural subjugation and socio-economic disparity, as described earlier with respect to the Aboriginal communities?

The police are in a difficult position in many ways. Should police officers look the other way when they see someone who fits all the descriptors of the last twenty drug dealers they arrested? If they look the other way, what are they doing about youth victimization and the drug trade? The challenge for officers is in maintaining balance and not losing their footing on the slippery slope from keen observation of criminal indicators to racial profiling. It is a very fine line. More important, however, is the fact that most citizens understand and appreciate the police doing their job aggressively in problem areas. What they often do not appreciate is being caught in the net and treated like a criminal because they happen to drive through a certain area.

In my entire career, I have rarely met a person who minded being pulled over for a traffic stop or spot-checked for a legitimate purpose as long as I was polite and honest about the reasons for the stop. Officers who become abrasive or make outright racist or inappropriate comments to people from any walk of life have crossed a line and become unprofessional.

At a national forum on policing in a diverse society, Deputy Chief Lawrence Hill (ret.), of the Ottawa Police Service described racial profiling as a pitfall that officers can fall into. In a radio interview Hill said, "Our members are not racist ... but we are no different than any other organization. Do stereotypes exist? Yes. Do things happen because we stereotype people? Yes" (McCooey 2003, 1). The average officer would have to admit, if they are being absolutely truthful, that they have on occasion taken a second look at someone because they are a visible minority. This does not, however, necessarily indicate racism.

Hill said that even officers who are members of visible minorities have become victims of racial profiling. However, except in the rarest of cases, racial profiling does not come from deep-rooted racist feelings that an officer brings to policing. It comes from experience. It is the exposure to daily experience that can taint an officer, the jaundice that can set in after several years of dealing with the more difficult citizens in our society that officers must guard against. At the First Nations Managers and Practitioners conference in Montreal in May 2012, Inspector Len Busch of the RCMP rightly pointed out that police officers carry the stress of dealing, day in and day out, with people who are at their "maddest, saddest, and baddest." Many officers go through periods, usually earlier in their careers, in which they must struggle to see the good in humanity. Thankfully, most are able to successfully regain faith in humanity.

What is commonly known as instinct is actually our natural subconscious reactions formed after years of experience. When an experienced police officer sees someone who walks, talks, acts, and dresses like the last twenty people they arrested, it gets their attention.

If I am driving down the street in a suburban neighbourhood and see a youth standing at the corner of a house, I will take a second look because I wonder if they are "standing six" (lookout), watching out for residents or the police while a confederate breaks into a residence. If the same kid looks even more out of place because he or she is member of a visible minority, most of whose members live in another neighbourhood, it may seem even more suspicious. Checking it out is just good police work. Taking it a step further and assuming they are doing something wrong or, even worse, treating them as a criminal without justification, is stepping away from professionalism and slipping into racial profiling; it is a fine line.

Some officers do succumb to biased policing, but it is not a brush that should be used to paint the entire police profession. In February 2011 the Quebec Human Rights Commission awarded $20,000 to Felix Fini and Christy Coulibaly as a result of a 2007 incident in which the couple was left standing in the cold with their infant child for forty-five minutes while their car was seized and towed away for lawful reasons. Fini came from the Ivory Coast as a student and now lives and works in Canada. When Fini asked to wait in the cruiser car, an officer allegedly declined, saying it was not a taxi (Scott 2011). The Montreal officer allegedly told the aggrieved Fini that if he did not like being stopped by the police, he should go back to his own country. This racist lack of compassion reflects poorly on policing, but it certainly doesn't represent the compassion that most officers demonstrate in carrying out their duties.

Besides basic police observation skills, a specialization in highway interdiction – stopping cars or trucks to look for drugs or weapons – has taken observation skills to an entirely new level over the past two decades. This specialty has evolved in the context of an ever-increasing illicit drug trade and the fact that tons of illegal drugs must be transported between where they are grown or manufactured and where they are distributed (Size 2012). Police officers hone the skills to detect the signs of such transport and catch drug and weapon traffickers. There is a fine line between pulling a vehicle over because it is suspicious for A, B, and C reasons or because it is driven by a certain visible minority group member dressed a certain way, in a particular type of car, etc.

In *So You Want to Find the Mother Load,* Andrew Hawkes reflects on seventeen years of highway interdiction experience in the United States, during which he made five hundred felony arrests and 5,100 pounds of street drug seizures. The book provides police officers with signs to watch for that indicate a person is transporting illegal drugs. From personal experience, I can say that such signs are learned through diligent observation and tenacity, but they could be mistaken for stereotyping or profiling. It is very much like the scenario I just described – a kid standing suspiciously by the side of a house can warrant a second look. Officers trained in interdiction look for the clues that a person is smuggling drugs. When they start to add up, suspicion grows until an officer forms grounds to suspect that a person is carrying illegal drugs. The person may be a visible minority, but the vehicle is stopped as the result of the observations of an officer who is taking all the circumstances into account. Sometimes an arrested person will have to wait until disclosure of the police report for their court case to learn exactly what the details were that caused an officer to form legal grounds to search or arrest them. Given this, it is no surprise that some people initially think they were the victims of racial profiling (Hawkes 2012).

In *Racial Profiling: Challenging the Myth of a Few Bad Apples,* Henry and Tator (2006) describe the systemic racial profiling that they feel occurs routinely in cities across Canada; they report that it affects Asians, Muslims, Arabs, Hispanics, Blacks, and especially Aboriginals. They argue that there is statistical evidence in the United States, Britain, and Canada that racial profiling is a routine part of policing (Ontario Human Rights Commission 2005; Satzewich and Shaffir 2009) and find that even if there are disagreements over the methods used to interpret statistical evidence, there are numerous anecdotal reports about racial profiling occurring (Harvey 2003; Ontario Human Rights Commission 2005; Wortley and Tanner 2003). Henry and Tator also note that police chiefs, police union representatives, and police boards generally deny that racial profiling is practised in Canada (Henry and Tator 2006; Wortley and Tanner 2003).

Canada has been praised internationally for its multicultural inclusion and yet it has a history of conflict related to racial discrimination (Henry and Tator 2005; Mosher 1998; Walker 2010; Wortley and Owusu-Bempah 2011). Wortley and Owusu-Bempah (2011) highlight the increasingly vocal input from Canada's growing black population about perceived persecution through racial profiling by the police. However, police agencies have often denied allegations of racial bias (Tanovich 2006; Tator and Henry 2006).

The results of many studies as well as the statistical analysis upon which police denials have been based have also been hotly debated (Gabor 2004; Melchers 2006). Wortley and Owusu-Bempah (2011) point out that many previous studies of racial bias by the police are based on anecdotal accounts or qualitative data derived from small samples and are, therefore, difficult to generalize to larger populations. They surveyed a larger sample in order to ascertain public perceptions in Toronto, Canada's largest and most ethnically diverse city and home to over half of Canada's black population. Their study found that blacks are more likely to view racial profiling as a problem in Canada. Caucasian and Asian respondents were more likely to view it as a useful crime-fighting tool. As mentioned earlier, the surveys found that black respondents were significantly more likely to report being stopped and searched by the police than were people from other ethnic groups (Wortley and Owusu-Bempah 2011).

Scholars have suggested that the language used to describe racism and racial profiling is important. It is no surprise that police officers deny racism, as the term has such negative connotations (Braithwaite 1989; Stenning 2011). Stenning (2011) points out "while racism often leads to racial discrimination, racial discrimination is not necessarily indicative of racism." Some scholars and commissions of inquiry have blurred the concepts of "racism" and "racial discrimination" as "systemic racism" (Henry and Tator 2011; Ontario 1995; Satzewich and Shaffir 2009). Sir William Macpherson's report on the inquiry into the London (England) Metropolitan Police Service's (MPS) investigation of the murder of Stephen Lawrence adopted the term "institutional racism" to describe systemic problems with racial bias in the MPS. That inquiry found that racial discrimination had occurred at the policy and procedural level and therefore it was important to include the term "racism" in characterizing what had occurred. Using the term "racism" removes any doubt that there were problems with racial bias that needed attention (Macpherson 1999).

Scholars have argued that the term "racist" should be included in descriptions of policies and behaviours where racial bias is alleged or suspected, because it is the only way that police agencies will take such accusations seriously (Tonry 2004). Others have argued that accusing police agencies of "systemic racism" or "institutional racism" has such negative connotations that it can make the agencies overly defensive and therefore such allegations can be counterproductive (Braithwaite 1989; Foster, Newburn, and Souhami 2005; Souhami 2007).

Overt racism by officers is an issue that can be judged and dealt with on a case-by-case basis while denying overt racism can cause agencies to overlook more subtle nuances that may be the bigger problem. The largest challenge for police agencies is at the policy level and involves organizational culture. For instance, the height restriction that was so commonly used as a hiring requirement twenty years ago discriminated against Asian people (and some women) who are typically shorter than the average white male of European descent. Height restrictions have now been abandoned, and greater cultural and gender diversity is being achieved. Stenning points out that these past practices did not result in agencies being accused of racism or sexism. They did, however, discriminate needlessly (Stenning 2011).

Stenning (2011) highlights two common reactions that police services have to allegations of racial profiling. The less credible reaction is "We don't do it." The more common defence is that "criminal profiling," occurs but the criteria are not racially based. This latter response, according to Stenning, acknowledges that systemic or unwitting or unintended discrimination may occur.

Stenning points out that officers may become confused when they receive mixed messages about diversity and race sensitivity. On one hand, they are taught to exercise their authority fairly and without regard to the race and ethnicity of the people they are dealing with. At the same time officers receive cultural sensitivity training that teaches them to account for cultural differences and discriminate in a positive way. Treating everyone exactly the same might be as dangerous as racism or prejudice, because no policy or procedure can be designed to be completely fair to all people from every different ethnic, age, gender, or other type of group.

Commissions of inquiry, task force reports, and scholarly research papers have suggested that minority groups are often "under-policed" as crime victims and "over-policed" as crime suspects and offenders (Satzewich and Shaffir 2009). Satzewich and Shaffir (2009) argue that, in the context of police subcultures, prejudice or discrimination against visible minorities may occur but without racist intent. Police officers may fall victim to strong organizational pressures that lead them to conform to accepted practices, including profiling (Chan 2011). Some research has found that many aspects of police culture have persisted throughout recent history, despite trends such as recent shifts to community-based policing (Loftus 2010).

An interesting twist on the debate about racial profiling is the fact that officers are routinely discriminated against on the basis of being police officers. One black officer with the Hamilton Police Service said, "When you get a call and you're a black person or a white person, Vietnamese, or whatever you are, you get called a pig just the same" (Satzewich and Shaffir 2009).

Throughout my entire career, I have had the uncomfortable experience, as have most officers, of being painted with the same brush as other police officers who have acted inappropriately, often in other agencies and even in other countries. Every police officer experiences this to varying degrees. The police officer cannot shed his or her professional identity any more than a member of a visible minority can shed their association with their cultural group. These experiences also contribute to the tendency to profile by developing an "us versus them" attitude. This is what police officers must guard against.

The process of being socialized into policing involves mastering skills and accepting the standards and beliefs of the organizational culture (Fine 1985). Police culture, just like any other profession, is defined by distinct norms and values, as well as ways of responding to situations (York 1994).

For all of the reasons described in the chapter on police demographics, today's new generation of police officers may be better equipped to avoid the pitfalls of racially biased policing. The new generation has been raised in a more multicultural society, with greater awareness of and sensitivity to culture and gender issues. One Hamilton Police Service officer said "new recruits not only come with more experiences relating to diversity, they are not willing to tolerate racist attitudes within the police force" (Satzewich and Shaffir 2009, 216). A female officer who was interviewed for the same study explained, "I do see an improvement with the younger people ... as opposed to twenty, twenty-five years ago when you finished high school, and you walked across the street to the police station and got hired ... recruits are older and are college and university educated" (ibid., 215).

Modern policing philosophies include intelligence-led, problem-oriented, hot spot, and community-based models (Caputo and Vallee 2005; Newburn and Reiner 2007; Seagrave 1996, 1997). O'Conner (2008) points out that, regardless of the policing model used, there has been an increasing emphasis on community involvement. Improved community engagement may be the key to reduced tension between police and visible minorities by reducing "us versus them" attitudes. It would be useful to have more research on which visible minority groups have negative views or relationships with the police and how those relationships may be improved. It would also be useful to have more research on age and gender as they relate to attitudes about policing. Hurst and Frank (2000) found that age is an important factor in police-community relationships, and research in this area is limited. O'Conner (2008) suggests that, without improved relations between the police and young people, community-based policing, which relies on partnerships, is not likely to succeed.

Diversity within police agencies is also important and has changed dramatically in recent decades. It is important for agencies to be representative of the communities they serve. The most significant change has been the increased inclusion of women, who comprise approximately 50 percent of the population. The next section examines the de-gendering of a male dominated profession, yet another aspect that has seen dramatic change in the past two decades.

WOMEN IN POLICING

Prior to the 1980s, policing was male-dominated and female officers had a continuous uphill battle to gain credibility and recognition, compounded by a high incidence of inappropriate harassment. In the past two decades, great strides have been made to open policing to women. Height, weight, and upper body strength requirements that were in place until the 1990s prevented many good female candidates from being hired (Stenning 2011). The resulting changes have enhanced the profession, as women bring an important balance and perspective that did not exist before.

In 1965, 190 or 0.6 percent of Canada's 30,146 police officers were female. By 1990, 3,573 of Canada's 55,008 police were female, 6.4 percent of the total. In 2011, there were 13,605 female officers who comprise 19.6 percent of Canada's 69,438 police officers (Statistics Canada 2011a). Statistics Canada reports that the number of female officers across Canada increased by 285 in 2011, while the number of male officers decreased by 97 (ibid.). (The decrease in the number of men is explained by the mass retirement of baby boomers mentioned earlier.) Quebec and British Columbia have seen the greatest increases in the numbers of female officers hired, while Manitoba, New Brunswick, and Prince Edward Island report the lowest increases. The number of female officers in the territories has been lower than in the provinces over the last few years (Statistics Canada 2011b).

Women have had an uphill battle in what has been commonly referred to as the testosterone-filled, male-dominated field of policing. The glass ceiling that exists in many industries is perhaps even more prominent in the policing profession. As a result, there is room for substantial change, although the percentage of women in non-commissioned officer and senior ranks has tripled in the past decade (Statistics Canada 2011a).

Substantial literature describes the variety of coping mechanisms that women have had to resort to in the gendered institution of policing (Eveline and Booth 2002; Hoschschild 1973; Jacobs 1987; Martin 1979; O'Connor, Morabito, and Tobin-Gurley 2011). Women have generally had unique challenges to face in overcoming workplace dynamics, including job performance as well as their relationships with fellow officers (Hochschild 1973; Martin 1979). Martin (1979) describes how early police women tended to display masculine job-related characteristics in order to fit in.

The same research from the 1970s found that women in those earlier years often maintained their femininity by gravitating to more administrative roles and non-patrol, less masculine, assignments (Martin 1979). Research has found that women who take on the traditionally more masculine assignments also have to take on some aspects of the masculine aggressive roles, which can make male officers feel threatened, while accepting non-patrol assignments, which are often less stressful, is not as good for career advancement (Berg and Budnick 1986; Garcia 2003; Martin 1979; Berg and Budnick 1986; Garcia 2003). Choosing subordinate roles also reduces the possibility of deconstructing and redefining gendered roles.

Attitudes about gender roles in policing have changed substantially in recent decades. Research in Britain has found that female officers who take on traditionally female tasks are often perceived by older officers (but not younger ones) as lacking commitment (Brown and Campbell 1991). Police women have seen themselves as being underrepresented in some police roles and as having had their assignments blocked by senior officers (Coffey, Brown, and Savage 1992).

American research from the 1980s found that about one in five patrol officers willingly worked with a female partner while one in five strongly resisted such a partnership (Brown and Carlson 1993). Working together for ten or more hours a day as a police team is a very intimate relationship. In the "old days" many officers used to say their wives would never stand for them working with a female partner. While it would be considered inappropriate to express such a sexist attitude today, it still occurs in isolated cases. Attitudes of superior officers were mixed, historically, but frontline male officers' attitudes towards police women were "almost uniformly negative" in the 1980s (Balkin 1988).

An Australian study found that sergeants and constables differed in their attitudes towards women police. Sergeants were found to believe that women are better at diffusing violent situations but that men's stronger physical presence deters violent situations. Twothirds of sergeants in 1994 felt that less than 10 percent of officers should be female, and the overwhelming majority felt that the police agencies should not do more to accommodate women having a family and children as well as a policing career (Centre for Police Research 1994).

The majority of constables surveyed in 1994 expressed no preference as to a male or female working partner and more than 70 percent felt that police services should do more to accommodate combining marriage and family with policing careers (Centre for Police Research 1994). This older research is mentioned as it highlights the prevalent attitudes that women have made significant strides in overcoming. It has been suggested that the passage of time alone may eventually eliminate this prejudice (O'Connor Shelley, Morabito, and Tobin-Gurley 2011).

Researchers have speculated that as male and female officers train and work together, prejudices will naturally be reduced (ibid.). I believe that this has already happened. Twenty years ago in Winnipeg, many supervisors felt that two female officers should never be assigned to work a cruiser car together. Now, gender is less of a consideration and two female members working together is not uncommon, although supervisors will often attempt to pair a female and male member because of the logistics involved – the male officer can search male suspects and the female partner can search female suspects. A same-sex team has to call for assistance every time they arrest someone of the opposite sex in order to protect the dignity and rights of both the citizen and the officers.

It has been reported that one of the greatest challenges that women find in policing is the work hours (Leighton and Syrett 1989; McRae 1990). As policing is generally conducted around the clock, there can be difficulties in balancing shift-work and family. The nature of the job is fluid and often requires flexibility around emergencies, overtime, and transfers, on top of the usual challenges of shifts that have to cover the clock, 365 days per year. Teamwork in specialty units often calls for a great deal of flexibility; officers who cannot work overtime due to childcare responsibilities may have a difficult time gaining acceptance in small specialized teams that require overtime on major projects. Imagine that the team makes a breakthrough on a major investigation and is serving search warrants and making arrests – and then one member has to leave.

Childcare has historically been viewed primarily as a female responsibility. However, relationships are changing and men are increasingly taking on childcare roles as well. As well, with an aging population, both men and women are increasingly looking after elderly parents as well as their children. Wilkinson (1994) found that the main reason women left policing was the perceived inflexibility of organizations to accommodate women trying to balance their responsibilities for childcare and policing. The same research found that challenges for women involved inflexibility in work arrangements as well as the lack of leaves of absence for child rearing. In Australia there are provisions for flexibility in many police agencies, as there are in Canada, but many officers feel that their career will be damaged if they take advantage of them. Wilkinson rightly points out that both the organization and the individual loses if an officer resigns due to family-work conflict.

Police shiftwork is a challenge that may eventually be viewed by the courts as an undue hardship for employees who are also caring for children or elderly family members. In 2010 a Canadian Border Services Agency officer filed a complaint with the Canadian Human Rights Tribunal, arguing undue hardship caused by the irregular shifts the agency had required her to work. A subsequent federal court decision requires workplaces to accommodate reasonable childcare-related requests from their employees (Canadian Press 2013). This decision, and others that are sure to follow, may have a massive impact on police and other emergency services that need people on active duty twenty-four hours per day, 365 days per year. Stuart Rudner, employment law specialist with Miller Thomson, said "This is likely the next frontier," (Canadian Press 2013, 1). Winnipeg's Discovery Children's Centre is one of the rare programs that offers childcare at odd hours (ibid.).

It is in the interest of both police agencies and individual officers to find innovative solutions to child care challenges. One solution I found was a practice we tried when I was coordinating the Missing Persons Unit. It was a very small unit and we routinely had emergency calls, such as international and interprovincial abductions, amber alerts, high-risk missing person cases, and homicides where we would be called to assist with unidentified remains. Several of our members had childcare issues and often could not stay for overtime, even if we had an emerging investigation. In order to offset this challenge, we took advantage of the fact that uniform patrol has overlap days when officers could be assigned to assist us with missing person investigations. We went out of our way to make this a regular occurrence and developed a pool of uniform officers with experience who could assist during emergent calls. This way, if we caught an emergency and some team members had to leave for family commitments, we could call in experienced uniform members to assist.

Our unit also made more use of members who were on restricted duties as a result of being pregnant than any other unit in our police service. Once a member declares that she is pregnant, she normally has to be restricted to office duties because fieldwork has too much risk of violence. Members would declare they were pregnant and then have restricted duties for several months until going on maternity leave. By giving them meaningful and challenging work to do while on restricted duty, they developed an appreciation of the nuances of missing persons work, and we benefited from their assistance.

Gender sensitivity has evolved in tandem with cultural diversity awareness over the past two decades. Human rights case law and agency liabilities have driven a great many changes in training, education, and policy through the 1990s and into the new millennium. In the past twenty years, the culture in the policing profession, like that in many industries, has changed. The work environment is much more professional and less gendered than it was in the late 1980s and early 90s.

Despite shifting attitudes and reduced tolerance for sexual harassment, it continues to occur. Isolated incidents happen in most organizations. However, the important challenge for police leaders is to ensure that the organizational culture is evolving in the right ways. Shifting organizational values is like turning a large ship at sea; it can be slow to respond at first but picks up momentum over time. The place of female officers in policing seems to have moved, generally in the right direction but occasionally taking a step backward.

Over the past decade Canada's largest police agency, the RCMP, with 30,000 members, has been beleaguered by harassment issues. One of the most prominent challenges is officer wellness. In 2011 over 1,700 members were receiving pensions for post-traumatic stress disorder (PTSD) related to a broad array of causes (Freeze and Baily 2011). When Corporal Catherine Galliford alleged that rampant sexism exists throughout the RCMP and that sexual harassment had ruined her health and career after she joined in 1991, it was a bombshell (Gillis and Macqueen 2011). Several other current and former RCMP members came forward to announce that they too had been subject to various forms of sexual and non-sexual harassment in the workplace (ibid.). Mike Webster worked as a psychologist with Canadian police officers for over thirty-five years; he reportedly said that more than a dozen other RCMP members had contacted him about harassment issues since Galliford went public and that two sexual harassment cases had been started before hers. Webster characterized the RCMP's policy of unlimited sick time as part of the problem: RCMP members are booking off sick due to stress-related issues or are sometimes placed on indefinite leave but their problems remain unresolved (Gillis and Macqueen 2011).

Given the size and massive jurisdiction of the RCMP, their issues may be in proportion with other police agencies across Canada. However, the RCMP's issues have become very public. After Commissioner Giuliano Zaccardelli resigned in 2006, during the Maher Arar affair, the government promised major reforms in response to numerous harassment allegations. For the first time in the agency's history, a commissioner, William Elliott, was appointed from outside the ranks of the RCMP (Gillis and Macqueen 2011).

In her PhD thesis on women in the RCMP, ex-RCMP member Bonnie Reilly Schmidt describes her ten years as one of Canada's first female RCMP members hired after 1974, over one hundred years after the agency's formation. Schmidt describes the difficult road that female officers had to travel in those earlier years, when they were challenged not only by the criminals they had to deal with but the male officers they served with. She describes how women have come a long way from the first troop of female members who graduated thirty-six years ago in high heels and pillbox hats instead of high-browns and Stetsons (Ryan 2011; Schmidt 2012).

David Brown, head of the 2007 task force on governance and culture within the RCMP, said in 2011 that the RCMP does not seem to be getting ahead of the allegations. Brown has reportedly said, "With the proper management structure and focus, much of this would not have happened. They are needless issues that can and should be rectified" (Gillis and Macqueen 2011, 3)

While isolated events or even systemic structural and organizational culture challenges raise concerns, and there are clearly some areas for improvement, it is important to point out that the vast majority of police officers are highly disciplined and professional. The proverbial "officer and gentle [wo]man" is, in my opinion, the rule rather than the exception in the RCMP and in police agencies across Canada. I have worked with the RCMP on numerous issues and the people I have worked with in every rank have generally impressed me as the embodiment of professionalism. That being said, the evidence points to a need to address major organizational issues in many areas. In 2011, Commissioner Bob Paulson was appointed from within the ranks and should have been well positioned to move the ship in the correct direction, address these problems, and improve morale within the RCMP (Kennedy and Quan 2011). The metaphor of organizational culture as a ship seems to fit, as it cannot be turned suddenly and requires momentum for meaningful change. In the case of the RCMP it is a particularly challenging task to change an organization that is steeped in tradition. By November 2012, Public Safety Minister Vic Toews was publicly chastising Commissioner Paulson and the RCMP for acting too slowly to deal with their persisting harassment issues and with female officer recruitment and promotions (MacCharles 2012).

The policing profession has come a long way in the last two decades. In my first posting, in Winnipeg's North End, there were over 150 general patrol officers and only a few were female. The female change room was a closet compared to the men's locker rooms and female supervisors were very rare. This was fairly typical of police agencies across Canada.

Now, female police officers hold key leadership positions across the country. Many women are high achievers in an aggressive profession that is just now losing the last remnants of its gendered past. The next chapter explores structure and governance, another dimension of policing that has seen much change as a result of changing attitudes.

9

Governance and Policing

MUNICIPAL GOVERNANCE

Canada's original provincial political boundaries were based on agriculture, rural communities, and trade routes. When the laws forming the provinces were first established, municipal levels of governance were not considered because cities did not exist. Now, however, cities have become the major population centres across Canada and the vast majority of services are provided at the municipal level. Large Canadian cities tend to be run more like corporations than as levels of government (Dunn 2002). The courts have ruled, however, that municipal governments have all of the obligations of other levels of government to provide fair and equitable services to all citizens (Frugg 1999). Municipal governance is unique in that, unlike ministers at the provincial and federal levels, city councillors are not directly responsible for city departments. While there is a doctrine of ministerial responsibility that defines accountability in the federal and provincial governments, municipal councillors rarely have to answer for actions taken by individual civic employees, although technically and legally city councillors are jointly answerable for the services the municipality provides. There is thus diminished individual responsibility for the decisions and actions of city councillors. Sancton (2002) observed that even mayors have no special authority, except in cases where it has been delegated by provincial statute.

While accountability differs between municipal and provincial and federal levels of government, it has also changed within those levels. Ministerial accountability is routinely debated at the federal and provincial levels. The debate centres on how a minister can be responsible for departments that are now so large and doing such technically complex work that he or she cannot possibly be aware of everything that is happening within them. Canadian scholars Kernaghan and Langford (1990) and Savoie (2003) have both described how provincial and federal ministers are still ultimately legally responsible for what happens within their departments. The debate continues, however, because the sheer complexity and sophistication of many modern government jobs puts individual employees in positions wherein only they truly understand, and can answer for, the details of the work they are doing. Thus civil servants are often the ones who are now called before parliamentary hearings and inquiries to answer for activities within their departments, because the minister is not the most knowledgeable in the area under consideration (Franks 2004). This is a departure from the past, when ministers would answer for government activities, keeping civil servants anonymous and protected.

Savoie (2003) has eloquently described this shift in accountability from politicians to civil servants. The same shifting of accountability is starting to apply at provincial and municipal levels. Accountability is also shifting internally, as police officers are increasingly facing challenges in open court about policies, procedures, practices, and tactics.

While municipal political governance structures differ from those of other levels of government, the administrative and working components operate under the same values, ethics, and structures across all three levels of government. All public servants are expected to serve both their political leaders and the public in an impartial, non-partisan, and neutral manner (Dunn 2002).

International, special interest, and local non-government organizations are increasingly engaged in governance and should be recognized for the significant roles they play in modern policy networks. In a globalized world, understanding the interplay between the various stakeholders that are now prominent in governance networks is critical to effectiveness. In the future, Aboriginal peoples may also come to be recognized as a fourth level of government in Canada (Canada, Indian and Northern Affairs 1996).

Simeon (2002) noted that international bodies, such as the World Trade Organization and the North American Free Trade Association, have become central policy actors as well in a world that is now affected on all levels by globalization. On a local level, non-government actors increasingly influence municipal administration, particularly in sectors such as the police where the current trend is to work more closely with the community, to form partnerships with non-government agencies, and to be subject to ever-increasing transparency and the accountability that comes with it.

Federal-provincial disputes over jurisdiction have existed since Confederation. Simeon (2002) describes how the provinces originally sought to pursue their own provincial economic development, while the federal government in Ottawa resisted in the name of nation-building. Arguably, municipal governments have been left to operate under the radar of Canada's larger political picture, despite the fact that they provide the majority of frontline services for most of Canada's population. Using Morgan's biological metaphor, Canadian cities can be characterized as independent organisms, operating within the larger ecosystem (Morgan 1997); they work and live independently, receiving occasional injections of financial sustenance from the provincial and federal governments.

Stoney and Graham (2009) point out that the federal government has many good reasons for not getting involved in municipal affairs, the most obvious one being that, constitutionally, the provinces are responsible for services provided in their jurisdictions. While the federal government has no direct role in the local delivery of many services, like policing, it does ultimately have a responsibility to support them. Lithwick has criticized the federal government's tendency to avoid taking responsibility for local challenges. He writes, "The federal government has used the constitution as an excuse to abstain from playing a responsible urban role, despite overwhelming evidence that it is the principal actor in the urban political reality" (Lithwick 1970, 577). Stoney and Graham write that Lithwick captures the "paradox" of federal-municipal relations in Canada, which is that the federal government has no authority over municipal governments, yet everything it does affects municipalities.

Municipal institutions operate separately from their provincial and federal counterparts; however, Sancton (2002) describes the three levels as inextricably intertwined. Simeon (2002) argues that the management of intergovernmental relations is a major part of any senior policy manager's job. This structure results in increased accountability and responsibility for modern civil servants, as they are required to interact directly with outside agencies and other departments.

This governance reality has significant effects on municipal police agencies, which also operate within a larger system with their counterparts in other jurisdictions and government levels. Much of the municipal police force's ability to secure resources and support from the larger system lies with its executives and their ability to negotiate with outside entities. This ability is connected, at least in part, to the education and experience described earlier as being an important part of police leadership, because being politically savvy and understanding how the system works is vitally important to a leader's ability to secure additional funds from other government levels and agencies.

TRICKLE-DOWN: GOVERNMENT FUNDING

While, constitutionally, the federal government is not directly responsible for the provision of frontline services in Canadian cities, some return on federal tax dollars needs to be apparent to the majority of citizens – and electors – who are now congregating in large urban centres. Stoney and Graham (2009) describe how rapid urbanization and population growth as a result of immigration has created infrastructure, housing, and transport challenges for Canadian cities and detail how urban costs are outstripping revenues. Estimated municipal costs were over $123 billion and growing steadily in 2007 (Federation of Canadian Municipalities 2007).

Tindal and Tindal (2004) note that although local governments have no constitutional link with the federal government they are, in reality, connected. Issues such as urban sprawl and crime are focused in urban centres and call for more collaborative, multilevel approaches. In many cases large amounts of government funding for frontline work is absorbed by provincial and federal bureaucracies. Pal (2006) provides dramatic examples of how higher-level bureaucracies can starve frontline service delivery by diverting resources. In the case of policing, the initial burden of responding to emergencies rests squarely on the shoulders of municipal emergency services and yet federal and provincial governments often absorb most of the available funding, leaving very little to trickle down to the frontline.

As a member of the disaster management team for the City of Winnipeg, I have witnessed this phenomenon firsthand. Hundreds of millions of dollars are spent by the federal government on emergency management and counter-terrorism intelligence and response programs. However, when an act of terrorism or a major industrial accident occurs in the centre of a city, it is the local emergency services that respond first.

A federal allocation of one billion dollars for updating the Public Safety Act, in preparation for the anticipated global flu pandemic in 2006, did not translate into improved capacity or expanded resources for local fire and police departments (Canadian Centre for Emergency Preparedness 2006). But, as one of the people who worked on the police and emergency response for my jurisdiction, I can say that the police role would have been extensive if the pandemic had become worse. The police would have played substantial roles in assisting the medical examiner's office to secure homes, record deaths, make death notifications, and manage the possible public hysteria. The police were to play a role in isolating and securing quarantined aircraft, public places, and buildings and in assisting emergency medical responders, who would surely be overwhelmed. All of this involved extensive plans to have numerous stakeholder agencies work together. Doing this takes training and practice, which requires another investment.

In the aftermath of the 9/11 terrorist attacks in the United States, billions of dollars were spent worldwide on emergency preparedness. The bulk of that money was spent on security, counter-insurgency, and intelligence agencies. The police officers and firefighters who are mandated to respond to an actual act of terrorism received very little from these massive new expenditures (Canadian Centre for Emergency Preparedness 2006). Municipal police and emergency services respond to any event that occurs within their jurisdiction. Shortly after the initial response by local services to a major event, special resources such as the national chemical, biological, radioactive, nuclear, radiological, and explosive (CBRNE) team may be deployed, but chances of their arrival, depending where in Canada the incident occurs, within a day or even several days are slim (RCMP 2012). In fact, even once special resources and teams arrive, their contribution is limited. For instance, if the national CBRNE team were deployed to support an operation, their role would be limited to their specific area of expertise, addressing the threat. The bulk of the work around a major event would be in assisting the community to mitigate the damage, recover, and regain a state of normalcy. Managing the actual explosion, or whatever the threat is, would constitute a much smaller aspect of the entire event than aiding the recovery of the community. While the police play only a small part in whole community recovery after a major event, it is still a significant draw on police resources.

Police executives must be astute in the dynamics of intergovernmental affairs and need to understand how funding is transferred from the federal and provincial governments to municipalities. They also must be able to negotiate effectively with municipal governments for their policing budgets. All Canadian provinces have ministries related to the frontline services, which can include transportation, education, health, income, maintenance, social services, natural resources, energy, agriculture, environment, economic development, and tourism. There is so much interplay between levels of government that most provinces now have ministries dedicated to intergovernmental provincial-municipal affairs (Sancton 2002).

Sancton characterizes provincial-municipal relations as being mainly about money. He describes how municipal governments provide the bulk of services that directly affect Canadians. They are responsible for police services, fire response, traffic management, animal control, infrastructure, parking, street lighting, transit, water, sewer and waste, land-use planning and regulation, building regulation and inspection, economic development, libraries, parks and recreation, culture, and emergency planning (Sancton 2002).

In many cases, provincial ministers are technically accountable for work provided by municipal agencies that they have no real connection to or control over. For instance, policing within Winnipeg is provided by constables who are appointed by the chief of police, who technically operates under authority of the Manitoba justice minister, under the Provincial Police Act (Manitoba, Provincial Police Act 2011). In reality, the proverbial "buck," as U.S. President Harry S. Truman described it, generally stops at the desk of the chief of police as far as activities of the Police Service goes and not at higher levels of government.

The provincial justice minister is rarely taken to task regarding issues arising out of local police forces, except perhaps over the level of financial support being provided by the province. As mentioned previously, the same independence appears to exist within municipal governance structures as well. While the chief of police answers to the city's chief administrative officer (CAO), the CAO is rarely if ever held to account for police activities.

Walsh and Conway (2011) have described the distinctive role that modern-day frontline police officers play in the administration of justice. The police role in law, authority, and discretionary power insulates them from outside political and bureaucratic interference. Common law evolved to protect the police from influence, as it is the police who must enforce the laws, even if it means arresting political leaders or senior bureaucrats. This independence extends to executive levels as well, meaning that politicians can only influence policing models and policies and not direct them. Municipal government controls funding, but has little influence regarding how justice is administered.

Leo (2007) points out the need for greater flexibility by the federal government in seeking municipal input in funding. Regional input is important because broad, national, or even province-wide policies may fail to consider local differences and needs. In my experience Leo's observations are correct, as the federal government seems even farther removed than the province. An example of this is when federal ministers came to Winnipeg in 2008 to announce new legislation addressing auto-theft (Canada, Prime Minister's website 2008). This was announced in Winnipeg, presumably because Winnipeg has had a significant auto-theft problem. However, the problem in Winnipeg stems much more from street-gang activity and joy riding than from commercial "chop shops" and organized crime, which was the focus of the new legislation. It appeared that the policy was meant to address a growing auto-theft problem in Canada but had overlooked local differences in Manitoba. It might have been more effective and appropriate to announce the legislation in a port city like Vancouver, where the car theft problem is known to be connected with international smuggling of stolen cars and parts.

In a limited sense, local emergency services have benefitted from federal funding through national training programs. Federal programs, such as the Joint Emergency Preparedness Program (JEPP), worked, in theory, as the federal government matched municipal investments in new emergency preparedness equipment and initiatives (Pal 2006). Unfortunately, municipal governments generally have all of their resources tied up in direct service delivery, leaving very little to finance programs. Yet the full responsibility (financially

and physically) for the initial response to a disaster rests with municipalities (Manitoba Government 2012b). JEPPs were a great deal
for municipalities that were in a position to pay half of the costs,
ensuring local needs were addressed. However part of the 2012 federal budget included closing the Public Safety College in Ottawa and
shutting down the JEPP program. In the case of emergency preparedness and response, municipalities can apply for federal and
provincial financial assistance, but only after an event. The immediate response remains a local responsibility.

The federal bureaucracy absorbs millions of dollars for federal
infrastructure protection, with very little trickling to the local frontline. For instance, the Public Health Agency of Canada and National
Microbiology Lab (NML) in downtown Winnipeg is a high-profile
facility that presents a potential risk in the case of human-induced or
accidental emergency events, protests, or high-risk emergency service calls. While its day-to-day activities are federally funded, any
emergency incident at the facility would be responded to by municipal services, at least during the initial response. When I met with my
counterparts in the NML to discuss improving responses by emergency services, we realized that false assumptions existed on both
sides about who is responsible for managing aspects of certain
events. We, in local emergency services, assumed that they would
have more federal resources for responding to emergencies and were
surprised to learn that they were operating on the assumption that
most types of emergencies at the lab would be responded to by local
emergency services, because the building is in the city's jurisdiction.
By working together, we gained a much better mutual understanding
of who can and who should do what in an emergency.

The tendency of agencies to operate in silos, with poor interagency
coordination of operations and resources and inadequate joint communication strategies, is a modern governance challenge. Another
growing challenge is the increasing reliance upon and integration of
government and private industry, discussed next.

PRIVATIZATION AND PUBLIC GOVERNANCE

Demands are outstripping government capacity in many areas,
including some aspects of policing. In recent decades, private industry has taken on greater responsibility for the provision of public
services that have historically been provided solely by government

(Rosen, Dahlby, and Smith 2003). The trend has been towards privatization, contracting out, and multilevel, multiagency collaboration. Everything is now so globalized and interconnected that no single agency or government can effectively address today's complex social problems independently. Walsh and Conway (2011, 61) describe how policing has changed "in response to the demands imposed upon it by an increasingly diverse, technological, urbanized, globalized, mobile, sophisticated, rights-conscious and knowledge-based society," placing greater emphasis on the need for police partnership with the private sector or outright private sector provision of some services.

Walsh and Conway (2011) note that the private security industry has been around for a long time, primarily serving the needs of private sector commercial clients; however, Walsh and Conway point out it is "rapidly expanding into more traditional public sector policing domains" (ibid., 72). Exclusive residential housing complexes often employ private police/security companies to supplement services they cannot get from the public police. Many police agencies are handing off to the private sector functions previously discharged by traditional government-run police services.

Stenning (2011) points out that private policing personnel are subject to laws and accountability mechanisms but will always be different from the public police. The main difference is that private forms are for hire, while the public police are not. Private corporations may be able to get a job done more cheaply, but at what cost? For instance, many private companies do not have the same diversity hiring policies as government. O'Leary (1994) highlights that private contractors may offer services and reduced short-term prices, but the intangibles must be considered. And even if private security firms offer short-term effectiveness, they are not necessarily more effective in the long-term; if security firms grow into larger monopolies, as private businesses tend to do, the benefits would diminish (O'Leary 1994). Challenges remain to determine how accountability and responsibility can be maintained when a mixture of traditional police structures and private sector resources is being used to provide services.

Increased reliance on the private sector for the provision of various public services exacerbates the need for cooperation between the three levels of government and between public and private sector agencies. In the wake of increased privatization and contracting out of services, Canada's hierarchical government bureaucracies, at all three levels, are giving way to more horizontal governance structures. Public servants are more likely to deal directly with their counterparts in other branches of government and with private contractors rather than going up and down the traditional command hierarchies. This raises questions about accountability for public servants as-well-as stewardship of funds in mixed public/private service sectors.

Good (2007) reports that private sector spending of public money constitutes over 15 percent of Canada's yearly federal budget; with such spending comes issues over administration, accountability, and governance. Mid-level managers working with partner agencies take on the responsibilities of indirect or direct oversight of government funding, moving this responsibility to mid-to senior-manager levels, rather than between executives, where the responsibilities have traditionally rested.

Public-private partnerships (P3s) are also becoming more common in order to finance large-scale capital projects that were historically funded solely by government. John Loxley of the University of Manitoba, in a presentation to IPAC in October 2010, emphasized that while P3s provide the financing for large projects that would otherwise not have the funding to proceed, they pose a different set of challenges for government. The details of P3 contracts are often treated as confidential and are guarded from public disclosure, leading to questions about accountability. While P3s can allow governments to defer payments and transfer risk for major projects to private-sector partners, they can also create deficits by locking future governments into long-term contracts (P3s are often in operation for decades) and giving partial control of large government projects to private interests (Price-Boase 2000). Leaders in government agencies, including the police, need to be alert to the pitfalls of such arrangements. When government agencies go into business with private corporations they run the risk of giving up control in certain areas, such as who does the work or how the product is marketed.

In 1995 the RCMP entered into an arrangement with the Walt Disney Company to market their logo. Some described the plan as a win-win scenario, as the deal was between a charitable organization associated with the RCMP, the Mounted Police Foundation, and Walt Disney Company (Canada) Ltd., which would bring Disney's considerable marketing expertise to the table. The proceeds were to be used to enhance existing RCMP community policing programs, such as crime prevention, victim services, and drug awareness (Pratt 1995). Some argue that it is Disney Canada and not a foreign company, while others have said Disney is Disney and the RCMP were dealing with an iconic American, corporate, Hollywood giant, even if the Canadian subsidiary managed the account (Vienneau 1995). Amid questioning over the program, RCMP spokesman Staff Sergeant Ken MacLean said, "We liked the idea of Mountie souvenirs that were made in Canada, but there wasn't a lot available," (Eggertson 1999, 1).

The five-year deal saw $1.5 million in royalties from the sale of teddy bears, T-shirts, insignia rings, and an assortment of other souvenirs split between Disney and the RCMP Foundation. The proceeds financed eighty-five community-policing projects (Eggertson 1999; Kenny 1995; Vienneau 1995).

Private security and expert consultants in a range of fields are no longer just supplements to the public police – in the twenty-first century they have become a large component of our public safety infrastructure and they are here to stay. Public policing leaders who understand justice economics will embrace private sector partners in order to provide more effective collaborative approaches to community problems. Both private and public sector service providers will improve their respective services if they can find innovative ways to work together rather than acting in opposition.

10

Transparency and Accountability

PRINCIPLES OF GOVERNMENT ACCOUNTABILITY

Accountability is important if government agencies are to maintain public trust. The public are much better informed than they were in the past, due in large part to the instant access to information that the Internet now provides. This transparency has made government agencies like the police much more accountable. However debates about privacy, security, freedom, and state control are as germane today as when the principles that make a good society were first debated. Current issues of accountability and allegations of corruption within government and policing agencies raise questions that can be traced back to early discussions of good governments by philosophers such as Thomas Hobbes (1588–1679), John Locke (1632–1704), and Jean-Jacques Rousseau (1712–1778) (Held 1996). Hobbes describes the need for governments to have extensive power and authority in order to prevent citizens from reverting to a violent state of nature, otherwise "the life of man [would be] solitary, poor, nasty, brutish, and short" (Hobbes 1651, xliii). This principle defines the need for organized policing, because without social control there would be chaos and uncontrolled violence. Having seen firsthand the violence that people are capable of, I have come to appreciate that Hobbes's statement is an immutable truth about the nature of people and the human condition.

Locke argues that citizens would be foolish to trust the government blindly and should resist any government that fails to represent them well. His position describes modern-day values of government accountability. He emphasizes the importance of fairness and people's right to self-preservation in his historic statement "Who sheddeth man's blood, by man shall his blood be shed" (Locke 1812, 342). Locke argues for the recognition of fundamental human rights, such as security and protection of property, which were later entrenched in laws. These principles lie at the heart of Canadian justice and the concept that people should be punished through court sentences, so that the victim feels retribution has been achieved to repair the damages caused by an offender's transgressions.

Locke argues that both men and governments are corruptible and need regulation; he captures the basic corruptible nature of humankind in stating, "absolute monarchs are but men" (1812, 345). This principle also stands at the heart of modern democracy, as Canadians are quick to hold politicians or other government representatives to account when they make mistakes or are dishonest. Citizens today criticize government and make public statements about the perceived incompetence of political leaders and public officials with no thought of the repercussions and persecution that they would have faced in other societies and earlier times. We should not take these hard-fought freedoms for granted as they came at great cost to our ancestors.

Rousseau's *On the Social Contract or Principles of Political Right* highlights the rights and duties of citizens in civil society. His writing has influenced much of what we take for granted in modern political thought. He argues the importance of public input to governance, stressing that citizens should only agree to be governed by just and fair government and laws, and that laws are only valid if they are for the common good. This principle resonates with much that I have presented throughout this book in the idea that collaboration and police-community partnership are the only effective strategies for addressing complex modern social problems. Rousseau's ideas resonate with Peel's principles that call for public approval, willing cooperation, and consent by people to be policed (Peel 1829).

The principle of public consent raises interesting questions about the role and authority of governments and police agencies. Should politicians and civil servants represent public opinion in their decisions or should they do what they think is good for the public, regardless of what citizens think? The common good theorists – Hobbes, Locke, Rousseau, and others – have stressed that governments are elected and given authority to represent public values and norms. Government officials, including the police, are entrusted with working for the public good, even when they cannot openly discuss all of their activities and operations. Doing the right thing includes protecting the vulnerable, protecting the rights and interests of society at large, not only elites or individuals.

It is important to emphasize that in this era of globalization and continuous technological advances, governments, by necessity, are entrusted with some duties whose elements must be kept confidential in order to operate effectively. At the same time, they should operate on the assumption that they will ultimately be open to public scrutiny and input. In policing, for example, investigation of crime and a wide range of operational activities require high security and secrecy in order to be effective. Where police agencies can stumble is in confusing the need for security with the right to make value judgments on behalf of the Canadian public. The public obviously cannot know about secret surveillance operations targeting criminal activity. They can, however, have input into how those targets are selected and prioritized.

Police officers are often burdened with carrying out politically volatile tasks, in secret, with little to no oversight. Policing with no or with inappropriate accountability measures is a potential recipe for loss of public credibility or worse. When criminal investigations are so secret that police officers can take liberties with the way they are carried out, or the police feel that they can take actions they believe will protect peoples' rights without any discussion or oversight, the police become self-governing and can be subject to criticism.

When investigations result in criminal prosecution, full disclosure of evidence must be made to defence counsel and prosecutors for cases to go to trial. Disclosure acts as a safeguard and a form of oversight, albeit long after police actions are taken. Investigations of complex issues, such as terrorism, are necessarily ongoing and long-term. Citizens can be investigated without a prosecution ever being mounted. The police must make decisions for the public good about actions they take in secret and that may deliberately or inadvertently invade the privacy of citizens.

In the ICE unit, for example, we served cutting-edge search warrants to investigate Internet-based activity and seize peoples' computers. At one point there was a debate within our unit about whether warrants were required to intercept, open, and read e-mails transmitted over the Internet. If the Internet counts as public domain, publicly accessible like a park or the street, and if there is no expectation of privacy, then search warrants are not required. Lawyers had mixed opinions because there was no case law on that particular scenario at that time. Yet, as police officers, we still had to decide whether to act without warrants or not, despite the fact that the lawyers were reluctant to offer an opinion.

Another difficult area that requires great discretion is the use and handling of informants. In this ethically tricky but very necessary police function, officers often must determine how much information to disclose. Protecting confidential informants is a fundamental police responsibility, as is transparency. Informants often know about criminal activity because they are involved themselves. If they are providing information that could solve a major organized crime while they are themselves committing petty crimes, is it ethical to overlook the petty crimes? There is a further complication – if an officer is aware of an offence but decides to overlook it, technically he or she is a party to the offence.

If officers tell a confidential informant they will seek a reward or request Crown consideration to drop or change charges in exchange for information about crimes, the informant may decide to get involved in crimes in order to gather information to pass to the police. Officers cannot direct an informant to commit crimes or gather information, because then they might be making the informant into an agent of the state, an agent provocateur. Nor can officers go undercover and act as provocateurs, inciting people to commit crimes and then arresting them. At a protest against the Security and Prosperity Partnership meeting at Montebello, Quebec, in August 2007, several protestors inciting the crowd to violence were identified as undercover police officers. The undercover officers were captured on video pushing the SQ riot-squad members, allegedly inciting violence. After several days of public pressure, the commissioner of the SQ admitted that the officers were in fact on duty but that they were not inciting criminal behaviour. Similar allegations arose around the 2010 G20 meeting in Toronto (Burrows 2010; CBC 2007). In these cases, the police are in the difficult position of needing to gather accurate information about protestors in order to work for public safety – and therefore needing to gain their confidence – while also balancing the right to freedom of speech.

These are the slippery slopes that officers must contend with. These types of issues come up fairly often and police officers have to make decisions on the fly about how to proceed. Such decisions involve the core values of policing. They are often not interpretations of the law but, rather, are ethical decisions that seek to represent what the average citizen would agree is right.

Principles of state power debated by the early philosophers are as salient today as when nation states were first formed. Police investigators and managers must determine if they should act in the public good, regardless of what the general public thinks, or attempt to find ways to seek oversight and public input. One can imagine Hobbes, Locke, and Rousseau ruminating over a Starbucks coffee about how they could have predicted many current policing scandals, which were due, at least in part, to ineffective external oversight and alleged lack of transparency and public input.

Experts and government officials carry a burden to protect the wellbeing of the greater society. Their burden as it regards public service can include knowledge of where the system is vulnerable and where there is potential for improvement. The challenges in protecting public safety and policing have become increasingly complex. While the investigation of issues such as terrorist threats and organized crime require high levels of security in order to be effective, officials also need to guard against the tendency to assume that average citizens are incapable of participating in such complex value judgments.

In the policing world, we are cognizant of the fact that the ultimate judge of our actions is the court of law, where a judge or a jury of citizens will review our actions. In an ideal world a jury of peers would also be involved in sensitive decisions during police operations. However, this type of civilian oversight and involvement is impossible to achieve while at the same time maintaining the speed and secrecy that police operations require. This is why police officers are entrusted with the authority and responsibility to act in good faith in their efforts to protect the community.

While investigations may be highly technical and complex, the final decisions about what is right and what is wrong are within the grasp of the average citizen and should be sought when possible. Again, Peel's principle that people are the police and the police are the people is highly relevant in the present day (Gayder 2008). One step towards better accountability is the increasing use of police commissions for police oversight. Most provinces across Canada have established police commissions and boards as a form of civilian oversight. These bodies can serve as both a bridge and a buffer between the police and political levels, helping to remove any perception of political interference and lack of accountability with respect to police agencies. Manitoba was one of the last provinces to establish a police commission. After a tragic incident in which an off-duty police officer struck and killed a civilian, the ensuing impaired driving (the cause of death) investigation was flawed and later came under intense scrutiny. As a result, a public inquiry was held and numerous recommendations were made (Salhany 2013). Manitoba's Police Act, which gives authority to police agencies, was re-written and a requirement included that every police agency must have a police board and the province must have a police commission. This governance structure will hire police chiefs and will have a mechanism for more independent investigations of alleged police misconduct. Police chiefs could potentially seek direction from such boards on strategic directions and they also provide a form of oversight for major policing issues. Ultimately, however, any system of accountability must rely on the integrity of the officers involved. If they seek advice or oversight from police boards, they will be expected to provide the true details and circumstances, otherwise effective oversight cannot be achieved.

When officers testify, they are expected to tell the truth. In cases where suspicions or allegations of perjury or withholding the truth do occur, police officers are usually vigorously investigated. A case in point is the perjury charges laid against several RCMP officers after their testimony at the Braidwood inquiry into the Taser-induced death of Robert Dziekanski at a Vancouver airport (Gillis and Macqueen 2011). The officers' testimony was alleged to have changed substantially between the initial reporting of events and what was said at the inquiry (Canadian Press 2011b). These types of incidents can undermine the public trust that is so crucial to policing.

A lack of transparency and failure to provide the public with information can result in a democratic deficit wherein people in power do not appear to represent the public they serve (Speers 2005). Transparency should therefore be a priority. If the police obtain knowledge about threats to the safety of citizens, they should advise people about the potential risks so that they can prepare themselves accordingly. Public consultation can help engage the community by making them part of the solutions, working together with the police and other government and non-government organizations to build community resilience.

Increased transparency is not achieved without cost. With increased transparency comes greater accountability and public servants may need protection. Government also has a responsibility to protect public servants who are willing to "blow the whistle" on corrupt practices or mismanagement when proper reporting channels have failed. Some recent RCMP cases illustrate that our current protections are not sufficient (Leblanc 2010). In one case, mishandled information from the RCMP resulted in a Canadian citizen, Maher Arar, being apprehended in New York and given over to Syria by the United States government, leading to his extended imprisonment and torture (Potter 2010). After allegedly attempting to sidestep allegations of pension fund misappropriation and the mishandling of the Arar case, the RCMP commissioner ended up resigning. A disturbing aspect is that the story never would have come to light without the courage and tenacity of whistle-blowers who risked their careers to expose the issues (Fitzpatrick 2007). Even more disturbing, however, was the apparent willingness of some elected members of Parliament to go along with attempted cover-ups (Martin 2007). These images of corruption can contribute to a public loss of confidence in politicians, senior officials, and government agencies, as national polls have illustrated (Weeks 2007). General loss of public trust and confidence in government can also translate into a loss of confidence in the police.

Kaariainen (2007) studied sixteen European countries and found that perceived government corruption directly correlated with decreased public trust in police agencies. The police cannot improve public opinion of their legitimacy unless they are seen to be fair and equitable in their enforcement of laws and deployment of resources. Research has also confirmed that people will not trust the police unless they believe they are enforcing laws that are aligned with community values (Hohl, Bradford, and Stanko 2010). If people feel that the police are not looking after their interests, they are not likely to trust them.

Every individual interaction between the police and the public can have a ripple effect in the community. A study of Chicago youth corroborates Peel's principles of fairness and impartiality, finding that perceptions and trust of the police were most often affected by personal experiences. The youth reported that if they saw a friend being treated badly or insultingly by the police, their trust declined (Flexon, Lurigio, and Greenleaf 2009). Such reports demonstrate the importance of building trust not just at the policy level but through the actions of individual officers carrying out their daily duties. The actions of one officer can have deep positive or negative effects that can ripple through a community, highlighting the need for police agencies to take allegations of misconduct seriously. Aggressive investigations and consequences for officers who are the subject of valid complaints effectively separates and insulates police agencies from "bad apples."

Maintaining morale is a great challenge for police executives, who must balance community trust with the appearance of supporting their officers in difficult, high-risk work. In a seminar on mediation and trust-building at the Cornerstone Institute in Cape Town, South Africa, in June 2011, Dean Peachey of the University of Winnipeg's Global College pointed out that one hurtful act in the process of mediation can move parties back to the starting position of distrust. Improved trust in policing requires fair, impartial, and consistent application of the law, guided by the principle that all members of society must be protected equally, as laid out by Peel. Accomplishing this grand goal requires alignment between the goals of police agencies and community values, which cannot occur unless people are clear about what those shared values are. Police leaders must therefore work to keep their agencies transparent and above reproach if they are to earn and retain public trust. Integrity and public trust are so important to policing that they must be a major aspect of professional and organizational culture.

POLICE CULTURE

In order to fully understand police organizations and the people in them, we must examine the elements that define police culture. Zwell (2000) defined culture as the language, beliefs, shared knowledge, and characteristics that bind groups so that they can work together. The unique demands and nature of police work set the stage for the development of a clearly defined organizational culture.

Research and literature about police culture has generally explored two different dimensions: the elements that define the profession and the differences between officers (Nickels and Verma 2008; Paoline 2004). (For the purposes of this discussion the terms "culture" and "subculture" are considered synonymous.) Police culture is generally understood as a set of beliefs and behaviours shared by all officers and supported by "socialization" (Crank 1998, 242) and "solidarity" (239). This culture has generally been understood to derive largely from aspects of the work that are common to police work everywhere (Niederhoffer 1967; Prenzler 1997; van Maanen 1974, 1978). Nickels and Verma (2008) note that these aspects commonly include danger and ambiguity, authority to use force, discretion, estrangement from civilians, bureaucracy, shift-work, routine contact with criminals, antagonism between frontline officers and managers, and vague and conflicting mandates.

Some researchers have explored the question of whether a police subculture exists at all or, if it does, to what extent. Their findings suggest that a police subcultures does exist; however, it is not necessarily the same for all police officers but varies among different groups within policing (Haarr 1997; Herbert 1998; Jermier et al. 1991; Manning 1995; Paoline, Myers, and Worden 2000). Much research has focused on the various kinds of police officers and how they adhere to various police subcultures (Brown 1991; Jermier et al. 1991; Wilson 1968). However these research projects are often based on subjective descriptions, making it difficult to measure their validity (Cochran and Bromley 2003).

Researchers have agreed that employees working in any field tend to develop specific subcultures based on the demands of their work (Manning 1995). People working in law enforcement, as well as in corrections, often display similar subculture characteristics as a result of their constant exposure to human misery, danger and uncertainty, and use of coercive authority and force in their work (Cochran and Bromley 2003; Crank 1998; Van Maanen 1974). I worked in the jails for several years in the 1980s as a sheriff's officer and now, with over twenty-three years in policing, I can say with certainty that these aspects are similar in both lines of work. The dry sense of humour and the way officers interact – honestly and directly – are very similar. Much has been written about law enforcement culture.

Police officers work in environments with rigid lines of authority, command, and control, commonly amid simultaneously conflicting guidelines, policies, and procedures (Lundman 1980; Neiderhoffer 1967). The cognitive dissonance caused by trying to help people who have been victimized or brutalized while operating within a framework of conflicting policies, laws, and structures causes many officers to feel frustration with the system. Many feel disillusioned after years of seeing the subtle, and sometimes not so subtle, effects of criminal behaviour on victims and the system's ineffectiveness at ending or rectifying them. Police officers are often characterized as cynical and authoritative with a tendency to isolate themselves from those who are not police officers (Carter and Radelet 1999; Davis 1969).

As I have matured and become more educated and experienced, I have come to realize that we often expect too much from the justice system. It is a blunt instrument that is meant to protect people from the brutality that Hobbes mentioned, the "nasty brutish and short" life that would come without overt social control of the police. As a blunt instrument, it does not deal well with the nuances of complex interpersonal relationships or the structural causes of conflict. The root causes of societal problems need intervention by all of society, not just the police and the courts.

The study of different policing styles did not really develop until the 1970s (Paoline 2004). Researchers then started to look at how officers vary in their adaptation to police work and at changing policing models such as community-based policing (Broderick 1977; Brown 1988; White 1972).

Paoline found that some characteristics are common to most or all police officers, mainly due to the culture and environment of the work. He writes, "these attitudes, values, and norms include a distrust and suspiciousness of citizens and a prescription to assess people and situations in terms of their potential threat (i.e., maintaining the edge)" (Paoline 2004, 207). He goes on to describe the tendency that officers have to develop a "we-versus-they" attitude with respect to the public. In my experience, the policing environment causes all of these tendencies, and officers have to guard against them throughout their careers.

In recent decades, research has focused on management styles, policing philosophies, traditions, changing contexts, demographics within police organizations, and training and officer development and careers. In the context of new policing strategies, such as decentralization and community-based models, researchers have found that police cultures are changing with the evolution of policing philosophies (Paoline, Myers, and Worden 2000; Scripture 1997). Different ways of testing have also allowed for more extensive research on officer differences based on gender, race, and education, in conjunction with changing policing models (Paoline 2004). My previous discussion on gender and race issues is a case in point.

A previously male-dominated profession has given way, over the last two decades, to a less gendered and more professional culture.

In her book, *I Love a Cop: What Police Families Need to Know* (2007) Kirschman, a police psychologist, describes the aspects of police work that will probably never change; these include shift work, long hours, crisis-driven and therefore unpredictable work, exposure of officers and their families to public scrutiny, frequent injuries, and occasional long deployments and separation from family. All of these points ring true for me as elements that have been there throughout my policing career. The sixth point, long deployments and separations, has become more pronounced, according to Kirschman, due to an increasing number of disasters, both human-induced and naturally occurring, and evolving methods of managing them. In my emergency preparedness and disaster management role, I have experienced long deployments with long hours and little rest. When people have been evacuated from their homes due to fire or flood, it becomes a low priority for police officers to get home to their own families, even if they have been affected. One of the lessons learned from Hurricane Katrina in New Orleans was that during a disaster officers need to know that their families are safe in order to focus on their work and fulfill their police roles effectively.

Once Hurricane Katrina hit the United States Gulf coast in 2005, the New Orleans Police Department spent the first several hours retrieving three hundred police officers from their own homes, where many were stranded on rooftops. After the disaster, sixty officers resigned, forty-five were fired, many for refusing to report for duty, and two committed suicide. In total, the New Orleans Police Department lost seven percent of its officers over Katrina and 70 percent of officers lost their homes (Anderson and Farber 2006). Officers were reluctant to leave their own families in danger in order to join the troops on duty. As a result of the Katrina experience many policing agencies have adopted policies of moving the families of police personnel to safety in hotels or making other such arrangements so that the officers can concentrate on their jobs.

People joining the policing profession come from diverse backgrounds, cultures, nationalities, work experiences, education levels, and age groups and then find themselves relying on each other in what are literally life and death situations. Police work requires people from diverse backgrounds to reach a consensus and carry out decisions about sensitive ethical, moral and legal issues in emotionally charged circumstances. The elements of trust, unique work demands, and core values that are oriented to helping people define a large portion of police organizational culture. But it is not always a smooth road to join and remain in that culture, especially if others perceive an officer as not conforming. Studies have confirmed that solidarity and secrecy are key values in police cultures (Barker 1994; Ferdinand 1980; Van Maanen 1974, 1978; Wilson 1968). The road can be very rocky for someone who is believed to have talked out of school or to not be solidly backing their fellow officers. Cancino and Enriquez (2004) conducted a study on peer retaliation and found that officers who are perceived to be non-conforming can be subject to a range of coercion from their peers, including everything from shunning to withholding backup and having their lives placed in danger.

Law enforcement personnel throughout the western world share similar core values of honesty, integrity, trust, honour, and respect. These are not abstract concepts from a more romantic era but are guiding principles in increasingly trying times. The Canadian public and justice systems entrust law enforcement officers with immense authority. Officers have their character tested routinely in their efforts to protect public safety, property, and the legal rights of complainants and offenders even when, in some circumstances, doing so is offensive and objectionable according to the officers' individual sensibilities. Neutrality is a strong value in policing, especially in Canada. The discipline of police officers is tested on a regular basis while they are protecting the rights of offenders, even after officers have been threatened, insulted, and/or physically assaulted.

Many distasteful and outright disturbing tasks also define the profession. Many officers have told me they could not work in units like the ICE Unit, examining horrendous images of child pornography, or in the Child Abuse Unit, dealing with children who have been hurt or sexually assaulted. Officers often say that they could not interview suspects who are accused of such heinous crimes. The work is a discipline that helps officers cope with the depravity they encounter. I have advised officers that they can take the repulsion they feel and redirect that energy into motivation to do a good and thorough job in obtaining proper confessions and strong evidence for convictions, enabling the courts to ultimately administer justice. The primary role of the police is to find the truth and report the facts, not to impose value judgments or pass sentences. I recall numerous suspect interviews in which I turned my feelings of disgust for the worst aspects of humanity into motivation to gain confessions, make solid cases, and achieve closure for victims.

One interview I am particularly proud of involved a thirty-year-old man, who had sexually assaulted his teenage niece when she was younger. She, many years later, had mustered the courage to tell others about the abuse. This put her in the tough spot of being the only witness to these historical offences. In the Child Abuse Unit, we were all acutely aware that, in many cases, if we can get a confession from the accused there is a high likelihood of a guilty plea and therefore a lower likelihood that a child will have to relive the assaults by testifying in court. In some cases people are traumatized by the process of examination by crown attorneys, and cross-examination by defence lawyers. For this reason investigators are highly motivated to gain confessions in a way that ensures that they will not be challenged. In this case, the girl had made the allegation and we now had her uncle in a police interview room.

He was not budging, as he had just been released from a lengthy prison sentence and had learned from having been previously convicted not to give confessions or any kind of admissions to the police. On camera, I watched a team of investigators talking to him for an hour, carefully observing his body language, noticing that he cringed a bit whenever talk of his childhood came up. Drawing on my interrogation training, I felt that he was an emotionally oriented offender and might respond to emotional triggers. (The opposite of that type is the logical offender who will only confess if you can convince them that you have a solid case and that it is in their best interest to negotiate a confession.)

To build trust, I started by talking at length about his background and divulging some of mine, being careful not to offer too much about myself. A large part of the interview and interrogation process involves establishing a relationship in which a person trusts you enough to feel that you will not abuse them if they disclose their innermost shame and admissions. In this case, once he trusted me, I kept bringing him back to the fact that he was a victim as well, and that we are all human, but that his niece now needed closure from what she had endured.

It is not easy, engaging in the intimate experience of interrogation and showing compassion, while warding off disgust, knowing that a camera is rolling on the other side of the one-way mirror with a group of fellow officers watching. This discipline is a big part of police culture that officers strive to develop. You could not force a confession out of a person who has already been hardened by prison, even if torture was legal. A confession has to be extracted with finesse and with genuine compassion, respect for humanity, and a legitimate passion for finding the truth.

This man eventually admitted to raping his niece dozens of times, for several years, from when she was seven years old onward. My motivation in that case was not to punish him but rather to protect people from him and provide closure for his victim so that she could work on her recovery and possibly start to get on with her life. He admitted to raping a child, knowing he was going back to prison for several more years and that he would be going as a "skinner" (prison vernacular for sex-offender) so that his life would be in danger if other prisoners learned what he had done.

Lawyers often suggest at court that it makes no sense for a suspect to admit crimes freely, inferring that a full confession must have been induced by torture or coercion. But those were certainly not involved in this case and the whole interview was videotaped. Such confessions are one of those mysteries of human behaviour; he was willing to clear his conscience and allow his niece a chance at recovery. Maybe he was also having a difficult time living outside prison, or perhaps he needed to unburden his feelings of guilt; we will never know. But the reality is, for whatever reason, people often do freely admit their offences.

Police officers often suppress the emotion they feel while managing situations by focusing on the discipline of completing the task at hand thoroughly and properly. Once the case is complete and forwarded for prosecution, it is out of their hands. Many do not want to know what happens later in court, even with their most significant cases. Early in my career I stopped looking up sentences that people received, partly because it served no purpose to frustrate myself by seeing serious offences plea-bargained to lesser crimes or lighter sentences. As well, I am generally far too busy, as most officers are, to burden myself with researching court findings. I have always seen my job as doing the absolute best investigations that I can, trying to find the truth and provide prosecutors with the best possible case and evidence for them to do their jobs.

My primary focus and mindset has been the protection of vulnerable persons, victims, and the community. Charges that are laid against an offender are, in my view, not so much in the interest of punishing the offender but rather in protecting the victim. For instance, in the Child Abuse and ICE units we prioritized investigations by the need to protect children. If we had five search warrants ready to go, we would go first on the one where young children were residing. We laid charges more in the interest of obtaining court-imposed conditions on offenders and separating them from potential victims. As long as the victims were protected and represented, I was not as concerned about the offenders' punishments; that is the role of the courts.

In fact, offenders are often victims of their own lives. Working in the Child Abuse Unit, I realized through the course of interrogations that many of those we dealt with had been sexually abused themselves as children. In some cases it became crystal clear during an interview and I would ask "Who did this to you?" Invariably they would tell me. While I believe offenders are victims too, we need to use police powers to protect them from themselves and from harming others when they have problems with aggression, substance abuse, violence, sexual compulsion, theft, and self-harm.

Suppression of bias while preserving and protecting citizens' legal rights, safety, and property is a defining characteristic of police culture. Unbiased, apolitical, detached objectivity in the search for truth defines police professionalism and is an attitude that most officers take great pride in.

Compassion for humanity is another common element of the police culture. It is one thing to believe that you are generally compassionate; it is quite another to protect and assist a man after he has led you on a high-speed pursuit through the city, needlessly and deliberately endangering the lives of innocent people. Imagine the discipline required to protect the safety, legal rights, and dignity of a person who is HIV positive, with a lengthy prison record, after he has violently attacked you and spat a mouthful of blood in your face. In moments like that you have an internal dialogue, reminding yourself why you are in this profession, that the offender is also a victim, and that everyone has rights. After this happened to me, I found myself more likely to look out for my colleagues who had been injured or assaulted on the job. As a peer support member for over a decade, I have found that these types of incidents take a toll on police officers and make them question if they should be risking their health in policing when their families need them.

Another phenomenon that illustrates police compassion as well as the stress of the profession is "suicide by cop." This is the deliberate attempt by people to force the police to kill them; it has been well documented and is much more common than people outside the profession may realize (Huston, Range and Anglin 1998; Parent and Verdun-Jones 1998; Perrou 1999; Wilson and Davis 1998). One study found that out of 707 incidents across North America between 1998 and 2006 in which police had to kill a subject, 36 percent were "suicide by cop" (Mohandie, Meloy, and Collins 2009). When it occurs, it is demoralizing and traumatizing for the officers involved. These officers are individuals who have dedicated their lives to helping people. When they are forced to take the life of a person who is distraught and reaching out for help, albeit in violent ways, it is extremely upsetting.

Research has revealed that the police have had to encounter and protect people with mental health issues more frequently in recent years (Bonovitz and Bonovitz 1981; Godfredson et al. 2010; Pogrebin and Poole 1987). This is a trend that is also being observed internationally (Fazel and Danesh 2002; Godfredson et al. 2010). In 2012 the number of people with mental health challenges being charged with criminal offences is so high in Canada that it is causing some to call for a Royal Commission to examine the issue (Brean 2012). It has been suggested that more training would be beneficial, particularly in multimodal approaches that engage mental health experts (Godfredson 2011). This observation aligns with my experience, as mental health issues have been a growing constraint on police resources.

In many cases, people who are involved in criminal activity and apprehended are found to be obviously suffering from varying degrees of mental illness. The tendency we have to guard against in policing is in stepping over the line and attempting to become psychiatrists, making on-the-spot diagnoses and assessments of culpability. Our role is to enforce the laws and let the Crown attorneys order a psychiatric assessment. More training would be beneficial, but there is a fine balance in how much more training we can do in all of the facets of policing. We could use more training in virtually every area.

"Suicide by cop" often involves mental health issues. As I was revising this manuscript, I was involved in such a case. A man with mental illness was no longer taking his medication and was acting agitated and delusional. His wife called for an ambulance and while the paramedics were in the apartment assessing him, he grabbed two butcher knives out of a kitchen drawer and ran at the paramedics. When we arrived, the paramedics were holding the door to the apartment shut from the outside. The man was inside yelling that he would cut himself and that he wanted to die. With the man's wife and a crowd looking on from down the hallway, two of us covered the doorway with our guns while a third, with a Taser, challenged the man to come out. We could not leave him alone in the apartment as he might try to kill himself.

He flung the door open and had a knife in each hand and another in his waistband. He was clearly agitated and was yelling things like, "I will kill you guys" and "I am going to [expletive] you up." After repeated demands to drop the knives he threw one out and then the other one, and then pulled another one out of his waistband. He refused to drop this knife and was threatening to come into the hallway. We could not let him go past us, as he might have hurt someone, including us. If he had run out, we would have been forced to shoot him. Fortunately a well-aimed shot with the Taser took him down and we were able to restrain him. After a struggle we handcuffed him and got a spit sock on his head because he was spitting everywhere – including at us. We then got him to the hospital for treatment. If we had been forced to shoot him, it would have been traumatic, not only because all the officers there would have felt conflicted about harming someone we were there to help but also because we know that the instant we pull the trigger, a major investigation (of us) commences. For years we would all be answering inquiries over our use of force.

When an officer-involved shooting occurs, officers are isolated from each other to prevent them from collaborating on their version of events and they are examined as a part of the crime scene. Their clothes are removed and seized, photographs are taken of their hands, along with swabs for lab examination, and they are generally in for a long stay at work before being allowed to go home. They are often placed on administrative leave for a few days, for their protection. Officers often do not like being sent home, as they prefer the company of their colleagues after a traumatic incident. We in the policing profession have, over the past two decades, come a long way in looking after officers' needs during and after traumatic events. However, the stress can only be diminished so much.

Compassion, respect for justice, and discipline are defining professional qualities and the reasons a common language exists among police officers everywhere. These unique elements of police culture make the prospect of bringing in non-police leaders for executive leadership positions problematic. Operational leadership is more effective when officers perceive their leaders as having paid their dues in sacrifice and public service. While not impossible, it is difficult for someone who has never faced the challenges of frontline police work to create and implement policy for others who have made these sacrifices. In the absence of direct experience it is difficult or impossible for police leaders to understand how unpredictable the job is.

Almost daily, even after decades of experience, I see things that I would not otherwise believe if I hadn't seen them with my own eyes. Recently, I was sent as the duty staff sergeant to assist a district shift supervisor in dealing with a unique situation. An arrested suspect had thrown off all of his clothes, flung excrement all over the inside of a police interview room, and was rolling in it, eating it, and also injuring himself by banging his head on the walls. Was this the result of mental health issues or was he doing this as a defence mechanism? For our purposes it didn't matter, we needed to protect him and everyone involved. Officers put on protective clothing and restrained him from hurting himself further but then the problem remained of what to do with him, the contaminated room, and the contaminated uniforms the officers were wearing, as well as how we could transport him safely. We did not want to use an ambulance because that would have taken it off the road for the rest of the day while it was being decontaminated, and ambulances are scarce resources. We ended up calling a janitor with special hazardous materials decontamination equipment and training and transported the man to the hospital in a cadet van – having it decontaminated afterwards.

The point here is that any experienced police commander would not be surprised at this bizarre incident because, after a few years of frontline police experience, you know that reality is stranger than fiction. That is not to say that civilian managers could not do the job, or that they could not enlist experts to provide advice. However, at some point commanders are called upon with regard to discipline issues, policy development, budgets, and any number of other challenges and need to understand that anything can and will happen. Having had experiences that are unique to the police can make dealing with these issues possible, or at least easier.

Exposure to the possibility of serious injury or even death is another shared experience that defines the police bond. I have travelled several times to the annual police memorial services on Parliament Hill in Ottawa. These are emotional experiences that really demonstrate the esteem that the general public feels for the police. Two particularly gut-wrenching funerals I attended for officers killed in the line of duty were for Constable Odette Pinard in Montreal and Constable Darren Beatty in Calgary.

Constable Pinard was thirty years old and had just returned to work with the Montreal Police after maternity leave for her third child. In November 1995, she was in a police storefront working on a report when someone shot her in the head at close range, killing her on the spot. Don Delorme and I were on the Winnipeg Police Association Board at the time and flew to Montreal for the state funeral. Police officers were there from all over North America. Don and I had decided not to bring heavy parkas, thinking the weather would be mild. A rank of police officers more than a mile long stood at attention for about an hour to honour Constable Pinard's family as the funeral procession passed. It turned out the weather was damp and freezing, the kind of cold that bites right to the bone. Don and I stood at attention in our tunics; most of the other officers wore heavy parkas. I mention this because this kind of discipline is part of the police culture. Don and I were freezing, literally almost hypothermic, but there was no way we would have broken ranks to get warm during the state funeral of a fallen fellow officer. Both of us would rather have landed in hospital than left our positions standing at attention waiting for the family of a fallen colleague to pass by. I will never forget the sound of the slow beat of the drum as Odette's service hat was marched slowly by. She had served for ten years and left behind three children and a husband.

Constable Beatty was twenty-nine years old and had served five years with the Calgary Police Service when he was shot and killed accidentally during training. In October 2001, Constable Beatty was training with the tactical unit to which he was assigned. They were using live rounds for one aspect of training, then took a break and returned to do exercises with blank rounds. During their exercise an officer fired an aimed shot and a live round from his service pistol struck Darren in the neck, killing him. When they switched from live ammunition to blanks, an officer had changed the magazines but failed to remove the live round that was in the chamber of the weapon, an easy mistake to make with pistols. This is the most painful and tragic sort of event, a friendly-fire incident. What made it heart-wrenching was that the officer who fired the fatal shot was Darren's close friend. I was in Calgary attending a police crisis negotiators' conference and volunteered to represent the WPA at the state funeral. As I stood in a rank of officers stretching over a mile along that Calgary roadway I recall thinking what a sad irony it is that officers are exposed to danger even while in training to protect people from violence. However, the only way to develop effective skills for dealing with reality is to create training scenarios that replicate situations that may actually happen.

Humour must also be mentioned in any description of police culture. Exposure to the dark underbelly of humanity in its lowest forms, day in and day out, requires coping mechanisms. Police officers, firefighters, paramedics, nurses, and military personnel are all exposed to things that are beyond the normal realm of experience, things that can trigger an emotional response that is beyond a person's control. I cannot even count the number of times that I have said to fellow officers that no one would believe what we are looking at unless they saw it for themselves. Sometimes it is bewildering, and sometimes it is funny.

One amusing incident that stands out in my mind is the time my partner, KMart, short for Kevin Martell, and I were sitting in a marked cruiser car, at a red light, facing westbound. It was a winter evening and there was no traffic on the road. A car travelling southbound started to take a wide turn to go east and then suddenly swerved and drove straight at our cruiser. I slammed the cruiser into reverse and buried the gas pedal. Not a word was spoken between KMart and me; we knew exactly what was happening, although we didn't know why, and that we had to get away. The tires spun on the ice and we watched helplessly as the car drove straight into my driver's door. It certainly looked like an intentional attack. I finally got the cruiser car moved back about ten feet, slammed it into park, and we jumped out before the car stopped moving. KMart and I ran over and dragged the lone occupant out from behind the driver's wheel. It turned out he was an accountant in his twenties and staggeringly drunk. When he realized he had run into a police car he started crying for his mother. I do not know if we had ever laughed so hard, but quietly, as we processed this unfortunate young man for impaired driving while he moaned about what a colossal loser he was, driving drunk into a police car. Some nights, when hilarious things like that are happening, you feel as if you own the streets, just being out there, protecting the city. An old police adage is that the only people out in the middle of the night are cops, drunks, criminals, and cabbies.

Police officers are pranksters. Practical jokes are a time-honoured tradition and a rite of passage for new recruits. One time, a senior officer who was field training a recruit on my shift told his recruit that a helicopter was coming down in distress in a shopping centre parking lot. He had the recruit running around in a big circle, in front of a crowd of people, waving his arms frantically with his flashlight on in the belief that the helicopter pilot needed him to mark where he could make an emergency landing. Of course, there was no helicopter.

Another time, my partner and I were pulling up to the drunk tank with an arrest. A team of younger officers zipped in front of us and took our place in line. They looked at us and laughed as they walked their prisoner in, knowing we would now have to wait for twenty minutes for our turn to enter. We noticed they had left their cruiser car unlocked and, without talking, we both knew it was a golden opportunity. We found a personal cell phone in the car and took it directly to the younger team's sergeant in the station and explained the situation. As expected, their sergeant and platoon-mates tormented them for the next few hours. The crew was led to believe a homeless person had stolen the phone and tried to negoti-ate its return in exchange for a case of beer or money, to no avail. When their shift mates and sergeant finally let them off the hook, they called my partner and me to concede that we had got them good. This kind of joking is part of the culture; it keeps police officers alert. For instance, if you leave yourself signed on to a com-puter, in an office or cruiser car, you can almost bet that an embar-rassing message will soon be sent to the entire police service under your name.

Humour permeates policing culture everywhere, I believe because of the nature of the work. The United Kingdom had an unusually snowy winter in 2010 and a number of Oxford's officers used their riot shields as sleds, earning them official reprimands but provoking stress-reducing laughter throughout the British police services. This type of humour is common in the policing world and is a valuable tool for psychological relief in a profession rife with stress and ten-sion (Morris 2010).

The humour is sometimes extreme and requires a commitment by managers to ensure and maintain respectful workplaces. There has been a distinct change over the past twenty years; the workplace is now much more respectful. Much of the distasteful, harsh humour of the past is now rare. Officers are aware of the ramifications of disrespectful acts and language, and they simply not tolerated in the modern workplace.

The high levels of stress that are common in the policing profession as a result of constant exposure to emotionally disturbing and traumatic, sometimes life-threatening, incidents can also result in alcoholism, failed relationships, and high suicide rates (Waters and Ussery 2007). Unfortunately, without effective coping strategies many officers become casualties of an emotionally demanding profession that requires stoicism and the ability to carry society's burdens (Ramos 2010).

The cumulative stress of seeing the things that people do to each other and dealing with the worst of humanity, death, and pain on a daily basis while feeling responsible for fixing problems or, even worse, feeling responsible for not being able to fix them, can damage a dedicated officer's soul. Officers often tend to use avoidance strategies in attempts to ease the psychological distress of their work (Gershon et al. 2009; Hem, Berg, and Ekeberg 2001; Pasillas, Follette, and Perumean-Chaney 2006). Orlando Ramos of the New Jersey State Police points out that officers sometime seek a permanent solution (suicide) to a temporary period of psychological distress: "Tragically, too many times suicide becomes the way officers deal with the horrors they have witnessed in daily performance of their duties" (Ramos 2010, 1). Training is critical to avoid these tragedies.

A high prevalence of Post Traumatic Stress Disorder (PTSD) associated with the policing profession has been increasingly recognized in recent years (Bonokoski 2012). While suicide is three times more prevalent in policing than in the community at large, PTSD is six times more common (Moore 2010). In 2009, according to Dene Moore of the Canadian Press, documents obtained under a freedom of information request from the federal government confirmed that 1,298 RCMP officers had received treatment for PTSD. In fall of 2009, Veterans Affairs Canada, which provides services for the RCMP, had 1,711 RCMP clients with psychiatric conditions including PTSD, anxiety, panic, and depression disorders; 1,051 of these individuals had been released from the force, and 660 were still serving (ibid.).

There has been greater awareness in recent decades of the inherent dangers of this unique profession. Mental health professionals are now a key part of every major police agency's staff as the police leadership has learned that early intervention can address many issues before they become chronic. Most modern police agencies have developed post-traumatic incident programs as well as support programs to help deal with the well-documented risks of the profession. Over the past twenty years, we have seen a great deal of change in attitudes about how traumatic incidents, and police members affected by them, are managed. For example, professional standards and internal investigations are now more respectful of the impact they have on police officers. It is extremely stressful for officers to be interviewed about criminal allegations that have been made against them. Twenty years ago, officers in Winnipeg would be arrested in the workplace or ordered to report for interview after working all night. Now, none of that happens. Internal investigators make interview appointments while officers are on duty, ensuring they have police association representation and that their rights are respected.

Management of trauma from stressful events has also evolved. Two decades ago, members were sent home with pay for three days and connected with mental health resources only after the most severe incidents, such as having to use lethal force. Now, supervisors are given sensitivity training and, in Winnipeg at least, senior management are concerned with members' well-being and support, bringing in resources to provide as much help as possible for members. After extremely stressful incidents that surpass the normal police experience, briefings are often held, a wellness officer is called in, and sometimes psychologists are engaged to ensure that the effects of severe stress are mitigated and the involved officers are back to their regular duties as soon as possible.

Human resource programs also monitor events such as high-speed pursuits, use of force, allegations of excessive force or misconduct, and sick days taken in order to spot potential difficulties. For instance, if an officer has numerous sick days and/or an inordinate number of violent fights, high speed pursuits, or a combination of other high risk incidents, they may be monitored by supervisors. This has become standard practice in North American policing in recent years.

There is a difference between a sudden severe traumatic event and the cumulative effects of continuous exposure to stress. We have come a long way from twenty years ago when supervisors were more likely to tell officers that they should leave their problems at home or "suck it up" if they talked about stress. This attitude has changed, but there is always still room for improvement. I contacted Sergeant Clarke Paris of the Las Vegas Metropolitan Police Department, who has created a seminar on police stress management that he is presenting across North America. His seminar is called "The Pain Behind the Badge" and seeks to bridge the gap between the stress that officers feel and the services provided by their agencies. Paris says PTSD cannot be fixed by the afflicted officer alone but requires professional intervention. Fifty-two percent of people diagnosed with lifetime PTSD have also been diagnosed with alcohol abuse or dependence, a rate twice that of the adult population. Other PTSD behaviour commonly includes abuse of power, sick humour, depression, disregard for safety, increased absenteeism at work, serious consideration of changing jobs, substance abuse, and contemplation of self-destructive actions. Paris reports that 48 percent of police suicides are related to failed relationships and that that officers with ten to fourteen years on the job are at greatest risk of suicide, a period that Paris refers to as the "Badge of Life" (Clarke 2011). In reflecting on my career, I have seen all of these symptoms from time to time in many of my colleagues. Awareness of police-related stress and the dangers inherent in this profession and culture is continually improving.

Kurtz (2009) found that female officers have more stress as they usually come home to a second job, running the family household, after a shift as a police officer, while many men have fewer domestic responsibilities. The same study showed that male officers often gather and tell war stories but not with their female counterparts. This means that many female officers are deprived of the therapeutic effect of debriefing, even if it is over beers. Personally I have not observed this, except with female members who have children and cannot justify going out very often after work with their colleagues. Social taboos, stricter laws, and reduced tolerance for drinking and driving has also significantly changed the way people party, beginning in the early 1990s, which I would characterize as a different era. The demographic shift described earlier has also affected the way police officers socialize. I realized I had slipped into the old guy category when I was taken aback by newer officers gathering around a television to play video-games during a shift party for my platoon. In the earlier days it was enough to have a beer and talk. Members would loosen up and newer members could hear the war stories and learn about organizational politics from the constables and sergeants.

Having worked in a number of specialty units, I have found that each unit develops its own culture and traditions. For a while in the Anti-Crime Tactical Unit we developed a tradition of meeting in member's garages for barbeques. We met at a different member's home each week. The ICE unit all went out for breakfast together every Friday morning. Every unit and platoon has its own traditions to recognize new members as well as retirements and transfers. Some have parties in public places, some meet at people's houses, some have cakes and coffee or potlucks in the office. While these traditions are common in all work places, I have to say that police officers generally regard "shifters," as such team gatherings are commonly known, as an important part of team building and an opportunity for debriefing among people who share unique stresses and demands. The traditional "choir practice," which historically involved the consumption of a lot of fermented beverages, has changed in recent decades as societal attitudes about alcohol and driving under the influence have changed. But the principle of being able to socialize, debrief, and decompress with peers is still strong.

This strong culture across policing stands out most for me when I recall occasions when I have met with officers from around the world. For instance, courses I have attended at the Canadian Police College are generally comprised of officers from across Canada, and there are usually a few in each class from other countries. These groups of strangers meet in the classes and mess halls and generally have such an instant affiliation that an outsider would not know that they are from different agencies, even different cultures. They share similar perspectives and speak the same policing language.

PERFORMANCE MEASUREMENT

Performance, like officer wellness, is difficult to measure and presents unique challenges in policing. Performance measurement is another aspect of government service that is evolving in Canada. In an age where the public has more information at their fingertips than ever before, it is no longer acceptable for government agencies like the police to tell the public that they have no business asking if their police resources are being used efficiently and effectively. People today want to know how the government is using their tax dollars.

Performance measurement in the public sector is more difficult than in the private sector where success is defined substantially by profits and the bottom line. How do we measure police performance? If you have a family member raped or murdered you want the best investigation possible, not the cheapest. This is where the use of private contractors, who are driven by the bottom line, is at odds with the values that drive public service.

Private corporations may be able to run a prison or process seized evidence at a lower cost than the government, but if we sent a contracted identification specialist to examine a break-and-enter scene in an elderly woman's home, will they be able to take the time to sit and comfort her? Or will they be driven to get that job done and move on to the next as quickly as possible because they are being paid by the job? It is the small acts of compassion that define success in the policing profession, in my opinion, and arguably should insulate it from being profit-driven. At the same time, government must provide good stewardship and seek the greatest performance possible from public resources.

There is a growing body of literature that describes challenges in public sector performance measurement (Osborne and Plastrik 2000). Speers (2005) emphasizes that reporting on public sector performance is challenging because it is difficult for a government, which is always concerned with voter confidence, to report on its own poor performance. The speed at which information travels coupled with demands for increased accessibility from the public has created an environment in which government agencies now must manage information that has already reached the public domain, as opposed to decades past when they focused more on deciding what information should be released.

Increased use by the public and media of access to information legislation underscores the need for government transparency. Public reporting of budgets is often viewed with cynicism (Mulvale and Hansen 2006). A more effective policy regarding performance concentrates on continually improving credibility through honest reporting of both good and bad outcomes of government programs. Law enforcement agencies can gain a great deal of credibility by reporting on their failures as well as on their successes. The key is to show the public that lessons were learned from failures and programs have been improved based on those lessons. Newcomer (2007) notes the challenges of public service measurement, emphasizing that there are endless opportunities for governments to improve performance reporting.

As mentioned earlier, corporate responsibility in Canada was partially addressed through the 2003 enactment of Bill-C45, which holds individual executives and officers within corporations criminally liable for decisions made on behalf of a company (Canada, Department of Justice 2003). This act demonstrates awareness within governments that corporate leaders cannot be granted complete trust to look after the welfare of the communities they operate in; there must be some accountability mechanisms. As the philosopher John Locke argues, citizens would be foolish to trust the government blindly and not make them accountable (Held 1996).

In a presentation to IPAC in 2007, Gilles Paquet of the Graduate School of Public and International Affairs, University of Ottawa, described the increasing accountability in Canada's decentralized, networked, governance system. Deeper scrutiny, from within and outside government, is increasing civil servant accountability and affecting organizational cultures. Civil servants now operate in a far more transparent environment than did their predecessors.

Horizontal, networked governance is, however, being managed in a far more technologically challenging and globalized environment than ever before. The level of complexity in many government jobs exceeds the expertise of senior managers, whose focus is more on administration. In many cases, this places a public servant in a position of having exclusive knowledge over program performance or inefficiencies. In contrast to twenty years ago, when senior police managers knew the constable's job, many jobs are now so complex and technologically advanced that senior executives must rely on their officers to report on what they are doing. In fact, even the frontline police general patrol job has changed so much that most senior managers could not jump into a cruiser car and work effectively without some mentoring on the changed computer systems, reporting processes and software, policies, and procedures.

There is ongoing debate about whether senior officials can be held truly accountable for mistakes made by employees several levels down in today's bureaucracies (Schafer 1999). In many cases, managers cannot know the technical aspects of all of the complex jobs they oversee and may not have a thorough understanding of performance and efficiencies in the operations over which they have authority. Therefore identifying inefficiencies, including those within police organizations, often falls to frontline workers. This has increased a focus on whistle-blowing at all levels of modern government. The implications of highly technical jobs on exclusive knowledge and whistle-blowing are an area of ongoing concern and highlight the importance and role of middle management, who tend to have a better understanding than executives of the technical tasks they oversee.

WHISTLE-BLOWING

As societies, economies, and governments have expanded and become more complex, regulatory governance and accountability systems have also expanded (Strick 2002). Public servants have a front row seat and are often the first to know when things go wrong in government agencies. As a result, they are often caught between their sense of duty to stop government waste while also protecting the agencies they serve. At a systemic level, the government walks a fine line between the need for secrecy and the democratic deficit that can result from restricting the public's right and the need to know what government agencies are doing.

A number of accountability mechanisms have evolved to prevent civil servants from complaining to outside sources (Delaney 2007). Public servants are constrained by corporate ethics and rules from divulging incompetence, waste, or even corruption within government. The fact that unauthorized disclosures or whistle-blowing occurs is, in itself, proof that existing internal reporting mechanisms are often inadequate. Government agencies that admit mistakes more freely, demonstrating transparency in dealing with incidences of alleged corruption and mismanagement, tend to inspire public confidence rather than distrust. It is important to know who is accountable within government and to whom civil servants should report wrongdoing if they see it. Both civic duty and principles of accountability must be considered. Many civil servants are caught in a struggle between simultaneous loyalties to their government and to the public (Kernaghan and Siegel 1999). Their sense of duty may be further complicated by dedication to a third set of values, the standards that guide their profession. These conflicts can be further exacerbated by the civil servant's sense of responsibility to their families: should they risk their livelihood and all they have worked for in order to expose an injustice or a mismanaged government program? Research has found that most civil servants are unwilling to risk their careers and well-being by becoming whistle-blowers. However, when internal reporting mechanisms fail, some individuals do choose to go public (Rowat 2004).

When is it appropriate to go outside of one's organization and blow the whistle? Some suggest that it should only be done when the matter being reported is contrary to peer group values (Laframboise 1991). This argument fails, however, as it may be collective peer group values that are the problem. The example of Canadian Airborne soldiers reporting the torture of Somali captives, including sixteen-year-old Shidane Arone, who was murdered, illustrates this point. The regiment may have developed a shared value that this behaviour was acceptable and if peer group values had dictated whether this unjust behaviour should have been reported, it would never have come to light.

The need to control information in order to protect lives makes military personnel and police officers interesting subjects for this discussion. Both groups work in dangerous environments where reliance on peers for safety creates strong shared values. Breaking ranks to report perceived wrongdoing could have extreme consequences. For example, unauthorized release of information on police operations can tip off suspects, who may choose to flee and escape arrest or lie in wait and ambush the police.

One famous, albeit dated, case of an officer standing up for major changes was Frank Serpico in the New York City Police Department (NYPD). Serpico, guided by his conscience, refused to take part in corrupt practices in the NYPD (Maas 1973). He testified in court about the experience and supported a government program attempting to correct widespread corruption in major American police organizations in the early 1970s. He became an outcast with his fellow officers and, tragically, was shot in the face when his peers neglected to back him up at a call for assistance in the line of duty.

Canadian police agencies have much less history of corruption; however, the Serpico case illustrates the dynamics that individuals may face in attempting to affect organizational change. Unpopular changes within the workplace are bound to be difficult without a critical mass of like-minded people, a strong chain of command, and effective leadership. Recent research, mentioned earlier in the section on culture, has confirmed the range of retaliation that police officers may receive at the hands of their peers when they are deemed to be non-conforming (Cancino and Enriquez 2004).

The act of whistle-blowing is seen as revolutionary; it undermines the effectiveness of an organization and therefore indirectly affects service to the public. In the police context, many unauthorized disclosures have been self-serving rather than for the public good. "Deep blue" media tips are sometimes given over issues like overtime and resource deployment in order to undermine collective bargaining efforts or to voice disagreement with a unit or program being shut down or members being redeployed.

Transparency can alleviate tensions within the community and increase credibility for police agencies. The previously discussed case of J.J. Harper, killed in 1989 by a WPS officer in the line of duty, illustrates the value of transparency. I was field-trained in Winnipeg's North End, which had a large Aboriginal community whose distrust of the police increased after the incident. As I mentioned earlier, this incident also led to the Aboriginal Justice Inquiry, which has affected many aspects of policing in Canada, and in Manitoba in particular (Hamilton and Sinclair 1991).

Following the Harper case, critical errors were made in providing honest information to the inquiry and to the public. As a result, many lessons were learned and more transparent accountability practices and policies resulted. For instance, some officers were embarrassed on the witness stand as a result of having followed deficient procedures and policies, including the way notes were made and the way evidence was handled during the investigation. The police chief was criticized for jumping too quickly to the defence of involved officers, before the completion of the investigation. Balance between the need to represent and support officers, retain impartiality, and provide truthful information to the public after sensitive events remains a challenge for modern police executives.

In his book, *The Corporation: The Pathological Pursuit of Profit and Power*, Bakan (2004) provides an intriguing analysis of privately owned corporations' profit-seeking motives which lead Western corporations, regardless of risks to public safety, the environment, or human exploitation, to employ morally dubious practices such as using Third World child labour in order to sustain their profit margins. Public safety is clearly one government responsibility that cannot be delegated entirely to private corporations. If profit is the goal of shareholders, managers of private corporations main interest must be to operate for profit. Of course, many non-government organizations are not profit oriented but the vast majority of large commercial corporations are. According to Bakan, if the share-holders of a corporation wish the manager to seek profit, then they must seek profit with all legal means. Private corporations may be able to provide emergency services or run a prison more cheaply than government, but using them raises questions about accountability. If laws exist that provide certain standards of service, it does not mean they are adhered to.

The existence of safety-related laws and regulations does not, in itself, ensure public safety. Laws do not protect anything unless resources are made available to enforce them. There are a myriad of laws in existence that are not enforced, either because they no longer fit the problem they were enacted to address or because they are not a priority. For example, numerous laws and acts regulate the railroad industry and yet over 1,000 derailments still happen in Canada each year (Transportation Safety Board of Canada 2006).

In some ways, the RCMP sets the standards for Canadian policing. They are the nation's largest police force, they manage the Canadian Police College, and they are connected politically on a national level. Until recently, the RCMP had a very favourable public image (Argititis 2007). A 2007 Ipsos Reid survey reported that two-thirds of Canadians have confidence in RCMP upper ranks, while one-third reported having little to no confidence in RCMP management (Weeks 2007). A series of scandals appears to be causing a growing loss of trust by the Canadian public in their national police (Argitits 2007). Problems for the RCMP organization seem to be increasing and gaining momentum (Clairmont 2007). It appears inevitable that more public inquiries will examine a variety of issues surrounding our national police agency. If the individuals involved in the Arar case, mentioned earlier, had dealt more openly with the issue when the error was identified, the impact on involved officers and the organization might have been mitigated.

The security of sensitive police investigations requires secrecy that makes public oversight problematic. It is this legal and proper need for secrecy that has encouraged organizational cultures of self-regulation and inevitably created problems in policing. Secrecy in highly sensitive investigations does not translate to a justification for denial of all oversight. Paradoxically, accountability mechanisms are also used to keep employees from making complaints of alleged corrupt practices to outside sources. This has allegedly occurred in the RCMP (Clairmont 2007; Delaney 2007; Martin 2007; Naumetz 2007a, 2007b).

The sudden resignation of RCMP Commissioner Zaccardelli in 2006 marked the end of an era within the RCMP and possibly the start of a new age of increased transparency and accountability. Confronted with a growing list of scandalous allegations, including internal grievances alleging everything from unfair labour practices to questionable business practices, the commissioner reportedly had no choice but to resign (CTV News 2006). In his article, "Mounties' Squeaky-Clean Image Blemished by Scandals," Argitis (2007) describes how the force had been beleaguered by allegations of defrauding the pension fund, botched investigations, and political interference. In his letter of resignation to the prime minister, Commissioner Zaccardelli stated that the continuing controversy made it difficult for him to fulfill his responsibilities (Zaccardelli 2006).

When newly appointed RCMP Commissioner Bob Paulson took office in November 2011, he stated he would push for swifter discipline against officers who commit plainly "outrageous" misconduct. In cases of significant lying, cheating or stealing, deliberate excessive force, or serious criminal conduct, said Paulson, the force will immediately suspend officers without pay and formally seek their dismissal. Paulson emphasized that he and senior officers need to protect the integrity of the RCMP by acting swiftly with regard to allegations of misconduct (Quan 2011, 2012). In 2012 it is apparent just how difficult it is to change organizational culture, especially in paramilitary organizations steeped in tradition like the RCMP (MacCharles 2012).

The modern environment is far less secure for public servants, who are often called to testify at public forums where, historically, ministers would have testified. For instance, a 2007 CanWest news piece described how ministers distanced themselves from recent RCMP scandals, illustrating why public servants may believe that they can no longer count on support from senior bureaucrats or their elected ministers when scandals arise (Fitzpatrick 2007). Public servants working within a system that is perceived to be mismanaged or corrupt have a difficult choice to make – remain silent and risk being accused of participating in the perceived corruption or mismanagement or blow the whistle and risk persecution for going public. In today's environment of increasing transparency, where the media are more likely to gain access to sensitive information and public servants see their colleagues left to face parliamentary committees or even criminal prosecutions, it seems wise to remain above reproach in work ethics, documenting and reporting on issues that may later come back to haunt them.

At a parliamentary committee investigating alleged mismanagement of the RCMP pension fund, Deputy Commissioner Barbara George adamantly denied, under oath, that she had ordered a detective off a case when he began uncovering material that was damning to the RCMP. In April 2008, she was admonished by a parliamentary committee for contempt of Parliament (CTV News 2008), reportedly the first person in Canada to be convicted of this offence in ninety-five years, the previous one being Louis Riel. George was a senior executive with power to affect careers and transfer frontline RCMP members (and their families) to remote outposts. The message the allegation sent to frontline officers who might consider disclosing embarrassing information or blowing the whistle was to be extremely careful. As she was removed from duty over the allegation and into retirement George has sought to have the public record cleared, insisting that she only became involved, as the head of human resources, late in the situation and did not transfer the officer in question. She remained adamant that she had not lied to Parliament. In 2012, MP Borys Wrzesnewskj, who led the original investigation – apologized publicly to George for making the allegation (Smith 2012).

In all of the stories about this scandal, or about any high-profile debacle, there is rarely a mention of what was done by government to protect informants. Those who go down the whistle-blowing road are likely to wind up on their own. The RCMP case over pension funds illustrates the jeopardy experienced by police officers at all levels. Accounts from a variety of whistle-blowers reveal that the first obstacle they encountered was credibility as they found it difficult to get others to take them and their information seriously. Secondly, there was the reaction of the affected parties, who are inevitably higher up in the organizational hierarchy. Martin (2007) describes how politicians distanced themselves from alleged RCMP wrongdoing when RCMP members came forward to accuse their superiors of covering up their allegations that the pension fund had been mishandled.

The RCMP represents a significant part of Canada's heritage. The extraordinary number of problems that it currently faces is largely systemic. Some individuals in the senior ranks clearly could have handled certain situations differently. However, this does not reflect on all of the dedicated people serving communities in every corner of Canada. More transparency and oversight might have prevented many of the RCMP's problems from becoming major issues.

Another relatively new aspect of whistle-blowing, blogging and Internet posting, is tied to increased use of social networking. Retired police officers are increasingly using these media formats to denounce and openly attack their former organizations, criticizing decisions, strategies, and policies that they could not speak publicly about while they were still working. News outlets, as well, now often have blogging sections attached to online articles and it is possible to follow the public reaction to stories. I have found that responses tend to be made anonymously, often by the same people who have something to say about everything. That being said, interesting ideas are often expressed and they are a potential way for public servants and politicians to get a sense of the public feeling over issues. Blogs and social networking sites are the contemporary version of the traditional letters to the editor, on steroids.

Future generations of Canadian civil servants, from the RCMP and other federal departments and Canadian police agencies, will have this period to look back on and learn from. Increasing access to information and the resulting accountability and need for transparency create an imperative for modern police agencies to adapt to changing community demands. This requires the ability to recognize when changes are required, as well as the ability to achieve them. These challenges will be discussed in the following chapter on changing police strategies.

11

Changing Police Strategies

MANAGING CHANGE

General principles of good public service underpin much of the debate about police resource deployment and change. Green and White (2007) write that the goal of the public service is efficient and effective program delivery and good stewardship over public funds. Police forces are among the government services that have been subject to new levels of scrutiny in recent years. They are also under considerable pressure to perform and to demonstrate efficiency and effectiveness in their operations. The public has joined the debate about how limited resources should be deployed and whether they are getting the best results from policing strategies. Productivity and morale have been affected by modern tendencies to do more with less. Feldheim (2007) writes that "downsizing" has become the most feared word in the contemporary workplace. These trends affect Canada's civil servants and the productivity of government agencies. In the policing context, there are continually increasing demands on officers from the frontline to middle management and executive levels.

The success of strategic change depends upon proper planning. Scholars have found that the biggest reason for the failure of organizational change is that little thought has been put into its impacts on people (Bridges 2003). Administrators must recognize both external factors that they have no or little control over and the psychological effect that change can have on people (Cameron and Green 2004). Lewin (1947) was a pioneer in managing organizational change, focusing on the human aspects that can cause initiatives to fail. He suggests that leaders must prepare people psychologically to understand the need for change (the "unfreezing" stage) and to improve the effectiveness of and anchoring change ("refreezing"). It is important to point out that awareness of these human resource issues and effective change management skills will enhance the success of future public sector and police leaders.

Strategy shifts, such as the move to more community-based approaches, come with the challenges involved in making organizations change (Glensor and Peak 1996). The tenacious adherence to core values, discipline, chain of command, and stability that define the policing profession have often created organizational cultures that are resistant to change. Research by Lewis, Rosenberg, and Sigler (1999) on acceptance of community-based policing approaches in the late 1990s found that resistance to change is a major barrier to innovation in policing. This study found that officers with higher education were often more accepting of new approaches. They found the same tendency to resistance to change among military personnel and recommend that police hire new recruits with less previous military experience in order to improve willingness to change in police organizations (Lewis, Rosenberg, and Sigler 1999).

In my own experience conducting recruit hiring interviews and reviewing applications, previous military experience was highly valued as it generally demonstrates an ability to operate in high stress, disciplined, team-oriented environments and within a chain of command. The more recent idea that new officers should demonstrate both flexibility and willingness and ability to learn and change as well as the historically sought-after conservative values of protecting the status quo and not questioning authority has created difficulties in finding individuals who can fulfill all these roles.

As a result of high professional standards, the police culture is often hard on its own members. Police officers who defend unpopular positions or implement new strategies sometimes risk being shunned or treated like outcasts by other officers. While this might seem like an overly dramatic description, it is accurate and an important consideration in discussing the elements of police culture and organizational change.

In his book *Soul of a Cop*, highly decorated NYPD officer Paul Ragonese described "putting on the grease," police vernacular for a situation in which a police officer is ostracized and shunned by his or her peers for talking openly about things that other members want to stay quiet (Ragonese and Stainback 1991). Michael Quinn served twenty three and a half years as a decorated Minneapolis police sergeant, one and a half years as the deputy director of the Minnesota Police Corps, and five years as a special deputy US marshal. In his book on the police code of silence, *Walking with the Devil: What Bad Cops Don't Want You to Know and Good Cops Won't Tell You* (2005), Quinn describes the culture of protection, often referred to as the code of silence or the blue wall, that is prevalent in policing organizations across America and the continuous ethical dilemmas that officers face throughout their careers. Many of these dilemmas involve whether or not to speak openly about policing issues or incidents or whether to blow the whistle on indiscretions they see.

Officers involved in major changes that are unpopular, who advocate unpopular ethical stands, or who are whistle-blowers risk being "put on the grease." As such, they often suffer for the changes that are made for the betterment of their police agencies. As stated earlier, major changes are bound to be difficult without a critical mass of like-minded people, a strong chain of command, and effective leadership.

Trice and Beyer describe the extreme difficulties often associated with introducing major organizational changes, given the natural resistance to them. Their research found that 90 percent of corporate strategy changes in American companies have failed (in Shafritz, Ott, and Jang 2005). In police agencies, natural organizational resistance to change is compounded by the slow moving cogs of justice. Where police have been willing to make changes, such as in those police services who have been at the leading edge of technological innovations, whether related to investigative techniques or processes such as electronic disclosure, they have often met with resistance in the courts. Despite superior court decisions supporting electronic disclosure, some crown prosecutors, lawyers, and judges historically resisted the wave of twenty-first century technology. In some instances the police provided cases on DVDs only to be ordered by the courts to produce the traditional binders of printed hardcopy paper evidence for defence layers, crown prosecutors, and judges. However things have changed drastically in twenty years. The 1990s saw the justice system beginning to shed its centuries-long strict commitment to low technology, paper, systems. The courts are changing, as new generations of progressive people are advancing into positions of authority within the systems.

Major changes are often resisted within police agencies as well, sometimes for the reasons outlined within the previous section on demographics. Officers who began their careers using manual type-writers can have difficulty adjusting to continually changing tech-nology. Leadership in modern police agencies requires the ability to deal with new technology and to lead others in the required continu-ous adaptation and change. I experienced these dynamics when par-ticipating in the implementation of new videotaped interview and interrogation policies and practices.

While establishing the Arson Strike Force in 2000, my teammates and I decided to videotape all of our interviews with suspects. At the time, youth were burning dumpsters and vacant houses in the core neighbourhoods of Winnipeg. We laid hundreds of criminal charges against dozens of youth and found that many of those charged had varying degrees of FASD. We decided as a team to videotape all of the interviews in order to ensure strong credibility and convictions in court. Videotaping reduces the opportunity for defence lawyers to raise doubts in court about the charged youth's understanding of their rights and the voluntariness of their confessions. That strategy resulted in a near 100 percent criminal conviction rate. Using video-taped interviews as a policing tool had only been used up to that point in certain specialty areas such as homicide and child abuse and was not yet an expected standard of evidence by the courts.

A forward-thinking commander brought me into the Crime Division years later, partially to implement videotaping interviews in the criminal investigation bureau. Some members were resistant to the change, which required learning new interview techniques that would withstand court scrutiny as well as discarding the off-camera interview techniques of the past. Some tense moments occurred between officers over decisions about whether or not to videotape certain suspect interviews and how these things should be managed.

On-camera interviews are a strong example of the progressive nature of policing and are one aspect of WPS culture that I am par-ticularly proud of. As an organization, we implemented the policy before the prosecutors and the courts came to expect it. I believe the change was made not only because it was inevitable but because it was the right thing to do. The practice improved transparency and increased the confidence of the courts, the legal community, and the public, despite being somewhat painful to initiate.

Scholars have described how important it is that public sector leaders understand what is worth protecting and what must change (Frechette et al. 2007). While for many decades policing was a static profession with little change, the past twenty years have seen a shift to a culture of continuous transformation, to the point where we must now guard against making change solely for the sake of change. We now must also guard against repeating past mistakes. Being slow to change has occasionally saved agencies from implementing programs that were adopted too quickly and failed elsewhere (Rasmussen 2000).

Some of the most common shifts in policing strategies are the continuous vacillation between centralizing and decentralizing operations, and between specialization and generalist philosophies. Executives can easily justify improvements through either route. Centralization improves communication and resource sharing within police services. For instance, when units are housed in the same building they communicate more. While this is potentially an area for further research, we have found anecdotally that communication between units diminishes when they are moved to separate buildings. I have experienced this myself on numerous occasions, working on task forces and projects that took groups of us away from proximity to other units. It takes a great deal of effort to maintain daily contact if you are working across town.

Centralized clerical and technical support serving numerous units can be more effective and efficient than having stand-alone operations in each corner of the organization. Decentralization, on the other hand, can improve public interface and community-based collaboration because the officers are situated in community offices that are highly visible and more accessible to the public. A new administration can focus on centralizing or decentralizing parts of an organization and demonstrate in either case that in their tenure they made positive changes.

Another common cycle of change involves policing philosophy. There seems to be a continuous shift between specialization and generalist approaches. One approach argues that officers who are highly specialized and extensively trained in a certain specialty can be more effective and efficient than generalist officers. Continuously advancing technology requires a high degree of training for officers to fulfill certain roles and functions, although in some cases it raises concerns about diminishing returns from expensive training, as discussed in previous chapters.

The generalist approach holds that better overall service occurs if frontline ranks are not depleted to create highly specialized detective positions. Rather than having an entire unit of detectives managing certain issues, general patrol officers handle the situation, perhaps calling an experienced specialist for guidance.

The generalist-specialist debate comes up most often, internally, at times when highly trained and specialized officers are transferred back into uniform operations. The argument is that we are all generalists and that uniform ranks are enriched by the unique skills that members bring back from special assignments. For example, after working in the Anti-Crime Tactical Unit for three years, I returned to uniform and taught surveillance courses for the uniform members in my district. Officers with gang and vice experience are a great resource on uniform shifts and expand the capacity of general patrol teams to finish complex investigations without handing them off to specialty units.

Police cultures have evolved, over the past twenty years, from being historically stable and resistant to change into cultures of continuous innovation. With changing technology and greater demands, police are specializing more. The days of the generalist police officer who can do it all are fading quickly, almost to the point where uniform emergency response, which is the basic police job, is evolving into a specialty. Increased demand for highly specialized skill sets and advanced training has resulted in many police organizations fragmenting into greater numbers of smaller, highly specialized units.

Police organizational cultural changes are reflected in the dramatically different manner in which major investigations are now handled. In the past fifteen years, Canadian police services have increasingly encountered cases that exceed the capacity of normal police resources. Investigations involving disasters, organized crime, Internet child exploitation and human trafficking, and a wide variety of other crime trends are complex and globalized; they require a wider range of cooperating agencies and place greater demands on the justice system and the communities they affect. New major case management systems are a drastic departure from historical, pre-1990s practices.

Cases such as Paul Bernardo and Karla Homolka's serial rape and murder of several young Ontario girls in the early 1990s and the Clifford Olson serial murder case in British Columbia highlighted the need for improved coordination and information sharing between agencies and the need for critical thinking in steering major investigations (Jenish 1996). Better coordination and information-sharing between regional police agencies might have identified suspects earlier and saved lives. The practice of dumping a murdered body in a neighbouring jurisdiction in order to confuse police agencies that may or may not communicate well with one another is common knowledge in the police world. The Pickton serial murder case in British Columbia and the arrest of Shawn Cameron Lamb for the alleged murder of three Winnipeg women with potential links to other parts of Canada have highlighted the need for greater cross-agency information sharing and cooperation (Canadian Press 2011a; McIntyre 2012).

Ontario police services are now mandated to use major case management systems that ensure critical thinking and effective management to control the speed, flow, and direction of major cases. Other police services are following suit before they are mandated to do so in order to maintain best practices and avoid the tunnel vision that can result in wrongful convictions. Best practices for major case management are outlined in a 465-page guidebook produced by the Canadian Police College (Canadian Police College 2002). Use of these systems requires that modern investigators and administrators have knowledge, skills, and abilities far exceeding what was demanded of them twenty years ago.

CRIME PREVENTION

As criminal sophistication and community-based problems have continued to increase, police agencies have been challenged to find innovative strategies to remain effective. Old paradigms are being challenged and adjusted. The new focus on evidence-based policing brings a new level of accountability in police management. Communities are increasingly critical of police programs and the choices made in the deployment of limited resources (Sinclair 2011).

Evidence-based policing and increased accountability first emerged in the policing discourse in the early 1990s with New York City Police Commissioner William Bratton's implementation of the COMPSTAT program (Bratton and Andrews 1999). COMPSTAT is a program that was developed to better utilize statistical analysis to direct police activities. As Willis, Mastrofski, and Weisburd (2003, v) point out, "Compstat shows promise of helping departments reduce crime through systematic data collection, crime analysis, and heightened accountability. Compstat's potential as a tool of police reform nonetheless depends on the extent to which it changes officers' routine activities."

Statistical crime analysis and weekly management meetings were implemented in New York City, and managers at all levels were challenged to solve crime-related social problems in their jurisdictions and to answer for the effectiveness of the programs under their commands. This increase in accountability marked a significant shift in strategy and changed the organizational culture of the NYPD. It created a culture of problem-solving and accountability that permeated the organization from the commanders to the front line officers. Bratton utilized crime analysis to determine "hotspots" and deployed resources accordingly. Crime fell by twelve percent in the first year, and another seventeen percent in·the second year (Duffy and Massimo 2007), which led to international recognition of the program. The changes were not painless, however, as numerous senior managers in command positions were replaced within the first few years of COMPSTAT's implementation after having been taken to task on the effectiveness of their strategies (Henry 2003). Bratton has said of the success of the COMPSTAT program in New York, "First, we had to remake the NYPD into an effective, focused organization. Second, we had to use this instrument actually to police the city by developing strategies and tactics that would prevent and uproot crime rather than just react to it" (Bratton and Andrews 1999, 1).

Elements of the COMPSTAT program are currently being adopted within many police departments across North America. Until the early 1990s, most detective sergeants had wall maps full of coloured pins representing whatever they were tracking: commercial or residential break-ins, robberies, thefts, or sexual assaults. Now, those pin-filled maps have been replaced with electronic charts, digital maps, and powerful analytical tools. When trained staff are available for data entry and analysis for major cases, highly complex and effective analytical software can be very effective. However, the police risk becoming increasingly ineffective if we have the software but cannot use it effectively due to lack of technical skills or support staff and no longer have experienced officers who have retained "old school" techniques for organizing complex investigations.

In 1996, I took the criminal intelligence analysis course offered at the Canadian Police College. It consisted of several workbooks sent by mail, with exercises to be completed. These exercises involved reading the information and intelligence provided and manually writing it into a printed matrix that allowed us to analyze it. For instance, in a stack of one hundred intelligence reports one name might come up repeatedly and in relation to several different players. Plotting information out and analyzing it made it possible to see relationships that otherwise might never have been uncovered. A person might be associated in different ways with every element of an organized crime network and thus might become a prime suspect rather than a peripheral or insignificant player.

Fast forward to 2005, when I took the intelligence analysis course again. It then involved learning how to use complex (and extremely expensive) analytical software. To use the software to its full potential, you need expensive plotter printers that can print up huge graphs and organizational charts displaying entire criminal networks. Large ones can take up entire rooms and can track hundreds of players and multiple pieces of intelligence associated with each one. Learning to use this software to its full potential can take a career, but when it is used with skill it is a powerful tool. The exercises in the 2005 version of the analysis course made the 1996 version appear primitive.

While effective analysis does not necessarily offer solutions, it reveals crime patterns so that they can be addressed. For instance, if a sexual assault occurred in a certain spot in a park and another one happened in the same spot the following month or the following year, it is possible that no one in the local police agency would notice. An analyst, however, might pull all crime reports from a certain area over a period of time and look for patterns. The analysis might reveal numerous sexual assaults in and around that particular spot. It might also reveal that the incidents were of increasing severity, with reported incidents of peeping, then of groping, followed by full-blown rape, as is common if a sexual assault suspect targets an area. The analysis might also reveal a pattern of offences happening at certain times of day, certain days of the week, and with certain periods of time between offences. This could provide an opportunity to warn the public and to set up surveillance around that location.

In one serial rape case in Winnipeg, we were puzzled by the apparently random location of similar sexual assaults throughout the city, until our analysis revealed patterns around a bus route that the suspect took from work. The value of analytical resources cannot be overstated – they can solve crimes and point to effective ways to deploy resources. They can also lead to better understanding of social problems, the root causes of crimes that we can work towards preventing.

Careful thought about crime inevitably leads to speculation over the value of preventive strategies. Schuck (2005) describes American crime prevention as being at a crossroad. While crime has generally decreased over the past ten years, this change may be the result of the increase in funding to police and prison systems. While statistical reports show reductions in some classes of crime, I would challenge the validity of any analysis that reports a reduction in violence and organized crime in Canada. One need not look far for information on the increase in street violence and crime severity (Blackwell 2010; Bolan 2009; Germano, McIntyre, and Giroday 2011). Drive-by shootings and gang-related killings used to be fairly rare but have now become far more common. The number of certain classes of incidents may have decreased statistically, but the events that occur are frequently more extreme; the numbers can be misleading, as I pointed out in the chapter on statistics.

Another change over the past two decades has been the preparation of crime statistics, maps, and reports for public consumption, illustrating the increased transparency and public accountability that I have stressed throughout this book. There is also an increasing focus on national security, use of technology, and information sharing among agencies, in particular after the terrorist attacks of 9/11. Given declining economic resources, many agencies are now renewing their focus on crime prevention. Increased globalization is creating the need for better cooperation and information sharing between law enforcement agencies and the broad spectrum of part-ner agencies and community stakeholders.

Schuck (2005) raises the issue of selective availability for new crime prevention technologies, noting that they are often prohibi-tively expensive and therefore unattainable by many local agencies or communities. Analytical resources are a case in point. Our federal partners often have the requisite staff support and equipment required to making full use of available tools, which is why joint task forces are often so successful. Municipal officers often provide the "boots on the ground" experience and tenacity while the RCMP brings the support resources, staff, and equipment required for mak-ing these teams truly effective.

Police resource deployment, however, should be a secondary consideration in crime deterrence. The main focus needs to be on finding ways to engage the entire community. Some research has revealed that 25 percent of overall crime deterrence is affected by family and community demographics (Wilson and Petersilia 2002). Stable families reduce crime. A greater emphasis on increasing community relationships with the police and supporting better parenting and stability in the family unit may also increase crime reduction and safety.

Aos et al. (2001) prepared a report entitled "The Comparative Costs and Benefits of Programs to Reduce Crime," based on their analysis of over four hundred crime-reduction programs in Canada and the United States over the past twenty-five years. Investments in interventions with high-risk youth resulted in a 2,000 percent saving in justice dollars over the long run. Imagine saving the cost of all of the related services that criminal activity leads to! The key finding by Aos et al. is that only some programs are a good investment for tax dollars so careful evaluations need to be made before funding is committed (Aos et al. 2001). This reinforces my earlier point about the importance of learning from previous mistakes.

New community-based policing strategies that have been adopted across North America are a reincarnation of the principles upon which Peel founded London's first professional metropolitan police force (Gayder 2008). With increased focus on community engagement and crime prevention rather than crime reaction, a critical mass may eventually be reached where the community becomes more resistant and resilient. Gladwell (2002) writes about how change takes place because of a build-up of critical mass. For example, he suggests that crime in New York dropped as a result of increased police attention to the seemingly less significant issues, such as broken windows and graffiti, until a tipping point was reached and overall crime was reduced. The argument is that if youth are dealt with when they are still at the stage of graffiti and petty thefts, they are less likely to progress into serious gang activity and major crimes (Bratton, Wilson and Kelling 2004; Gladwell 2002).

Kochel (2011) points out that American police agencies have sought to address rising crime and to improve public confidence through a variety of approaches, such as team policing, broken-windows policing, community policing, and problem-oriented policing in recent decades. Similar approaches in Canada have followed the American trends. One example of intelligence-led policing is the "hot-spots" strategy that identifies high-crime areas and then floods them with police resources (Kochel 2011). Its first documented use was in 1988-89 in Minneapolis, Minnesota, and it quickly became popular across the United States (Eck et al. 2005; Sherman and Weisburd 1995). A survey in 2000 found that 70 percent of American police agencies with one hundred officers or more map crime data to identify hot-spots (Weisburd et al. 2003). A survey in 2006 revealed that 81 percent of police executives claimed that targeting hot-spots of crime and disorder is an important strategy and 83 percent claimed they had used hot-spots policing (Kochel et al. 2006). What exactly the police resources do is less clearly defined, but generally they involve increased traffic enforcement, problem-oriented policing strategies, and zero tolerance of the targeted problem (Braga 2001).

Braga (2001) found there is considerable evidence that the hot-spots approach reduces crime. Hot-spots policing strategies are, however, short-term solutions that beg the question of whether they actually reduce crime or merely push problems into adjacent neighbourhoods or other areas. Prostitution is an excellent example of this. We have found over and over again that crackdowns on street prostitution merely push prostitutes into the next neighbourhood. More recently, we have seen street prostitution drastically reduced but there has been an increase in underground illegal massage parlours and escort services as well as advertising on Internet-based marketing services such as Craigslist. As well, the hot-spots approach may lead to the police becoming perceived as oppressive and to accusations of racial profiling. Sending a small army of officers into a neighbourhood to spot-check everything that moves can easily exacerbate these impressions. While attacking hot-spots might address major problems in the community quickly, the police could just as quickly lose public confidence.

Community involvement could ultimately be a more effective direction on which to concentrate than a focus that only analyzes police resource deployment in crime prevention. While long-term effectiveness is more difficult to measure, it is clear that approaches designed to improve community resilience and prevent crime are the best investment of police resources.

The past three decades in North America have shown that continuously assigning more resources to the justice system is not solving crime problems. The massive and continuous growth of the prison system, especially in the United States, is a case in point. The focus should be on crime prevention and not on reaction. Offenders need to be engaged and involved in their communities and not warehoused in prisons, except where public safety is at stake.

Silver (2005) studied three different inner-city neighbourhoods in Winnipeg and found that they had varying degrees of success in introducing community involvement initiatives to improve quality of life. The most successful neighbourhood was the one with sufficient long-term funding, high citizen involvement, and a sense of ownership within the community.

In previous research Silver identified a problem with some members of the community who lacked a sense of involvement (Silver, Hay, and Gorzen 2004). He found that many Aboriginals were marginalized and felt relatively unconnected to mainstream society. With increasing numbers of Aboriginal peoples becoming urbanized, this is a serious twenty-first century problem. The key to empowering individual communities must lie in improved citizen involvement and ownership. Empowerment must include economic security and pride, which flows largely from education, employment, and engagement.

The main challenge of police involvement in crime prevention strategies is the difficulty that police agencies have in shifting crime reaction resources into prevention efforts. The natural resistance to organizational change that was previously described exacerbates this fundamental problem of policing and helps explain the challenges associated with shifting from reactive to proactive models, even in the face of strong evidence that crime prevention is a more economically sound long-term approach to justice in Canada (Henry 2003).

The missing persons example illustrates this. The WPS had a problem with chronic missing person reports. We found that 70 percent of over 5,000 missing person calls per year involved chronic repeat runaways. We embarked on a process to use intensive resources and attention to intervene with these youth in an attempt to reduce their self-destructive and criminal behaviour and to protect them from sexual predators. We tried to prevent future runaway behaviour in order to reduce the strain on frontline uniform police resources created by responding to runaway reports. We also gained an understanding of how these runaways were being sought out, groomed, and exploited by predators. We were thus attempting to reduce the long-term strain on the police service while impacting and even saving lives of high-risk youth.

We found that we could assign extraordinary resources to a few select individuals out of the many who needed them. However, by focusing on high-risk cases, we ended up creating more work for detectives in the Missing Persons Unit as well as frontline uniform officers. We flagged the high-risk youth in our report system so that uniformed officers who encountered them received special instructions to speak with their assigned detective before returning them to the group home or facility they had run from. We did this because we knew if they were returned to the same facility they would run out the back door and be back taking drugs or being exploited in the sex trade within minutes. This created work at the front end, as uniformed officers would have to babysit these individuals or wait for other facilities to be arranged. The argument was that this preventative approach would reduce our long-term involvement – the assigned detectives would work with a team of people from the health system, social work, education, probation, and numerous other systems to create safety plans to keep the girls safe.

It is difficult to take frontline units and assign them to preventative program work when, as mentioned earlier, there is always a backlog of service calls and urgent investigations that need attention. But this approach felt like the right thing to do and social workers advised me that lives were saved because of it.

Many of the issues discussed in this book are already on the radar and being worked on, while others require renewed focus in order to meet evolving community needs. Clearly, there is room for improved coordination and use of resources between police and partner agencies. The biggest challenge, however, is in making use of the largest partner of all, the community at large. Viable and potentially effective strategies for improved community involvement with police support may rest with the relatively new and evolving field of alternative dispute resolution or peace and conflict studies.

PEACE AND CONFLICT STUDIES

In chapter 7, I discussed restorative justice and community forums as potentially effective models to enhance the justice system. Alternative dispute resolution models offer other means of effective conflict resolution, which in turn has implications for improvements to

Canadian justice. These approaches rely on multisystem cooperation that can deepen community involvement and strengthen the social fabric. Keeping young people out of jail can potentially save dollars that would have been spent on reactive responses from the justice, health, and social welfare sectors.

Throughout this book, I have focused attention on resource deployment and the importance of multisystem collaboration in addressing social problems. When considering conflict, one must be aware of the complex nature of human interactions, whether we are analyzing the cause of disputes between individuals or the structural causes of conflict in society at large. Structural causes can include social problems such as racism or the barriers to mobility and socio-economic disparities that contribute to the social ills that police forces must contend with. There is a great deal of room in the policing profession for deeper analysis of how and when the blunt instrument of justice should be deployed in addressing complex social problems.

In some cases, enforcement of laws can aggravate a situation, whereas other forms of dispute resolution may potentially prove more effective for all involved. For example, following the public inquest into the 2000 domestic murder of two sisters in Winnipeg, the WPS responded by implementing a policy that made all domestic violence–related service calls "priority one" (CBC News 2000). Once that policy was implemented, the line of pending service calls became even longer than it had been in the past, as domestic violence calls trumped calls with lesser priority. The number of domestic violence service calls increased, as did the number of arrests, so domestic violence calls basically overwhelmed frontline police resources for a period.

The priority one policy also emphasized the policy of zero tolerance for domestic violence that had resulted from a 1995 case in which a Winnipeg man killed his wife and then committed suicide (Schulman 1997). The inquiry report resulted in training for all police officers on the cycle of domestic violence and on the zero tolerance policy. The public inquiries into these murder cases were stressful for the officers who had to testify in such high profile public forums, but the experience was traumatizing for some civilian police staff, who are not used to testifying and being challenged under oath in a very public and adversarial way. Dispatchers, for instance, had to testify as to their handling of the emergency calls made by victims before they were murdered and found this very stressful.

The zero tolerance and priority one policies led to a culture of caution in the WPS, as people became very careful not to bend any rules when dealing with domestic violence cases for fear of being called to account if something went wrong later (for instance, if charges are not laid and then one of those involved returns and commits murder). The culture of caution persists to this day, even as the memories of these public inquiries fade.

While implementing the newly created policy of high priority for domestic violence, I have witnessed many families who first suffered the trauma of domestic violence and then were separated from their families when the police were required to arrest one of the parents. Then, after the aggressor is removed and charged, he or she is ordered to have no contact with the family, leading to further separation. If only we had processes that could temporarily separate families after a violent incident and offer effective community support to help fix the problem and keep the family together. Services could be provided to address the underlying issues, such as anger management and substance abuse, and to assist people in overcoming structural barriers to obtaining education, social skills, and jobs. Instead, we have processes through which families are broken up. Domestic violence is a serious social problem that needs intervention, but more multi-disciplinary approaches could potentially serve victims and offenders better and work more effectively to keep families intact.

The field of peace and conflict studies examines the underlying causes of conflict while providing more comprehensive solutions to address root causes. Alternative models could, in many cases, potentially reduce the need for the police and the courts and consequently improve social justice. A deeper analysis of conflict in society reveals that true peace is more than simply the absence of war or crime. Conflict resolution expert Johan Galtung (1996) delineates the differences between negative peace, which is the absence of war or crime reduction, and positive peace, which includes the elimination of poverty and improved education and social welfare. The goal of policing should not be simply crime reduction or responding to violence but should instead be to play a part in creating a system that produces improved living conditions, positive peace and social justice, a society with equal access to education, health, and opportunities for happiness and prosperity. Police cannot bear full responsibility for serious social problems such as domestic violence but they can be a catalyst for change. They can be influential advocates for dispute resolution and collaborative problem-solving approaches and leaders in community partnership.

Dispute resolution can assist people in understanding their situations, interactions, and reactions. Overall, alternative dispute resolution models can assist conflicting parties in uncovering and addressing the root causes of conflict, preferably before violence occurs. On an individual level, this can mean effective conflict mediation and resolution. On a community level, it can mean exploring and understanding the complex social cube that Sean Byrne of the Mauro Centre for Peace and Justice, University of Manitoba, uses as a metaphor to describe the immense complexity of human conflict. The social cube illustrates the multiple interacting dimensions that can help us understand the root causes of conflict and provide solutions. You cannot fix the problem until you analyze and understand the causes (Byrne and Senehi 2012). Some argue that crime and interpersonal violence will end when the social structures that cause death, poverty, malnutrition, and inequality have been transformed (Jeong 1995). If we understand the root causes, we stand a better chance of intervening before the violence happens. This is why I have dedicated my research interests to understanding the root causes of social problems and intervening with multi-disciplinary approaches. In my current PhD level studies at the Mauro Centre for Peace and Justice, University of Manitoba, I am striving, as are others, to find research paths that will add new knowledge to the field while implementing practical solutions to help vulnerable people in the community.

In Canada, increasing youth gang involvement and the associated street violence are challenging and growing problems. Gang activity is far too massive a social problem to be dealt with by the police, who play a small, albeit visible and significant, part in the larger system. Police are trapped in a cycle of arresting and re-arresting gang members, while the home situations of these youth continues to enable and encourage criminal involvement. Young people become involved in gangs because that is where their human needs are met. When their needs are met at home, gang involvement diminishes. It is short sighted to think that gang problems end when the police lay charges or when the courts send someone to prison.

Our processes need to be changed so that we can interrupt the cycle of criminal involvement, court, prison, and criminal involvement again. We need to recognize and acknowledge what is not working and build upon the ideas that do work. One example is the high-risk victim strategy that I described earlier. We kept a victim-centred approach, bringing multiple disciplines together with a focus on the needs of each individual youth, adjusting policies to fit the needs of each child rather than letting them get lost in policy gaps between mandated agencies. This approach was labour intensive, but a greater investment of resources up front exponentially reduces costs down the road.

Another example is the Winnipeg auto-theft suppression strategy, which followed a similar approach in focusing on the offenders and finding ways to intervene in their high-risk, anti-social lives. This model was very successful because it involved strategic planning that brought the right resources together. Since 2006 we have seen a reduction of eighty-one percent in car thefts, going from 14,000 per year to below 2,600 per year (Linden 2013). Paul reports that "auto theft dropped 83 percent and overall crime rates dropped with the work of the task force, a multi-pronged initiative that combined extra police, probation, and Crown attorneys, along with social services for families, entire communities, and schools. Authorities kept high-risk offenders under surveillance and anti-theft devices were installed" (Paul 2011, 1). In the fall of 2011 the program pioneered the use of GPS ankle bracelets to track offenders (Owen 2011c). This is a good example of a regulatory tool that can be implemented in support of better collaboration between the community, police and partner agencies. But its use needs to be planned strategically so everyone is working together.

Rick Linden of the University of Manitoba, co-chair of the auto-theft suppression program and the chair of Manitoba's new Police Commission (established in 2013), has called for more strategic approaches to combat Winnipeg's increasing street violence. In response to a weekend of violent shootings in October 2011, Linden stated "until someone is put in charge of crime control [to coordinate all agencies, not just the police], with a budget, staff, and a plan, we'll continue to have crimes like this" (Paul 2011, 1). Society will not make true headway in addressing complex problems until we work together as a cohesive community, pooling and focusing our resources and overcoming the barriers that prevent us from working toward ensuring social justice.

Lederach (1996), in his analysis of conflict transformation, emphasizes the need for citizens to be empowered to enable them to participate more fully in solving society's problems. This seems to me to be the most effective mindset for making changes. The key to success will be in effective strategies that build and draw on the strengths of all of the players. But working collectively can raise additional problems. Senge (2006) highlights how the phenomenon of groupthink that I described earlier can result in smart people collectively coming up with poor strategies. Senge also points out that we often think of the captain steering the ship as the most important actor, when in fact it is the designer who actually has the greatest impact on the ship's performance. If we learn from our mistakes and from what works, we can design effective strategies and systems. However, we must be willing to continue to learn and improve in order to achieve success. The next and last section explores the process of learning and how policing might adapt effectively to continuously changing demands.

REFLECTIVE PRACTICE

The ability to learn is critical in creating and maintaining systems that work, because society is always changing. Schon and Argyris (1996) describe the process of learning from mistakes and adapting strategies using "double loop learning," which emphasizes reflection in every stage of a process. It seems common sense, but all too often we continue doing things because "that is the way we've always done it," when we should be reflecting on every action we take, assessing whether it is working and correcting our approaches. As well, we often abandon principles and practices that have been proven effective. A large body of research has underlined the importance of reflective practice that focuses on improved professional skills through continual self-reflection on work performance. Entire scholarly journals are now dedicated to reflective practice, so there has been a large amount of work in the area since the ideas were first generated by the pioneers in this growing field of study, such as Gibbs 1988, Johns 1995, Kolb 1984, Schon 1983. Self-reflection can motivate and inform learning within organizations such as the police, helping to improve inclusion and collaboration with the community and ultimately empower the multi-stakeholder systems of service providers. Our goal should be to empower and support those who can help create effective, multidisciplinary, collaborative teams and systems that continually learn and refocus in order to remain aligned with changing community needs. All of the different stake-holders and agencies in society must synchronize their resources if efficiency and effectiveness of the whole system are to be achieved. Reflective practice may improve the ability of agencies to contribute and work together (Schon 1983).

Once more, Peel's principles of good policing are a case in point (Lentz and Chaires 2007). These principles can inform police practices of inclusion and the transformation of justice systems to better represent the populations they serve. As stated several times throughout this book, Peel's seventh principle, that "the police are the people and the people are the police," emphasizes that all citizens share responsibility for public safety and that the police are an extension of the public and should be protecting community values, not only elite interests. While the police are only a small player in a large multi-agency system, they can play a leadership role in creating social change. No single agency can tackle today's complex problems alone. A justice system that is perceived to be of the people and for the protection of society at large, contributes to public trust and confidence. Creating this legitimacy, however, requires police officials and citizens to agree on community values and on how they should be enforced.

While inclusion is critical to effective policing, it is equally important that the police guard against developing organizational cultures that could lead them to believe that their main emphasis should be on serving minority groups alone, and not the population as a whole. Some groups, such as Aboriginal peoples, refugees, children, and the elderly are vulnerable in society and need and deserve special resources and attention, but the police have a responsibility to keep all citizens safe.

Many professional service agencies do not have a formal understanding of organizational learning and a focus on continuous improvement. Checkland (1981) describes how flexibility is required to allow for continuous adaptation, based on reflection and continuously improved practices.

Community trust must also be addressed. The police can play a critical role in coordinating numerous community stakeholders to achieve better collaboration and partnership, but only if they are trusted. A major aspect of trust-building is the ability of agencies such as the police to take advantage of the lessons learned and adapt and change. Continuous learning through reflective practice should result in transformation and improved partnership between all parties involved and increased trust in the police.

In refugee and newcomer communities, there is also much room for improved service and for research on how the police can improve their practices. Refugees, by definition, come from countries where atrocities have occurred, often at the hands of police, military, and other government bodies. Bureaucrats and police officers need to guard against the highly ethnocentric idea that refugees will have the same trust in the police that mainstream society in their adopted country does. Trust is earned; it cannot be assumed. Confidential sources in the refugee community have told me about incidents in which the police seemed insensitive, often through an apparent lack of understanding of the refugees' perspectives. This has compelled me, as a senior police manager, to think about ways of improving practice.

Improved social justice requires both structural changes and the engagement of marginalized peoples to overcome the effects of oppression caused by violence, colonization, or war. It is critical that current service agencies improve engagement through trust-building, transformation, partnership, and empowerment. Trust in the police by the refugee community, as well as by the Aboriginal community, will be increased through greater inclusion.

Crisis management is another area that can be improved through reflective practice. Researchers have stressed the vital need to improve multi-agency cooperation in disaster management, particularly given the increasing global threat of borderless wars and terrorism (Boyd and Sullivan 2000). Reflective practice can be used to monitor performance and improve practices in dealing with all of these social problems, which are now so complex and globalized that no one agency can tackle any of them alone.

While the police have opportunities to act as change agents, they cannot be solely responsible for any of these major social issues. My argument, however, is that the police role is much broader than just law enforcement. The police have a responsibility to contribute to public safety, crime prevention, and, ultimately, to improved equality and social justice. The police are a small but significant part of a governance system that includes many larger elements such as social and child welfare, medical and education institutions, and the citizenry. With that in mind, the police are highly visible and often influential leaders in social justice issues. While the police have legitimate authority bestowed upon them by government, the public they serve validates their legitimacy.

Action research is another tool that can be used in the process of reflective practice, performance measurement, and continuous improvement. It diverges from traditional research methods in its emphasis on assisting practitioners to engage in the improvement of their own organization's response to specific problems (Avison et al. 1999; Wood-Harper and Baskerville 1996). While actively participating in organizational improvement, the action researcher seeks to contribute to existing theory and literature as a participant observer, while also addressing the problem at hand (Checkland 1981; Elden and Chisholm 1993). Research can sometimes challenge the status quo, mainly by criticizing organizational practices and policies. This can put the practitioner/researcher in an awkward position, as an active member of the organization about which they are gathering evidence, even if their work is focused on trying to improve the organization.

As a police officer, I have experienced this dynamic when questioning policies or strategies. Action researchers need to embark on such inquiries with their eyes open, realizing that the "gate-keepers" of the status quo, as Olesen and Myers (1999) aptly term them, may not be open to the feedback or criticism you are offering. In the regimented policing context this can put a participant researcher in an awkward position. In a progressive organization, on the other hand, inflection and objective truthful analysis can be highly valued.

While action research uses the entire range of quantitative or qualitative measurement instruments, a common element in their use, which defines the approach as action-oriented, is the focus on continuous change and improvement, guided by constant reflection. Such research is therefore very context specific and the problems it deals with may change as the research affects it by improving policies, systems, and practices. We need to be cognizant of the way we look at our work and reflect on our practices. If we learn from our mistakes, we should be able to remain aligned with changing demands and continually improve.

Afterword

Canadian police agencies are experiencing significant changes in the new millennium. Criminal sophistication, advancing technology, and evolving societal demands continually challenge police officers and administrators in new ways. Terrorism, organized crime, Internet-based child exploitation, human trafficking, and a host of other borderless crimes have globalized law enforcement, requiring interagency cooperation and information and resource sharing on a level never seen before.

In response, police services are undergoing fundamental shifts in strategic planning. They are being challenged to replace long-practiced reactive tactics with proactive, evidence-based strategies that target the root causes of social problems and not just the symptoms. Increased accountability is driving innovation as individual officers, and whole systems, adapt to new challenges almost daily.

Mass retirements are changing the demographic makeup of police organizations, causing a loss of critical corporate knowledge and forcing a new focus on recruitment, retention, and mentoring. Effective managers are now aware of the dynamics of age, gender, and ethnic diversity that were unheard of twenty years ago. Physical distance and communication barriers are collapsing so quickly that we may barely recognize their impact or know how to respond effectively. Police, and all public servants, must be vigilant in dealing with the change that is occurring all around us. We must be aware of technological advances and their implications and be prepared to take full advantage of them rather than being overwhelmed.

In the past twenty years Canadian policing has changed from a culture of change-resistance to a culture of continuous innovation and increased transparency, often brokering change with others in the broad spectrum of service agencies. While criminals operate in an increasingly borderless and globalized world, without the constraints that affect the police – such as the need to act lawfully, respect jurisdictions, and work with limited resources administered by bureaucracy – they are still not winning the war. New frontiers of policing lie in increasing community engagement and approaches that can help resist the tendency to revert to reactive strategies of the past. New methods of analysis and reflective practice hold the potential for helping police agencies to remain aligned with changing community needs and continuously adapt for optimum effectiveness.

The narrative within communities and among the agencies of justice needs to evolve to engage all of society to work together to reduce crime and improve quality of life (Byrne et al 2009; Byrne and Senehi 2012). The police can play critical roles in this discourse, but they are only a small part of a larger system. The implications for the future are considerable – police agencies that fail to work in whole-community teams risk failing to contribute to the solution of significant social problems.

The evolution from the use of manual typewriters to today's globally connected digital world does not redefine the ageless fight between good and evil – it only changes the weapons and the battleground.

References

Aldhous, Peter. 2007. "Criminal justice: Are you ready for the science bit?" *New Scientist* 193, 2590, 11, 1.

Amnesty International. 2004. "Stolen sisters: A human rights response to discrimination and violence against indigenous women in Canada." http://www.amnesty.ca /campaigns/sisters_overview.php.

Anderson, Willoughby, and Daniel Farber. 2006. "This isn't representative of our department: Lessons from hurricane Katrina for police disaster response planning." http://www.law.berkeley.edu/library/disasters/Anderson.pdf.

Aos, Steve, Marna Miller, and Elizabeth Drake. 2006. "Evidence-based public policy options to reduce future prison construction, criminal justice costs and crime rates." Washington State Institute for Public Policy. www.wa.gov/wsipp.

Aos, Steve, Polly Phipps, Robert Barnoski, and Roxanne Lieb. 2001. "The comparative costs and benefits of programs to reduce crime." Washington State Institute for Public Policy, www.wa.gov/wsipp.

Argitis, Theopolis. 2007. "Mounties' squeaky-clean image blemished by scandals." *Bloomberg*, 17 May.

Ashley, Stacey. 2010. "Hells Angels clubhouse seized in Winnipeg." CTV News, 29 July. http://winnipeg.ctv.ca/servlet/an/local/CTVNews/20100729/wpg_hells_clubhhouse_100729/20100729/?hub=WinnipegHome.

Astwood Strategy Corporation. 2004. "2002 Canadian police survey on youth gangs." Ottawa, ON: Public Safety and Emergency Preparedness Canada.

Auf der Heide, Erik. 1989. *Disaster Response: Principles of Preparation and Coordination*. St. Louis, MO: C.V. Mosby.

Austin, Ian. 2012. "Vancouver's Con Air fugitive program expanding to remainder of B.C." *The Province*, 5 March.

Avison, David E., Francis Lau, Michael Myers, and Peter Axel Nielsen. 1999. "Action research." *Communications of the ACM* 42, 1, 94–7.

Backhouse, Constance. 1999. *Colour-Coded: A Legal History of Racism in Canada*. Toronto, ON: University of Toronto Press.

Bakan, Joel. 2004. *The Corporation: The Pathological Pursuit of Profit and Power*. Toronto, ON: Penguin Books.

Balkin, Joseph. 1988. "Why policemen don't like policewomen." *Journal of Police Science and Administration* 16, 1, 29–38.

Ballingall, Alex. 2012. "Omnibus crime bill C-10 passed; A Conservative election promise kept." *Maclean's*, 13 March.

Barker, Thomas. 1994. "Peer group support for police occupational deviance." In Barker, T. and Carter, D., eds, *Police Deviance*., 9–21. Cincinnati, OH: Pilgrimage.

Barlow, Kevin. 2003. "Examining HIV/AIDs among the Aboriginal population of Canada in the post-residential school era." http://www.ahf.ca/downloads/hiv-paper.pdf.

Baum, Daniel. J. 1934. *The Canadian Criminal Justice System: Discount Justice*. Toronto, ON: Burns and MacEachern.

Bayoumi, Ahmed M., and Gregory S. Zaric. 2008. "The cost-effectiveness of Vancouver's supervised injection facility." *Canadian Medical Association Journal* 179, 11, 1143.

Beattie, Sara, and Amy Mole. 2007. "Police resources in Canada, 2007." Statistics Canada, Canadian Centre for Justice Statistics, http://www.statcan.ca.

Beehr, Terry A., Lana Ivanitskaya, Katherine Glaser, Dmitry Erofeev, and Kris Canali. 2010. "Working in a violent environment: The accuracy of police officers' reports about shooting incidents." *Journal of Occupational and Organizational Psychology* 77, 2, 217–35, June.

Bell, Stewart, and Patrick Kelly. 2006. "Global terror war hits Canadian front." *Winnipeg Free Press*, 4 June.

Bellemare, D. A., and Rob Finlayson. 2004. "Report on the prevention of miscarriages of justice." Department of Justice, Canada. http://www.justice.gc.ca/eng/dept-min/pub/pmj-pej/pmj-pej.pdf.

Benda, B., and C. Tollett. 1999. "A study of recidivism of serious and persistent offenders among adolescents." *Journal of Criminal Justice* 27, 2, 111–26.

Berg, Brunce L., and Kimberly Joyce Budnick. 1986. "Defeminization of women in law enforcement: A new twist in the traditional police personality." *Journal of Police Science and Administration* 14, 314–19.

Bergslien, Elisa. 2006. "Teaching to avoid the CSI effect." *Journal of Chemical Education* 83, 5, 690–1.

Beton, Randal, Andy Stergachis, Mark Oberle, Elizabeth Bridges, Marcus Nemuth, and Tamlyn Thomas. 2005. "The Sarin gas attacks on the Tokyo subway – 10 years later/lessons learned." *Traumatology* June, 11, 2, 103–19.

Bittle, Steve, Nathalie Quann, Tina Hattem, and Danielle Muise. 2002. "A one-day snapshot of Aboriginal youth in custody across Canada." Justice Canada. http://www.justice.gc.ca /eng/pi/rs/rep-rap/2001/ yj1-jj1/index.html.

Blackstock, Cindy, and Nico Trocme. 2005. "Community-based child welfare for Aboriginal children: Supporting resilience through structural change." *Social Policy Journal of New Zealand* 24, 12–33.

Blackstock, Cindy, and Nico Trocme. 2004. "Child maltreatment investigations among Aboriginal and non-Aboriginal families in Canada. *Violence Against Women* 10, 8, 1–16.

Blackwell, T. 2010. "Gang violence increases as law-enforcement steps up: Study." *National Post*, 22 March.

Blake. L., and R.T. Coupe. 2001. "The impact of single and two-officer patrols on catching burglars in the act: A critique of the audit commission's reports on youth justice." *British Journal of Criminology* 41, 2, 381–96.

Bolan, Kim. 2009. "As drug-gang violence increases, so does challenge to police." *Postmedia News*, 6 June.

Bonokoski, Mark. 2012. "Police recognizing PTSD scourge." *Winnipeg Sun*, 14 October.

Bonovitz, J. C., and J.S. Bonovitz. 1981. "Diversion of the mentally ill into the criminal justice system: The police intervention perspective." *American Journal of Psychiatry* 138, 973–6.

Borer, Tristan Anne. 2006. *Telling the Truths: Truth Telling and Peace Building in Post-Conflict Societies*. Notre Dame, IN: University of Notre Dame Press.

Borins, S. 2002. "Transformation of the Public Sector: Canada in Comparative Perspective." In Dunn, C., *The Handbook of Canadian Public Administration*, 3–17. Don Mills, ON: Oxford University Press.

Boyd, A., and J.P. Sullivan. 2000. "Emergency preparedness for transit terrorism." Office of Critical Infrastructure Protection and Emergency Preparedness Canada.

Boylen, Max, and Robert Little. 1990. "Fatal assaults on United States law enforcement officers." *Police Journal* 63, 1, 61–77.

Braga, Anthony. 2005. "Hot spots policing and crime prevention: A systematic review of randomized controlled trials." *Journal of Experimental Criminology* 1, 317–42.

Braithwaite, John. 1989. *Crime, Shame, and Reintegration*. Cambridge, UK: Cambridge University Press.

Brass, Mervi. 2004. "Starlight tours." *The National Magazine*, CBC News, 2 July. http://www.cbc.ca/news /background/aboriginals/starlighttours. html.

Bratton, William J., and William Andrews. 1999 "Crime & Punishment: What We've Learned About Policing." *City Journal* 23, 1, 1–3. http://www.city-journal.org/html/9_2_what_weve_learned.html.

Bratton, William J., James Q. Wilson, and George L. Kelling. 2004. "This works: Crime prevention and the future of broken windows." Policing Center for Civic Innovation, Manhattan Institute. http://www.manhattan-institute. org/html/cb_36.htm.

Brean, Joseph. 2012. "Mentally ill may be at risk of jail under new crime bill: Society has hard time coming up with workable solutions." *National Post*, 18 February.

Bridges, William. 2003. *Managing Transitions: Making the Most of Change*, 2nd edition. Cambridge, MA: Perseus Publishing.

Broderick, J.J. 1977. *Police in a Time of Change*. Morristown, NJ: General Learning Press.

Brooks, S. 2002. "Policy analysis in Canada." In Dunn, Christopher., ed., *The Handbook of Canadian Public Administration*, 192–203. Don Mills, ON: Oxford University Press.

Brown, Craig. 2002. *The Illustrated History of Canada*. Toronto, ON: Key Porter Books.

Brown, J., and G. Campbell. 1991. "Less than equal." *Policing* 7, Winter, 324–33.

Brown, Jodi M., and Patrick A. Langan. 2001. "Policing and homicide, 1976–98: Justifiable homicide by police, police officers murdered by felons." Washington DC: United States Bureau of Justice Statistics.

Brown, M.K. 1988. *Working the Street: Police Discretion and the Dilemmas of Reform*. New York, NY: Russell Sage Foundation.

Brown, M., and Carlson, R. 1993. "Do male policemen accept women on patrol yet?: Androgyny: Public complaints and dad." *Journal of Police and Criminal Psychology* 9, 1, 10–14.

Brunacini, Alan V. 1985. *Fire Command*. College Park, MA: YOS Productions.

Buiza, Ruby, and Justin Thompson. 2003. "Wrongfully convicted." CBC News Online, 15 May.

Bumstead, J.M. 1999. *Aboriginal*. Winnipeg, MB: University of Manitoba Press.

Burrows, Terry. 2010. "The Toronto G20 riot fraud: Undercover police engaged in purposeful provocation at tax payers' expense." *Global Research*, 27 June.

Byrne, Sean, and Jessica Senehi. 2012. *Violence: Analysis, Intervention, and Prevention*. Athens, OH: Ohio University Press.

Byrne, Sean, Dennis J.D. Sandole, Ingrid Sandole-Staroste, and Jessica Senehi. 2009. *Handbook in Conflict Analysis and Resolution*. Oxford, UK: Routledge.

Calgary Herald. 2007. "Commission backs one-officer cars." *Calgary Herald*, 27 June.

Calverley, Donna. 2007. "Youth custody and community services in Canada, 2004–2005." *Juristat* 27, 2.

Cameron, Esther, and Mike Green. 2004. *Making Sense of Change Management: A Complete Guide to the Models, Tools, and Techniques of Organizational Change*. Sterling, VA: Kogan Page.

Canada, Department of Justice. 2012a. Youth Criminal Justice Act website, http://www.justice.gc.ca/eng/pi/yj-jj/ycja-lsjpa/ycja-lsjpa.html.

Canada, Department of Justice. 2012b. Website on restorative justice, http://www.justice.gc.ca/eng/dept-min/pub/jc/vol7/no2/page5.html.

Canada, Department of Justice. 2011a. "Applications for ministerial review: Annual report 2011 Minister of Justice." http://publications.gc.ca/collections /collection_2012/jus/J1-3-2011-eng.pdf.

Canada, Department of Justice. 2011b. "Backgrounder: Legislation to repeal the 'faint hope' clause." http://www.justice.gc.ca/eng/news-nouv/nr-cp/2011/doc_32590.html.

Canada, Department of Justice. 2003. "A plain language guide: Bill C-45 amendments to the Criminal Code Affecting the criminal liability of organizations." www.justice.gc.ca.

Canada, Department of Justice. 1982. "Constitution Act." http://lois.justice.gc.ca/en/charter/.

Canada, Government of. 2006. "Regulations respecting applications for ministerial review-miscarriages of justice." *Canada Gazette* 136.

Canada, Government of. 2005. "Police resources in Canada." Canadian Centre for Justice Statistics. Ottawa, ON: Statistics Canada.

Canada, House of Commons Standing Committee on Aboriginal Affairs. 1990. *Unfinished Business: An Agenda for All Canadians in the 1990's.* Ottawa, ON: Queen's Printer.

Canada, Indian and Northern Affairs Canada. 1996. "People to people, nation to nation: Highlights from the report of the Royal Commission on Aboriginal Peoples." http://www.aadnc-aandc.gc.ca/eng/1307458586498.

Canada, Prime Minister's website. 2008. "PM announces new legislation that targets auto theft and property crime." www.pm.hc.csa.

Canada Gazette 2012. Firearms Act, Firearms Information Regulations (Non-restricted Firearms) 146,15 (18 July).

Canadian Centre for Emergency Preparedness. 2006. "A perspective on emergency management in Canada." *Emergency Management Canada* 2, 2.

Canadian Charter of Rights and Freedoms. 2011. Government of Canada website, http://laws.justice.gc.ca/eng/Charter/.

Canadian Police College. 2002. "Major case management manual, 6th edition." Canadian Police College. http://www.cpc/ccp.gc.ca/fr/cpclibrary/gouvernance-et-police.

Canadian Press. 2013. "Employers told they must accommodate staff's child-care requests." *The Canadian Press*, 5 February. http://www.cbc.ca/news/canada/story/2013/02/05/court-ruling-employers-family-life.html.

Canadian Press. 2011a. "Hearings attempt to explain why justice system failed Robert Pickton's victims." *Winnipeg Free Press*, 11 October.

Canadian Press. 2011b. "Mounties face perjury charges in Taser death." *Winnipeg Free Press*, 8 May.

Canadian Press. 2003. "Sophonow cashes $2.3 M cheque for wrongful conviction, buys mansion in BC." *The Canadian Press*, 7 March.

Cancino, Jeffrey Michael, and Roger Enriquez. 2004. "A qualitative analysis of officer peer retaliation: Preserving the police culture." *Policing: An International Journal of Police Strategies and Management* 27, 3, 320–40.

Caputo, Tullio, and Michel Vallee. 2005. "Life after community policing: The future of policing in Canada." Paper presented at the annual meeting of the Academy of Criminal Justice Sciences, Chicago, IL.

Carlson, G.P. 1983. "Incident command system, fire protection publications." Stillwater, OK: Oklahoma State University.

Carnoy, Martin. 1984. *The State and Political Theory*. Princeton, NJ: Princeton University Press.

Carter, David L., and Louis L. Radelet. 1999. *The Police and the Community*, 6th edition. New York, NY: Prentice-Hall.

Castillo, Dawn N., and Lynn E. Jenkins. 1994. "Industries and occupations at high risk for work-related homicide." *Journal of Occupational Medicine* 36, 2, 125–32.

CBC News. 2011. "A timeline of residential schools, the Truth and Reconciliation Commission." http://www.cbc.ca/news/canada/story/2008/05/16/f-timeline-residential-schools.html.

CBC News. 2010. "Man's abuse claims false." CBC News, 17 December, http://www.cbc.ca/news/canada/manitoba/story/2010/12/17/mb-starlight-tour-allegations-addressed-maud-winnipeg.html.

CBC News. 2008. "Residential schools: Aggressive assimilation." 16 May. http://www.cbc.ca/news/canada/story/2008/05/16/f-faqs-residential-schools.html.

CBC News. 2007. "Montebello protest. " http://www.cbc.ca/news/canada/montreal/story/2007/08/22/ot-police-070822.html.

CBC News. 2000. "Man charged with 24 arsons." 29 February. www.cbc.ca/news/story/2000/02/29/arsoncharges.html.

Centre for Police Research. 1994. "Police officer perceptions of the role of women in policing." Unpublished, Edith Cowan University.

Chacko, James, and Stephen Nancoo. 1993. *Community Policing in Canada*. Toronto, ON: Canadian Scholars Press.

Chan, Janet. 2011. "Racial Profiling and Police Subculture." *Canadian Journal of Criminology and Criminal Justice* 53, 1, 75–8.

Chandler, Michael. J., Christopher E. Lalonde, Bryan W. Sokol, and Darcy Hallett. 2003. "Personal persistence, identity development, and suicide: A study of native and non-native North American adolescents." *Monographs of the Society for Research in Child Development* 68, 2, 1–141.

Charles, Michael T., and Anne G. Copay. 2003. "Acquisition of marksmanship and gun handling skills through basic law enforcement training in an American police department." *International Journal of Police Science and Management* 5, 16–30.

Chartrand, Paul, Wendy Whitecloud, Eva McKay, and Doris Young. 2001. "Aboriginal Justice Implementation Commission Final Report." ajic.mb.ca.

Checkland, Peter. 1981. *Systems Thinking, Systems Practice*. New York, NY: John Wiley and Sons.

Cheldelin, Sandra, Daniel Druckman, and Larisa Fast. 2003. *Conflict: From Analysis to Intervention*. New York, NY: Continuum.

Chrisjohn, Roland, and Tanya Wasacase. 2009. "Half-truths and whole lies: Rhetoric in the 'apology' and the Truth and Reconciliation Commission." In Gregory Younging, Jonathan Dewar, and Mike DeGagné eds., *Response, Responsibility, and Renewal: Canada's Truth and Reconciliation Journey*. Ottawa, ON: Aboriginal Healing Foundation.

Churchill, Winston. 2011. Statistics quotation. www.iwise.com/LxWHj.

Clairmont, Susan. 2007. "Hamilton cop takes over troubled RCMP unit." *The Hamilton Spectator*, www.Hamiltonspectator .com.

Clarke, Paris. 2011. "The pain behind the badge.com." www.thepainbehindthebadge.com.

Clement, Douglas. 2002. "Private vs. public: The prison debate: Can private prisons save tax dollars? The evidence is inconclusive." *Fedgazette* 14, 1, 8 January.

Cochran, John, and Max L. Bromley. 2003. "The myth of the police subculture." *Policing: An International Journal of Police Strategies and Management* 26, 1, 88–117.

Coffey, Sara, Jennifer Brown, and Stephen Savage. 1992. "Policewomen's career aspirations: Some reflections on the role and capabilities of women in policing in Britain." *Police Studies* 15, 1, 13–19.

Collin, Chantel, and Hilary Jensen. 2009. "A statistical profile of poverty in Canada." Library of Parliament, http://www.parl. gc.ca/Content/LOP/ResearchPublications /prb0917-e.pdf.

Colwell, Lori, Holly Miller, Phillip M. Lyons, Jr, and Roland S. Miller. 2006. "The training of law enforcement officers in detecting deception: A survey of current practices and suggestions for improving accuracy." *Police Quarterly* 9, 275–90.

Comack, Elizabeth, Lawrence Dean, Larry Morrisette, and Jim Silver. 2010. "If you want to change violence in the 'hood you have to change the 'hood: Violence and street gangs in Winnipeg's inner city." *Canadian Dimension* 44, 2, 19–24.

Comack, Elizabeth, Lawrence Dean, Larry Morrisette, and Jim Silver. 2009. "If you want to change violence in the 'hood you have to change the 'hood: Violence and street gangs in Winnipeg's inner city. A report presented to Honourable Dave Chomiak, Manitoba Minister of Justice and Attorney General, September 10." Winnipeg: Canadian Centre for Policy Alternatives–Manitoba. http://www.policyalternatives. ca/offices/manitoba.

Commission on Systemic Racism in the Ontario Criminal Justice System. 1995. *Final Report of the Commission on Systemic Racism in the Ontario Criminal Justice System*. Toronto, ON: Queen's Printer for Ontario.

Conference Board of Canada. 2011. Conference Board of Canada website. www.conferenceboard.ca/Files/hcp/pdfs /hot-topics/caninequality.pdf.

Conti, Norman, and James J. Nolan. 2005. "Policing the platonic cave: Ethics and efficacy in police training." *Policing and Society* 15, 166–86.

Conway, Rosalind. 2011. "A criminal mind: Judges show conflicting thoughts on enhanced credit." www.lawtimesnews.com.

Corbelia, Licia. 2010. "Crime is down in Canada? That's not the case." *The Windsor Star*, 18 August.

Cornall, Robert. 2005. "New levels of government responsiveness for all-hazards: The management of natural disasters and emergencies." *Australian Journal of Public Administration* 64, 2.

Correctional Investigator of Canada. 2012. "Annual Report of the Office of the Correctional Investigator 2011–2012." http://www.oci-bec.gc.ca/rpt/pdf/annrpt/annrpt20112012-eng.pdf

Correctional Service of Canada. 2008. Correctional Service of Canada webpages. http://www.csc-scc.gc.ca.

Correctional Service of Canada (CSC). 2001. "National action plan on Aboriginal corrections." Ottawa, ON: Aboriginal Issues Branch, Correctional Service of Canada.

Cotler, Irwin. 2010. "Still getting it wrong on wrongful convictions." *The Ottawa Citizen*, 3 September.

Crank, John. 1998. *Understanding Police Culture*. Cincinnati, OH: Anderson.

Criminal Intelligence Service Saskatchewan (CISS). 2005. "2005 Intelligence trends: Aboriginal-based gangs in Saskatchewan." *CISS* 1, 1, 1–8.

Criminal Law Quarterly. 2007. "Understanding and preventing wrongful convictions." *The Criminal Law Quarterly* 52, 2.

Crowley, Brian Lee. 2011a. "We must be honest about crime to develop smart policies." *Calgary Herald*, 5 March.

Crowley, Brian Lee. 2011b. "Counting crimes." *National Post*, 28 February.

CTV News. 2008. "MPS vote to find Mountie in contempt of Parliament." http://www.ctv.ca/servlet/ArticleNews/story/CTVNews/20080410/mountie_contempt.

CTV News. 2006. "RCMP's Zaccardelli resigns over Arar testimony." www.ctv.ca/servlet/ArticleNews /story/CTVNews/20061205.

Cuttler, Michael J., and Paul M. Muchinsky. 2006. "Prediction of law enforcement training performance and dysfunctional job performance with general mental ability, personality, and life history variables." *Criminal Justice and Behavior* 33, 3–25.

Dallas Police. 2011. Dallas Police Child Exploitation Unit website. http://www.dallaspolice.net/index.cfm? page_ID=3114.

Dauvergne, Mia, and John Turner. 2010. "Police-reported crime statistics in Canada, 2009." *Juristat* 30, 2.

David-Evans, Maria. 2012. "The hidden potential." *Public Sector Management* 23, 1.

Davis, Kenneth C. 1969. *Discretionary Justice: A Preliminary Inquiry.* Baton Rouge, LA: Louisiana State University Press.

Dedel, Kelly. 2006. "Juvenile runaways. Center for problem-oriented policing." http://www.popcenter.org/problems /runaways/.

Dehn, Kelly. 2008. "CTV special report: Crime fighting." http://winnipeg. ctv.ca/servlet/an/local/CTVNews/20080213/wpg_crime_fighters_080213/20080214/CSI.

Dei, George, J. Sefa, Leene Karumanchery, and Nisha Karamanchery-Luik. 2007. *Playing the Race Card: Exposing White Power and Privilege.* New York, NY: Peter Lang.

Delaney, Joan. 2007. "Whistleblower legislation needs more work, say critics." Victoria, BC *Epoch Times.* http://en.epochtimes. com/news/7-5-17/55413.html.

Delattre, Edwin J. 1989. *Character and Cops: Ethics in Policing.* London, UK: University Press of America.

Del Carmen, Alejandro, and Lori Guevara. 2003. "Police officers on two-officer units: A study of attitudinal responses towards a patrol experiment." *Policing: An International Journal of Police Strategies and Management* 26, 1, 144–61.

Denov, Myriam, and Kathryn Campbell. 2005. "Criminal injustice: Understanding the causes effects and responses to wrongful conviction in Canada." *Journal of Contemporary Criminal Justice* 21, 224.

DeRiviere, Linda. 2005. "An examination of the fiscal impact from youth involvement in the sex trade: The case for evaluating priorities in prevention." *Canadian Public Policy* 80, 2.

DeVries, Laura. 2011. *Conflict in Caledonia: Aboriginal Land Rights and the Rule of Law.* Vancouver, BC: UBC Press.

Dinse, Charles, and Kathleen Sheehan. 1998. "Competence and character: Developing leaders in the LAPD." *The FBI Law Enforcement Bulletin,* January, 18–23.

Donohue, John J. 2007. "Economic models of crime and punishment." *Social Research* 74, 2. 379–412

Dooley, S., Welsh, A., Floyd, R., Macdonald, S., and T. Fenning 2005. "Aboriginal youth justice: Emerging strategies for program development." Vancouver Police Department. Surrey, BC: Kwantlen University College.

Duffy, Michael, and Massimo Calabresi. 2007. "The NYPD chief who did his job too well." *Time Magazine*, 15 November.

Duhaime, Lloyd. 2008. "Canada's criminal code: A history." http://www.duhaime.org.

Dunn, Christopher. 2002. *The Handbook of Canadian Public Administration*. Don Mills, ON: Oxford University Press.

Duran, Phil. 2003. *Developing the Survival Attitude: A Guide for New Officers*. New York, NY: Looseleaf Law Publications.

Drizin, Steven A., and Richard Leo. 2004. "The problem of false confessions in the post-DNA world." *North Carolina Law Review* 82, 891–1007.

Dror, Itiel. 2006. "Contextual information renders experts vulnerable to making erroneous identifications." *Forensic Science International* 156, 74–8.

Dynes, Russel R. 1970. *Organized Behavior in Disaster*. New York, NY: Heath.

Eck, John, Spencer Chainey, James G. Cameron, Michael Leitner, and Ronald E. Wilson. 2005. *Mapping Crime: Understanding Hot Spots*. Washington DC: United States Department of Justice/National Institute of Justice. http://discovery.ucl.ac.uk/11291/1/11291.pdf.

Edwards, Terry D. 1993. "State police training programs: An assessment of course content and instructional methodology." *American Journal of Police Science and Administration* 13, 1–9.

Eggertson, Laura. 1999. "Disney deal all but over, RCMP says: Force will-control product licensing via foundation." *Toronto Star*, 25 September.

Ehrich, Lisa Catherine, and Brian Hansford. 1999. "Mentoring: Pros and cons for HRM." *Asia Pacific Journal of Human Resources* 37, 3, 92–107.

Eichinger, Robert W., Michael Lombardo, and Dave Ulrich. 2004. *100 Things You Need to Know: Best Practices For Managers and HR*. Minneapolis, MN: Lominger Limited

Eisenberg, Terry. 2005. "Successful police chief mentoring: Implications from the sub-culture." *Public Management Magazine* 87, 11.

Elden, Max, and Rupert Chisholm. 1993. "Emerging varieties of action research: Introduction to the special issue." *Human Relations* 46, 2, 121–42.

Esbensen, Finn-Aage, and D. Wayne Osgood. 1999. "Gang resistance education and training (G.R.E.A.T.): Results from the national evaluation." *Journal of Research in Crime and Delinquency* 36, 2, 194–225.

Esbensen, Finn-Aage, D. Wayne Osgood, Terrance J. Taylor, Dana Peterson, and Adrienne Freng. 2001. "How great is G.R.E.A.T.? Results from a longitudinal quasi-experimental design." *Criminology and Public Policy* 1, 1, 87–118.

Evans, Ron. 2011. "The high cost of incarceration." *Winnipeg Free Press*, 17 January.

Eveline, Joan, and Michael Booth. 2002. "Gender and sexuality in discourses of managerial control: The case of women miners." *Gender, Work, and Organization* 9, 556–78.

Fazel, Seena, and John Danesh. 2002. "Serious mental disorder in 23,000 prisoners: A systematic review of 62 surveys." *Lancet* 359, 545–50.

Federal/Provincial/Territorial Heads of Prosecutions Subcommittee. 2011. The path to justice: Preventing wrongful convictions. Public Prosecution Service, Canada. http://www.ppsc-sppc.gc.ca/eng/pub/ptj-spj/index. html

Federation of Canadian Municipalities. 2007. "Danger ahead: The coming collapse of Canada's municipal infrastructure." Ottawa, ON: FCM. http:/www.fcm.ca/CMFiles/mdeficit1OPT-792008-3425.pdf.

Feldheim, Mary Ann. 2007. "Public sector downsizing and employee trust." *International Journal of Public Administration* 30, 249–70.

Fellows, Michael, Greg Flanagan, and Stanford Shredd. 1997. *Economic Issues: A Canadian Perspective*. Toronto, ON: McGraw-Hill Ryerson.

Ferdig, Mary Alice Speke. 2001. "Exploring the social construction of complex self-organizing change: A study of emerging change in the regulation of nuclear power." Doctoral dissertation, Benedictine University, Lisle, IL.

Ferdinand, Theodoore N. 1980. "Police attitudes and police organizations: Some interdepartmental and cross-cultural comparisons." *Police Studies* 3, 46–60.

Findley, Keith A., and Michael Scott. 2006. "Multiple dimensions of tunnel vision in criminal cases." *Wisconsin Law Review* 2, 291–397.

Fine, Gary Alan. 1985. "Occupational aesthetics: How trade school students learn to cook." *Urban Life* 14, 3–31.

Fisher, Roger, William Ury, and Bruce Patton. 1991. *Getting to Yes: Negotiating Agreement Without Giving In*. New York, NY: Penguin.

Fitzgerald, Paul. 2002. "Fishing for stories at Burnt Church: The media, the *Marshall* decision, and representation." *Canadian Dimension* 36, 4, 29.

Fitzpatrick, Meagan. 2007. "Former ministers distance themselves from RCMP scandal." *CanWest News Service* www.canada.com/ montrealgazette.

Flexon, J., Arthur Lurigio, and Richard Greenleaf. 2009. "Exploring the dimensions of trust in the police among juveniles." *Journal of Criminal Justice* 37, 180–9.

Forst, Brian. 2000. "The privatization and civilianization of policing." Washington DC: United States Department of Justice. http://www.ncjrs. org/criminal_justice2000/ vol_2/02c2.pdf.

Foster, Janet, Tim Newburn, and Anna Souhami. 2005. "Assessing the impact of the Stephen Lawrence Inquiry Home Office Research Study 294." London, UK: Home Office.

Franks, (Ned) C.E.S. 2006. "From Gomery to the Accountability Act: The devil is in the details." *Policy Options* June, 46–52.

Franks, (Ned) C.E.S. 2004. "Putting accountability and responsibility back in the system of government." *Policy Options* October, 64–6.

Frechette, Louise, Tony Dean, Moya Green, and Hugh Segal. 2007. "5 Trends that are transforming." http://www.ppforum.ca/ common/assets/ publications/en/ 5_trends_e.pdf.

Freeze, Colin. 2006. "U.K. spymaster raises alarm." *The Globe and Mail*, 10 November. www.theglobeandmail.com/servlet/story/RTGAM. 20061111.

Freeze, Colin, and Ian Bailey. 2011. "Female RCMP officer delivers damning indictment of her employer." *Globe and Mail*, 10 November.

Fricker, Ronald, D., Jerry O. Jacobson, and Lois Davis. 2002. "Measuring and evaluating local preparedness for a chemical or biological terrorist attack." Santa Monica, CA: Rand Corporation.

Frittelli, John. 2005. "Transportation security: Issues for the 109th Congress." Library of Congress, US Government. http://fpc.state.gov/documents/ organization/59935.pdf.

Frontier Centre for Public Policy. 2001. "One officer vs two officer cars in Winnipeg." www.fcpp.org.

Frugg, Gerlad. E. 1999. *City Making: Building Communities without Building Walls*. Princeton, NJ: Princeton University Press.

Gabor, Thomas. 2004. "Inflammatory rhetoric on racial profiling can undermine police services." *Canadian Journal of Criminology and Criminal Justice* 46, 457–70.

Galley, Valerie. 2009. "Reconciliation and the revitalization of Indigenous languages." In Gregory Younging, Jonathan Dewar, and Mike DeGagné, eds, *Response, Responsibility, and Renewal: Canada's Truth and Reconciliation Journey*. Ottawa, ON: Canada: Aboriginal Healing Foundation.

Galloway, Gloria. 2011. "First Nations chief wants to disband Aboriginal Affairs Department." *Globe and Mail*, 12 July.

Galtung, Johan. 1996. *Peace by Peaceful Means: Peace and Conflict, Development and Civilization*. Thousand Oaks, CA: Sage.

Garcia, Venessa. 2003. "Difference in the police department: Women, policing, and doing gender." *Journal of Contemporary Criminal Justice* 19, 330–44.

Garrett, Brandon. 2008. "Judging innocence." *Columbia Law Review* 108, 55–142.

Gayder, John. A. 2008. "Founding principles of Canadian policing." www.2ampd.net/Articles/Gayder/Founding _Principles_of_Canadian_ Policing.htm.

Germano, Daniela, Mike McIntyre, and Gabrielle Giroday. 2011. "Triple shooting feared latest episode in Winnipeg gang war." *Winnipeg Free Press*, 15 August.

Gershon, Robyn M., Briana Barocas, Allison Canton, Xianbin Li, and David Vlahov. 2009. "Mental, physical, and behavioral outcomes associated with perceived work stress in police officers." *Criminal Justice and Behavior* 36, 275–89.

Gibbs, Graham. 1988. *Learning by Doing: A Guide to Teaching and Learning Methods*. Oxford, UK: Oxford Polytechnic.

Gillis, Charlie, and Ken Macqueen. 2011. "A Royal Canadian Disgrace." *Maclean's*, 28 November.

Giroday, Gabrielle. 2010. "OxyContin robberies hit four pharmacies." *Winnipeg Free Press*, 6 December.

Gladwell, Malcolm. 2002. *The Tipping Point*. New York, NY: Back Bay.

Glensor, Ronald W., and Ken Peak. 1996. "Implementing change: Community-oriented policing and problem solving." *FBI Law Enforcement Bulletin* 65, 7.

Global News. 2012. "Timeline: Evolution of Canada's long-gun registry." *Global News*.

Goar, Carol. 2006. "UN's criticism of Canada's record on human rights, poverty is ignored." *CCPA Monitor* 12, 8, 38.

Godfredson, Joel W. 2011. "Police perceptions of their encounters with individuals experiencing mental illness: A Victorian survey." *Australian and New Zealand Journal of Criminology* 44, 2, 180–95.

Godfredson, Joel W., James R.P. Ogloff, Stuart D.M. Thomas, and Stefan Luebbers. 2010. "Police discretion and encounters with people experiencing mental illness: The significant factors." *Criminal Justice and Behavior* 37, 1392.

Goldsmith, Andrew. 2005. "Police reform and the problem of trust." *Theoretical Criminology* 9, 4, 443–70.

Good, David A. 2007. *The Politics of Public Money: Spenders, Guardians, Priority Setters, and Financial Watchdogs Inside the Canadian Government*. Toronto, ON: University of Toronto Press.

Gordon, Robert. 2000. "Criminal business organizations, street gangs and 'wanna-be' groups: A Vancouver perspective." *Canadian Journal of Criminology* 42, 1, 39–60.

Green, Ian, and Jodi White. 2007. "Canada's public service in the 21st century: Discussion paper." www.ppforum.ca /common/assets/ publications/en/public_service _21st_century_en.pdf.

Green, Joyce. 2006. "From Stonechild to social cohesion: Anti-racist challenges ahead for Saskatchewan." *Canadian Journal of Political Science* 39, 507–27.

Grekul, Jana, and Patti LaBoucane-Benson. 2006. "When you have nothing to live for, you have nothing to die for: An investigation into the formation and recruitment processes of Aboriginal gangs in Western Canada." Ottawa, ON: Aboriginal Corrections Policy Unit, Public Safety Canada.

Griffin, Iris. 2001. "The practical application of traditional Aboriginal healing practices as a restorative justice process: A case study of the Helen Betty Osborne story." Ottawa, ON: National Library of Canada.

Gudjonsson, Gisli H. 2003, 1992. *The Psychology of Interrogations, Confessions, and Testimony*. Chichester, UK: Wiley.

Guy, John 2008. "Report of the Provincial Court of Manitoba on the Fatality Inquiries Act inquest into the suicide of Tracia Owen." http://www.manitobacourts.mb.ca/pdf /tracia_owen.pdf.

Ha, Tu Thanh. 2012. "Toronto police officer in stable condition after being stabbed in neck." *Globe and Mail*, 16 April.

Haarr, Robin N. 2001. "The making of a community policing officer: The impact of basic training and occupational socialization on police recruits." *Police Quarterly* 4, 402–33.

Haarr, Robin N. 1997. "Patterns of interaction in a police patrol bureau: Race and gender barriers to integration." *Justice Quarterly* 14, 53–85.

Haberfeld, Maria R. 2002. *Critical Issues In Police Training*. Upper Saddle River, NJ: Pearson Education

Hallett, Bruce, Nancy Thornton, and Donna Stewart. 2006. "Aboriginal people in Manitoba." Manitoba Aboriginal Affairs Secretariat. Canada: Her Majesty the Queen in Right of Canada.

Hamilton, Alvin C., and Murray Sinclair. 1991. *Report of the Aboriginal Justice Inquiry of Manitoba: The Justice System and Aboriginal People*. Manitoba: Queen's Printer.

Hamilton Spectator. 2012. "Three charged in Caledonia protest incident." 26 April.

Haney, Craig. 2001. "From prison to home: The effect of incarceration and re-entry on children, families, and communities, the psychological impact of incarceration: Implications for post-prison adjustment." Santa Cruz, CA: University of California. http://aspe.hhs. gov/hsp/ prison2home02/index.htm.

Harris, Chandler. 2011. "The evidence doesn't lie: Genre, literacy and the CSI effect." *Journal of Popular Film and Television* 39, 1, 2–11.

Harvey, Edward. 2003. "An independent review of the *Toronto Star* analysis of criminal information processing (CIPS) data provided by the Toronto Police Service." www.torontopolice.on.ca/publications/ 2003.02.20-review/ pptpresentation.pdf.

Hawkes, Andrew. 2012. "So you want to find the mother load." *Interdiction Weekly* 24, 2nd edition.

Hedges, Charlie. 2002. "Missing you already: A guide to the investigation of missing persons." London, UK: Home Office. http://re-search.org. uk/hedges-missing-you-already.pdf.

Held, David. 2004. *Global Covenant: The Social Democratic Alternative to the Washington Consensus.* Cambridge, UK: Polity Press.

Held, David. 1996. *Democracy and the Global Order: From the Modern State to Cosmopolitan Governance.* Palo Alto, CA: Stanford University Press.

Hellriegel, Don, John W. Slocum, R.W. Woodman, and S.N. Bruning. 1998. *Organizational Behavior: Canadian Eighth Edition.* Toronto, ON: Thompson Publishing.

Hem Eriend, Anne Marie Berg, and Oivind Ekeberg. 2001. "Suicide – A critical review." *The American Association of Suicidology* 31, 2.

Henry, Frances, and Carol Tator. 2011. "Rejoinder to Satzewich and Shaffir on racism versus professionalism: Claims and counter-claims about racial profiling." *Canadian Journal of Criminology and Criminal Justice* 53, 65–74.

Henry, Frances, and Carol Tator. 2006. *Racial Profiling in Canada: Challenging the Myth of a Few Bad Apples.* Toronto, ON: University of Toronto Press.

Henry, Frances, and Carol Tator. 2005. *The Colour of Democracy: Racism in Canadian Society.* Toronto, ON: Nelson.

Henry, Vincent. E. 2003. *The Compstat Paradigm: Management Accountability in Policing, Business and the Public Sector.* New York, NY: Looseleaf Law Publications.

Herbert, Steve. 1998. "Police subculture reconsidered." *Criminology* 36, 2, 343–69.

Herz, Denise C. 2001. "Improving police encounters with juveniles: Does training make a difference?" *Justice Research and Policy* 3, 57–77.

Higgins, Myles. 2008. "Cultural genocide: A Canadian tradition." *Canadian Press* 12 June, http://www.canadafreepress.com/index. php/print-friendly/3479.

Highway of Tears website. 2012. http://www.highwayoftears.ca/.

Hill, Kim, and Michael Clawson. 1988. "The health hazards of street level bureaucracy: Mortality among the police." *Journal of Police Science and Administration* 16, 4, 243–8.

History of the Royal Canadian Mounted Police. 2012. Mounted Police Post, http://www.mountieshop.com/new/history.asp.

Ho, Taiping. 2004. "Recruiting police officers and education standards: College versus high school applicants." *Law Enforcement Executive Forum* 4, 2.

Hobbes, Thomas. 1651. *Leviathan*. Oxford, UK: Oxford University Press.

Hochschild, Arlie. 1973. "Making it – marginality and obstacles to minority consciousness." *Annals of the New York Academy of Sciences* 208, 179–84.

Hohl Katrina, Ben Bradford, and Elizabeth A. Stanko. 2010. "Influencing trust and confidence in the London Metropolitan Police." *British Justice and Criminology* 50, 491–513.

Huber, J. 2008. "More youths joining gangs across Canada." *Postmedia News*, 13 April.

Huber, Marg. 1995. "Native mediation model for urban communities." In Mark Umbreit, ed., *Mediating Interpersonal Conflicts: A Pathway to Peace*, 263–72. West Concord, MN: CPI Publishing.

Human Resources and Skills Development, Canada. 2012. "Indicators of wellbeing in Canada: Work – unemployment rate." Website: www4. gc.ca/.3ndic.1t.4r@-eng.jsp?iid=16.

Hurst, Yolander G., and James Frank. 2000. "How kids view cops – the nature of juvenile attitudes toward the police." *Journal of Criminal Justice* 28, 3, 189–202.

Huston, H. Range, and Dierdre Anglin. 1998. "Suicide by cop." *Annals of Emergency Medicine* 32, 6.

Indian and Northern Affairs, Canada. 2006. Indian and Northern Affairs website. ainc-inac.gc.ca/index_e.html.

Indian and Northern Affairs, Canada. 1996. "People to people, nation to nation: Highlights from the Report of the Royal Commission on Aboriginal Peoples." www.ainc-inac.gc.ca/ ch/rcap.

Ingraham, Patricia W., Guy Peters, and Donald Moynihan. 2000. "Public employment and the future of the public service." In Guy Peters and Donald Savoie, eds., *Governance in the Twenty-First Century: Revitalizing the Public Service*, 385–427. Montreal, QC: McGill-Queen's University Press,

Innis, Harold Adams. 1930. *The Fur Trade in Canada: An Introduction to Canadian Economic History*. New Haven, CN: Yale University Press.

Iocobucci, Frank. 2010. "Canada's response to terrorism." *Review of Constitutional Studies/Revue d'dtudes constitutionnelles*. 187. http://www.thefreelibrary.com

Jackson, Jonathan, and Ben Bradford. 2010. "What is trust and confidence in the police?" *Policing* 4, 3, 241–8.

Jacobs, P. 1987. "How female police officers cope with a traditionally male position." *Sociology and Social Research* 72, 4–6.

Janis, Irving. 1971. *Groupthink: The Desperate Drive for Consensus at Any Cost*. Sussex, UK: Sussex Publishers.

Jenish, D'arcy. 2006. "Bernardo investigation lawed." *Maclean's*, 22 July.

Jeong, Ho Won. 1995. *Peace and Conflict Studies: An Introduction*. Burlington, VT: Ashgate.

Jermier, John M., John W. Slocum, Louis W. Fry, and Jeannie Gaines. 1991. "Organizational subcultures in a soft bureaucracy: Resistance behind the myth and facade of an official culture." *Organization Science* 2, 170–94.

Johns, Christopher. 1995. "Framing learning through reflection within Carper's fundamental ways of knowing in nursing." *Journal of Advanced Nursing* 22, 2, 226–34.

Jones, David, Liz Jones, and Tim Prenzler. 2005. "Tertiary education, commitment, and turnover in police work." *Police Practice and Research* 6, 1, 49–63.

Joyce, G. 2003. "Police agencies tested by huge numbers of missing and murdered women." *Canadian Press*, 19 December, http://www.missing-people.net/police_agencies_tested_by_huge_n.htm.

Kaariainen, Juha Tapio. 2007. "Trust in the police in 16 European countries: A multilevel analysis." *European Society of Criminology* 4, 4, 409–35.

Kassin D.M., and G.H. Gudjonsson. 2004. "The psychology of confession evidence: A review of the literature and issues. *Psychological Science in the Public Interest* 5, 35–69.

Kassin, Saul. 2010. "False confessions." *Albany Law Review* 73, 4, 1227–34.

Kassin, Saul M. 1997. "The psychology of confession evidence." *American Psychologist* 52, 221–33.

Kelling, George L. 1999. "Broken windows and police discretion." United States Department of Justice, National Institute of Justice. https://www.ncjrs.gov/App/Publications/abstract.aspx?ID=178259.

Kennedy, Mark. 2011. "Crime bill not too expensive: PM." *Winnipeg Free Press*, 7 November.

Kennedy, Mark, and Douglas Quan. 2011. "Deputy Commissioner Paulson to head RCMP; Former B.C. Mountie to take over force suffering from low morale." *The Vancouver Sun*, 16 November.

Kennedy, Paul E. 2009. "Police investigating police – The final public report." http://www.cpc-cpp.gc.ca/prr /rep/rev/chair-pre/pipR/index-eng.aspx.

Kenny, Eoin. 1995. "RCMP marketing alliance with Disney 'outrage.' " *Kingston Whig-Standard*, 29 June.

Kernaghan, Kenneth, and David Siegel. 1999. *Public Administration in Canada*, 4th edition. Toronto, ON: Nelson, Thompson Canada.

Kernaghan, Kenneth, and John W. Langford. 1990. *The Responsible Public Servant*. Halifax, NS: Institute for Research on Public Policy.

Kessler, David A. 1985. "One-or-two-officer cars? A perspective from Kansas City." *Journal of Criminal Justice* 13, 1, 49–64.

Kettl, Donald. 2007. *System Under Stress: Homeland Security and American Politics*. Washington, DC: CQ Press.

Kirschman, Elle. 2007. *I Love a Cop: What Police Families Need to Know*. New York, NY: Guilford Publications.

Kitaeff, Jack. 2011. *Handbook of Police Psychology*. New York, NY: Routledge.

Kives, Bartley. 2011. "Thugs put cops in cross-hairs." *Winnipeg Free Press*, 1 February.

Klein, Gary. 1998. *Sources of Power: How People Make Decisions*. Cambridge. MA: MIT Press.

Klein, Malcolm. W. 1995. *The American Street Gang*. New York, NY: Oxford University Press.

Kochel, Tammy Rinehart. 2011. "Constructing hot spots policing: Unexamined consequences for disadvantaged populations and for police legitimacy." *Criminal Justice Policy Review* 22, 350.

Kochel, Tammy Rinehart, Stephen Mastrofski, E. Maguire, and James Willis. 2006. "COMPSTAT and community policing: Complementary or conflicting?" Paper presented at the American Society of Criminology Conference, Los Angeles, California.

Kolb, David A. 1984. *Experiential Learning: Experience as the Source of Learning and Development*. Englewood Cliffs, NJ: Prentice Hall.

Kramer, William M., and Charles W. Bahme. 1992. *Fire Officer's Guide to Disaster Control*, 2nd ed. Saddlebrook, NY: Fire Engineering Books and Videos.

Kraus, Jess F. 1987. "Homicide while at work: Persons, industries, and occupations at high risk. *American Journal of Public Health* 77, 10, 1285–9.

Krotki, K.J., and J. Henropin. 2006. "Baby boom." The Canadian Encyclopedia, Historica Foundation of Canada.

Kuban, Ron. 1993. "Crisis management: An analysis of the management of communal catastrophe." Doctoral dissertation, University of Alberta.

Kurtz, Don. 2009. "How male, female police officers manage stress may accentuate stress on the job." *Feminist Criminology*.

Kusch, Larry. 2006. "Help (desperately) wanted: Province in dire need of workers to fill positions." *Winnipeg Free Press*, 8 July.

Ladner, Kiera, and Leanne Simpson. 2010. *This Is an Honour Song: Twenty Years since the Blockades*. Winnipeg, MB: Arbeiter Ring Press.

Laframboise, H. 1991. "Vile wretches and public heroes: The ethics of whistleblowing in government." *Canadian Public Administration* 34, 1, 73–7.

Lanning, Kenneth V. 2001. "Criminal justice responses to the prostitution of children." http://www.sapsac.co.za /crim_just_report.pdf.

Lassiter, G. Daniel. 2004. *Interrogations, Confessions, and Entrapment*. New York, NY: Kluwer Academic.

Law Commission of Canada. 2006. "In search of security: The future of policing in Canada." Ottawa, ON: Her Majesty the Queen in Right of Canada. www.lcc.gc.ca.

LeBeuf, Marcel-Eugène. 2011. "The role of the Royal Canadian Mounted Police during the Indian residential school system. On behalf of the Royal Canadian Mounted Police (RCMP)." 29 October. http://www. rcmp-grc.gc.ca/ aboriginal-autochtone/irs-spi-eng.htm.

Leblanc, Daniel. 2010. "RCMP set for shakeup as Ottawa stands by commissioner." *Globe and Mail*, 6 September.

Lederach, John. 1996. *Preparing for Peace: Conflict Transformation Across Cultures*. New York, NY: Syracuse University Press.

Lee, Ian. 2011. "Scholars behaving badly; Obsessed with advancing a 'socially just' agenda, Canada's criminologists are ignoring hard facts about the national crime rate." *National Post*, 21 March.

Leighton, Patricia, and Michael Syrett. 1989. *New Work Patterns: Putting Policy into Practice*. London, UK: Pitman Publishing.

Lentz, Susan A., and Robert H. Chaires. 2007. "The invention of Peel's principles: A study of policing textbook history." *Journal of Criminal Justice* 35, 1, 69–79.

Leo, Chris. 2007. "Deep federalism: What do we have to do in order to protect community difference in national policy." blog.uwinnipeg.ca/ ChristopherLeo/archives/ 2007/01/deep_federalism.html.

Leo, Richard A., and Richard J. Ofshie. 1998. "The consequences of false confessions: Deprivations of liberty and miscarriages of justice in the age of psychological interrogation." *Journal of Criminal Law and Criminology* 88, 429–96.

Lesce, Tony. 1988. *Plainclothes and Off-Duty Officer Survival: A Guide to Survival for Plainclothes Officers, Undercover Officers, and Off-Duty Police Officers.* Springfield, IL: Charles Thomas Publishers.

Lewin, Kurt. 1947. "Frontiers in group dynamics." *Human Relations* 1, 2, 143–53.

Lewis, Scott, Helen Rosenberg, and Robert T. Sigler. 1999. "Acceptance of community policing among police officers and police administrators." *Policing: An International Journal of Police Strategies and Management* 22, 4, 567–88.

Li, Geoffrey. 2008. "Private security and public policing." http://www. statcan.gc.ca/pub/85-002-x/2008010/article /10730-eng.htm.

Lindell, M.K., Perry, R.W. and Prater, C.S. 2005. Organizing Response to Disasters with the Incident Command System/Incident Management System. International Workshop on Emergency Response and Rescue, Hazard Reduction and Recovery Center, Texas A & M University. mlindell@tamu.edu.

Lindemann, E. 1944. "Symptomatology and management of acute grief." *Journal of Neurons and Mental Disease* 181, 11, 709–10.

Linden, Rick. 2013. "Winnipeg Auto Theft Suppression Strategy." https:// justice.alberta.ca/ programs_services/safe/events/Documents/ Rick%20Linden%20Presentation_files/frame.htm.

Linden, Rick, Donald Clairmont, and Chris Murphy, C. 2001. "Crime prevention in Aboriginal communities." Winnipeg, MB: University of Manitoba. www.restorativejustice.org/articlesdb/articles/2015.

Lithwick, N. Harvey. 1970. *Urban Canada: Problems and Prospects.* Ottawa, ON: Canada Mortgage and Housing Corporation.

Locke, John. 1812 [1690]. *The Works of John Locke in Ten Volumes,* 11th ed. London, UK: W. Otridge and Son. .

Loftus, Bethan. 2010. "Police occupational culture: Classic themes, altered times." *Policing and Society* 20, 1, 1–20.

Lonsway, Kimberly, Susan Welch, and Louise F. Fitzgerald. 2001. "Police train-ing in sexual assault response: Process, outcomes, and elements of change." *Criminal Justice and Behavior: An International Journal* 28, 695–730.

Lowenthal, Werner. 1981. "Continuing education for professionals: Voluntary or mandatory." *Journal of Higher Education* 52, 5.

Lowry, Carmen Stephen Littlejohn. 2003. "Dialogue and the discourse of peacebuilding in Maluku, Indonesia." *Conflict* 23, 4, 409–26.

Lugosi, Nicole V.T. 2011. "Truth-telling and legal discourse: A critical analysis of the Neil Stonechild inquiry." *Canadian Journal of Political Science* 44, 2, 299–315.

Lundman, Richard J. 1980. *Police and Policing: An Introduction.* New York, NY: Holt Rinehart and Winston.

Lynskey, Edward J. 2001. "Higher education and early retirement in the New Jersey state police." Doctoral dissertation, Seton Hall University.

Maas, Peter. 1973. *Serpico.* New York, NY: Viking.

MacCharles, Tonda. 2012. "Public Safety Minister Vic Toews slams RCMP head Bob Paulson for inaction on gender bias." *The Star*, 23 November.

Macleod, Ian. 2011. "Crime rate swoons, police ranks swell; Annual oper-ating costs in Canada top $12.3 billion, Statistics Canada finds." *Ottawa Citizen*, 9 January.

Macpherson, Sir William. 1999. "The Stephen Lawrence Inquiry (Cm. 4262–1): Report of an inquiry by Sir William Macpherson of Cluny." London, ON: HMSO.

Malm, Aili, Nahanni Pollard, Paul Brantingham, Paul Tinsley, Daryl Plecas, Patricia Brantingham, and Bryan Kinney. 2005. "A 30 year anal-ysis of police service delivery and costing." Abbotsford, BC: Institute for Criminology and Criminal Justice, University College of Fraser Valley.

Manishen, Jeffrey. 2006. "Wrongful convictions, lessons learned: The Canadian experience." *Journal of Clinical Forensic Medicine* 13, 296–9.

Manitoba. 2011. "Provincial Police Act." web2.gov.mb.ca/laws/statutes/ccsm/p150e.php.

Manitoba, Emergency Measures Organization. 2011. www.gov.mb.ca/emo/.

Manitoba, Law Enforcement Review Agency. 2010. www.gov.mb.ca/justice/lera/.

Manitoba Government. 2012a. "The Inquiry Regarding Thomas Sophonow." http://www.gov.mb.ca/justice/publications/sophonow/intro/thefacts.html.

Manitoba Government. 2012b. "Emergency Measures Act." http://web2.gov.mb.ca/laws/statutes/ccsm/e080e.php.

Manitoba Government. 2008. "Peguis First Nation provincial circuit court officially opened." Province of Manitoba e-mailed news release, 27 October.

Manning, P.K. 1995. "The police occupational culture." In Bailey, W. ed., *Encyclopedia of Police Science*, 472–5. New York, NY: Garland Publishing.

Mantell, Michael R. 1994. "Ticking bombs." *Psychology Today*, January/February, 20–1.

Marshall, Robert. 2011. "Full disclosure, the good, bad, ugly." *Winnipeg Free Press*, 30 April.

Martin, Don. 2007. "Whistles blew on RCMP months ago, pension fund scandal: Committee suppressed accusations." *National Post*, 4 April.

Martin, Nick. 2011. "Tears flow from U of M apology." *Winnipeg Free Press*, 4 November.

Martin, Susan. 1979. "Policewomen and police *women*: Occupational role dilemmas and choices of female officers." *Journal of Police Science and Administration* 7, 3, 314–23.

Martin, Susan. 1978. "Sexual politics in the workplace: The interactional world of policewomen." *Symbolic Interaction* 1, 44–60.

Maslach, Christina. 1982. *Burnout: The Cost of Caring*. New York, NY: Prentice Hall.

Maslach, Christina, and Susan Jackson. 1979. "Burned out cops and their families." *Psychology Today* 12, 58–62.

Maslow, Abraham H. 1954. *Motivation and Personality*. New York, NY: Harper and Row.

Mayeda, Andrew, and Mark Kennedy. 2011. "Conservative majority would bundle crime bills." *Vancouver Sun*, 8 April.

McCooey, Paula. 2003. "Profiling remark angers police officers." *The Ottawa Citizen*, 1 March.

McCracken, Molly, and Claudette Michell. 2006. "Literature review of post-secondary education/skills training and Aboriginal people in Manitoba." Canadian Centre for Policy Alternatives–Manitoba.

McFerran, John. 2006. "Companies can learn from Gates' departure." *Winnipeg Free Press*, 15 July.

McIntyre, Mike. 2012. "Accused serial killer speaks in interview." *Winnipeg Free Press*, 22 July.

McIntyre, Mike. 2011. "Decade later, jury finds police acted properly." *Winnipeg Free Press*, 10 November.

McRae, Susan. 1990. *Keeping Women In: Strategies to Facilitate Their Continuing Employment in Higher Level Occupations*. London, UK: Policy Studies Institute.

Melchers, Ron. 2006. *Inequality before the Law: The Canadian Experience of Racial Profiling*. Ottawa, ON: Research and Evaluation Branch, Royal Canadian Mounted Police. http://cpc.phippsinc.com/cpclib/pdf/60756e.pdf.

Mellor, Brian, Leslie MacRae, Monica Pauls, and Joseph Hornick. 2005. "Youth gangs in Canada: A preliminary review of programs and services." Prepared for Public Safety and Emergency Preparedness Canada. Calgary, AB: Canadian Research Institute for Law and the Family. http://www.securitepublique.gc.ca/res/cp/_fl/ygreport_2005-en.pdf.

Menzies, Peter. 2009. "Homeless Aboriginal men: Effects of intergenerational trauma." Toronto, ON: University of Toronto. www.homelesshub.ca/FindingHome.

Mitchell, Jeffrey T. 1983. "When disaster strikes: The critical incident stress debriefing process." *Journal of Emergency Medical Services* 8, 1, 36–9.

Mitchell, Jeffrey, and George Everly. 1993. *Critical Incident Stress Debriefing: An Operations Manual for the Prevention of Traumatic Stress among Emergency Services and Disaster Workers*. Ellicott City, MD: Chevron Publishing.

Mohandie, Kris, J. Reid Meloy, and Peter Collins. 2009. "Suicide by cop among officer-involved shooting cases." *Journal of Forensic Science* 54, 2. 456–62.

Moore, D. 2010. "RCMP struggling with post-traumatic stress disorder within its ranks." *Canadian Press*, 20 December.

Morgan, Gareth. 1997. *Images of Organization*. Thousand Oaks, CA: Sage Publishing.

Morris, Steve. 2010. "Laughing policemen in trouble for sledging using a riot shield." guardian.co.uk, 14 January.

Morrison, Gregory B. 2006. "Police department and instructor perspectives on pre-service firearm and deadly force training." *Policing* 29, 226–45.

Mosher, Clayton James. 1998. *Discrimination and Denial: Systemic Racism in Ontario's Legal and Criminal Justice Systems, 1892–1961*. Toronto, ON: University of Toronto Press.

Mulvale, Jim, and Yolanda Hansen. 2006. "Democracy and dollars: Citizen participation in determining government budgets." Canadian Centre for Policy Alternatives, policyalternatives.ca.

Murphy, Paul. 2006. Intelligence and Security Committee Report into the London Terrorist Attacks on 7 July 2005. London, UK: British Government

Nafekh, Mark. 2002. An Examination of Youth and Gang Association within the Federally Sentenced Aboriginal Population. Ottawa, ON: Correctional Service of Canada.

Nafekh, Mark, and Yvonne Stys, Y. 2004. A Profile and Examination of Gang Affiliation within Federally Sentenced Inmates. Ottawa, ON: Correctional Service of Canada.

National Institute of Justice (NIJ). 1998. Research in Brief. Preventing Crime: What Works, What Doesn't, What's Promising. Washington DC: Office of Justice Programs, US Department of Justice.

National Working Group on Crime Prevention. 2007. *Building a Safer Canada: First Report of the National Working Group on Crime Prevention.* Ottawa, ON: Institute for the Prevention of Crime.

Native Women's Association of Canada. 2009. Voices of Our Sisters in Spirit: A Report to Families and Communities. 2nd Edition. http://www.nwac.ca/media/release/29-04-09.

Naumetz, Tim. 2007a. "Former Mounties ethics officer says RCMP filled with bad behaviour." *CanWest News Service* www.canada.com/nationalpost/news.

Naumetz, Tim. 2007b. "Mounties clash at inquiry into pension fund." *CanWest News Service* www.canada.com/montreal gazette/news.

Nay, Rob. 2008. "Missing: 50 mysteries and the folks trying to solve them." *Winnipeg Sun*, 9 November.

Nemeroff, Teddy. 2008. "Generating the power for development through sustained dialogue: An experience from rural South Africa." *Action Research* 6, 2, 213–32.

Newark, Scott. 2011. "Why Canadian crime statistics don't add up: Not the whole truth." The Macdonald-Laurier Institute for Public Policy: True North in Canadian Public Policy. http://macdonaldlaurier.ca/files/pdf/MLI- Crime_Statistics_Review-Web.pdf.

Newburn, Tim, and Robert Reiner. 2007. "Policing and the police." In Maguire, M., R. Morgan, and R. Reiner, eds, *The Oxford Handbook of Criminology*, 4th ed. New York, NY: Oxford University Press.

Newcomer, Kathryn E. 2007. "Measuring government performance." *International Journal of Public Administration* 30, 307–29.

Nickels, Ernest, and Arvind Verma. 2008. "Dimensions of police culture: A study in Canada, India, and Japan." *Policing: An International Journal of Police Strategies and Management* 31, 2, 186–209.

Niederhoffer, Arthur. 1967. *Behind the Shield: The Police in Urban Society.* New York, NY: Doubleday.

Noor, Ebrahim. 2011. *Noor's Story: My Life in District Six*. South Africa: I M Publishing.

Norris, Mary Jane, D. Beavon, E. Guimond, and M. Cooke. 2000. "Migration and residential mobility of Canada's Aboriginal groups: An analysis of census data." Paper presented at the Population Association of America (PAA) meeting, San Francisco.

Norris, Mary Jane, Don Kerr, and Francois Nault. 1995. "Summary report on projections of the population with Aboriginal identity, Canada, 1991–2016, prepared by Population Projections Section, Demography Division, Statistics Canada, for the Royal Commission on Aboriginal Peoples." Canada Mortgage and Housing Corporation.

O'Connor, Christopher. 2008."Citizen attitudes toward the police in Canada." *Policing: An International Journal of Police Strategies and Management* 31, 4, 578–95

O'Conner, Tara Shelley, Melissa Schaefer Morabito, and Jennifer Tobin-Gurley. 2011. "Gendered institutions and gender roles: Understanding the experiences of women in policing." *Criminal Justice Studies: A Critical Journal of Crime, Law and Society* 24, 4, 351–67.

Officer.com. 2012. http://forums.officer.com/showthread.php?43687-History-(definition)-of-the-word-quot-COP-quot.

Office of the Auditor General of Canada. 2007. "Report of the Auditor General of Canada: National Defence-NATO Flying training in Canada." www.oag-bvg.gc.ca/domino/reports.

O'Leary, Dennis. 1994. "Reflections on police privatization." *FBI Law Enforcement Bulletin*.

Olesen, Karin, and Michael D. Myers. 1999. "Trying to improve communication and collaboration with information technology: An action research project which failed." *Information Technology and People* 12, 4, 317–32

Olson, David, Brendan D. Dooley, and Clarence Kane. 2004. "The relationship between gang membership and inmate recidivism." *Research Bulletin* 2, 12, Illinois Criminal Justice Information Authority.

Ondeck, Deborah. 2002. "Diversity discussion: Intergenerational issues in the workplace." *Home Health Care Management and Practice* 14, 5, 391–2.

Ontario. 1995. *Report of the Commission on Systemic Racism in the Ontario Criminal Justice System*. Toronto, ON: Queen's Printer.

Ontario Human Rights Commission. 2005. *Paying the Price: The Existence of Racial Profiling*. Toronto, ON: Ontario Human Rights Commission.

Osborne, David and Peter Plastrik, P. 2000. *The Reinventor's Fieldbook: Tools for Transforming your Government*. New York, NY: Jossey-Bass.

Owen, Bruce. 2011a. "Our justice system's revolving door." *Winnipeg Free Press*, 8 May.

Owen, Bruce. 2011b. "Provinces, feds bicker over cost of crime bill." *Winnipeg Free Press*, 2 November.

Owen, Bruce. 2011c. "Expansion of program to track car thieves." *Winnipeg Free Press*, 2 November.

Pablo, Carlito. 2012. "Ex-Mountie says RCMP is a toxic workplace." Straight.com.http://www.straight.com /article-612481/vancouver/ exmountie-says-rcmp-toxic-workplace.

Pablo, Carlito. 2009. "Regional police force not a priority." Straight.com, http://www.straight.com/ article-236595/regional-police-force-not-priority.

Pal, Leslie. 2006. *Beyond Policy Analysis: Public Issue Management in Turbulent Times*, 3rd Edition. Toronto, ON: Nelson, Thompson Canada.

Paoline, Eugene A. III. 2004. "Shedding light on police culture: An examination of officers' occupational attitudes." *Police Quarterly* 7, 2, 205–36.

Paoline, Eugene A. III, Stephanie Myers, and Robert E. Worden. 2000. "Police culture, individualism, and community policing: Evidence from two police departments." *Justice Quarterly* 17, 3, 575–605.

Paperney, Anna Mehler. 2012. "Toronto tries Saskatchewan's method for stopping crime before it starts." *The Globe and Mail*, 19 July.

Parent, Richard B., and Simon Verdun-Jones. 1998. "Victim-precipitated homicide: Police use of deadly force in British Columbia." *Policing: An International Journal of Police Strategies and Management* 21, 3, 432–48.

Parsons, Jennifer R.L. 2004. "Occupational health and safety issues of police officers in Canada, the United States and Europe: A review essay." http://www.safetynet.mun.ca/pdfs/Occupational%20H&S.pdf.

Pasillas, Rebecca, Victoria M. Follette, and Suzanne Perumean-Chaney. 2006. "Occupational stress and psychological functioning in law enforcement officers." *Journal of Police and Criminal Psychology* 21, 1.

Paul, Alexandra. 2012. "First Nations suicides reflect youth despair. *Winnipeg Free Press*, 23 June.

Paul, Alexandra. 2011. "Crime can be stopped: Professor says methods used to curb auto theft work." *Winnipeg Free Press*, 31 October.

Paulin, Mel. 2003. "Weapons of mass destruction: The first responder." Eastern Michigan University, School of Fire Staff and Command.

Peel, Sir Robert. 1829. New Westminster Police Service website, www. newwestpolice.org/peel.html.

Peel Regional Police. 2012. Peel Regional Police website, www.peelpolice. on.ca/en/aboutus/abriefhistory.asp.

Perrou, Barry. 1999. "Crisis intervention: Suicide in progress – a working document." Public Safety Research Institute. http://www.lancasterpsri.org.

Pesare, Anthony, Robert McKenna, Chris Menton, and Robert Engvall. 2003. "Overlapping the actual with the academic: The education-training continuum." *Law Enforcement Executive Forum* 3, 3.

Pogrebin, Mark R. and Eric D. Poole. 1987. "Deinstitutionalization and increased arrest rates among the mentally disordered." *Journal of Psychiatry and Law* 15, 117–27.

Police Sector Council. 2012. Website, www.policecouncil.ca/pages/policing.html.

Police Sector Council. 2006. "National diagnostic on human resources in policing, Police Sector Council, Government of Canada." http://www.surveyhost.com/haygroup/police/.

Polk, O. Elmer, and David A. Armstrong. 2001. "Higher education and law enforcement career paths: Is the road to success paved by degree?" *Journal of Criminal Justice Education* 12, 1, 77–99.

Pona, Steve. 2012. "Aging population will strain the economy: Bank of Canada." *Winnipeg Free Press*, 5 April.

Potter, Mitch. 2010. "RCMP goes global with Maher Arar torture probe." *The Star*, Washington Bureau, 14 June.

Pratt, William. 1995. "A winning deal for RCMP, Disney." *Edmonton Journal*, 17 July.

Prenzler, Tim. 1997. "Is there a police culture?" *Australian Journal of Public Administration* 56, 4, 47–56.

Price-Boase, Joan. 2000. "Beyond government? The appeal of public-private partnerships." *Canadian Public Administration* 43, 1, 75–91.

Prothrow-Stith, Deborah, and Howard Spivak. 2004. *Murder Is No Accident*. San Francisco, CA: John Wiley and Sons.

Public Safety Canada. 2012. Aboriginal Policing website, www.public-safety.gc.ca/prg/le/ap/1index-eng.aspx.

Public Safety Canada. 2011. Integrated Proceeds of Crime Program website, http://www.publicsafety.gc.ca/prg/le/oc/ipc-eng.aspx.

Pugliese, David. 2003. "Police warn of presence of potential terrorists in Canada." *Postmedia News*, 8 July.

Puryear, Edgar.F. (Jr.). 2003. *American Generalship*. New York, NY: Random House.

Puxley, Chinta. 2011. "Third World living conditions for First Nations should be election issue: Chief." *Canadian Press*, 1 October.

Quan, Douglas. 2012. "Top Mountie promises to weed out bad apples." *Winnipeg Free Press*, 29 May.

Quan, Douglas. 2011. "New RCMP Commissioner Paulson vows swift justice for misbehaving Mounties." *Montreal Gazette*, 6 December.

Quinn, Michael. 2005. *Walking with the Devil: The Police Code of Silence: What Bad Cops Don't Want You to Know and What Good Cops Won't Tell You*. Minneapolis, MN: Quinn and Associates

Quinet, Kenna, Samuel Nunn, and Nikki Kincaid. 2003. "Training police: A case study of differential impacts of problem-oriented policing training." *Police Practice and Research* 4, 263–83.

Qureshi, Faiza, and Graham Farrell. 2006. "Stop and search in 2004: A survey of police officer views and experiences." *International Journal of Police Science and Management* 8, 83–103.

Ragonese, Paul, and Berry. Stainback. 1991. *The Soul of a Cop*. New York, NY: St. Martin's Press.

Ramos, Orlando. 2010. "Police suicide: Are you at risk?" *FBI Law Enforcement Bulletin* May, 21–4.

Randerson, James. 2007. "Study questions reliability of fingerprint evidence." *The Guardian*, 23 March, www.guardian.co.uk/science/2007.

Rasmussen, Ken. 2000. "The Manitoba Civil Service: A quiet tradition in transition." In E. Lindquist, ed., *Government Restructuring and Career Public Services*. Toronto, ON: The Institute of Public Administration of Canada.

RCMP. 2012. Chemical Biological Radiological Nuclear Explosive (CBRNE) team website, http://www.rcmp-grc.gc.ca/fsis-ssji/fis-sij/cbrne-eng.htm.

RCMP. 2004. Royal Canadian Mounted Police website, http://www.rcmp-grc.gc.ca/aboriginal-autochtone/apo-reg-eng.htm.

Reber, Susanne, and Robert Renaud. 2005. *Starlight Tour: The Last Lonely Night of Neil Stonechild*. New York, NY: Random House.

Regester Michael, and Judy Larkin. 2005. *Risk Issues and Crisis Management: A Casebook of Best Practice*, 3rd edition. London, UK: Kogan Page.

Reid, John. 2006. Addressing Lessons from the Emergency Response to the 7 July 2005 London Bombings: What We Learned and What We Are Doing about It. London, UK: British Government.

Richardson, Cathy, and Natasha Blanchet-Cohen. 2000. Survey of Post-Secondary Education Programs in Canada for Aboriginal Peoples. UNESCO: University of Victoria.

Roach, Kent. 2000. "Changing punishment at the turn of the century: Restorative justice on the rise." *Canadian Journal of Criminology* July, 249–80.

Robbins, Stephen P. 2003. *The Truth about Managing People and Nothing but the Truth*. Upper Saddle River, NJ: Prentice Hall.

Robson, John. 2011. "What crime statistics don't tell you." *The Ottawa Citizen*, 13 February.

Rorty, Richard. 1979. *Philosophy and the Mirror of Nature*. Princeton, NJ: Princeton University Press.

Rose, Barbara. 2006. "Preparing for the baby boomer brain drain." *Chicago Tribune*, 2 May, 1–3.

Rosen, Harvey, Bev Dahlby, and Roger S. Smith. 2003. *Public Finance in Canada*. 2nd Canadian edition. Toronto, ON: McGraw-Hill Ryerson.

Ross, Jeffrey. 1995. "The historical treatment of urban policing in Canada: A review of the literature." *Urban History Review* 24, 1, 36–43.

Rotman School of Management. 2002. "Leadership program trains police executives at University of Toronto: Rotman School of Management." Gale Group, 2 May.

Rousseau, Jean-Jacques. 1913. [1767]. *On the Social Contract or Principals of Political Right*. London, UK: J.M. Dent.

Rowat, Donald. C. 2004. "Canada needs a law and independent commission to protect whistleblowers." *Policy Options* October, 60–3.

Royal Commission on Aboriginal Peoples (RCAP). 1996. Report of the Royal Commission on Aboriginal Peoples. Ottawa, ON: Indian and Northern Affairs Canada.

Rubenstein, Ed. 1995. "The economics of crime: The rational criminal." *Vital Speeches of the Day* 62, 19, 3.

Russell, Harold E., and Allan Beigel. 1990. *Understanding Human Behavior for Effective Police Work*. New York, NY: Basic Books.

Ryan, Denise. 2011. "Greatest mancatchers alive." *Vancouver Sun*. http://www2.canada.com/edmontonjournal/news/sundayreader/story.html?id=232aff3f-e69e-4099-b99d-f6f439777648

Salhany. 2013. "Taman Inquiry into the investigation and prosecution of Derek Harvey-Zenk." http://www.tamaninquiry.ca

Sancton, Andrew. 2002. "Provincial and local public administration." In Christopher Dunn, ed., *The Handbook of Canadian Public Administration*, 249–62. Don Mills, ON: Oxford University Press.

Sanders, Carol, and Mary Agnes Welch. 2011. "When trouble is just one slip away." *Winnipeg Free* Press, 9 March.

Satzewich, Vic, and William Shaffir. 2009. "Racism versus professionalism: Claims and counter-claims about racial profiling." *Canadian Journal of Criminology and Criminal Justice* 10, 51.2, 199–26.

Saunders, Harold. H. 2003. "Sustained dialogue in managing intractable conflict." *Negotiation Journal* 19, 1, 85–95.

Savoie, Donald. 2004. "Searching for accountability in a government without boundaries." *Canadian Public Administration* 47, 1, 1–26.

Savoie, Donald. 2003. *Breaking the Bargain: Public Servants, Ministers, and Parliament.* Toronto, ON: University of Toronto Press.

Schafer, Arthur. 1999. "A wink and a nod: A conceptual map of responsibility and accountability in bureaucratic organizations." *Canadian Public Administration* 42, 5–25.

Scheck, Barry, Peter Neufeld, and Jim Dwyer. 2000. *Actual Innocence.* New York, NY: Doubleday.

Schicor, David, and Dale Sechrest. 1996. *Three Strikes and You're Out: Vengeance as a Public Policy.* Thousand Oaks, CA: Sage Publications.

Schmidt, Bonnie Reilly. 2012. "Women in Red Serge: Female Police Bodies and the Disruption of the Image of the Royal Canadian Mounted Police." Pending, PhD dissertation, Simon Fraser University, Burnaby, BC. http://blogs.sfu.ca/people/bschmidt/?page_id=3

Schön, Donald. 1983. *The Reflective Practitioner, How Professionals Think in Action.* London, UK: Basic Books.

Schon, Donald, and Chris Argyris. 1996. *Organizational Learning II: Theory, Method, and Practice.* Westminster, MD: Addison-Wesley.

Schuck, Amie M. 2005. "American crime prevention: Trends and new frontiers." *Canadian Journal of Criminology and Criminal Justice* 47, 2.

Schulenberg, Jennifer L., and Deirdre M. Warren. 2009. "Content and adequacy of specialized police training to handle youth-related incidents perceptions of trainers, supervisors, and frontline officers." *Criminal Justice Review* 19, 456–77.

Schulman, Perry. 1997. Commission of Inquiry into the deaths of Rhonda Lavoie and Roy Lavoie: A Study of Domestic violence in Manitoba. Winnipeg, MB: Queen's Printer.

Schultz, Eric C. 2004. "Training for higher education: The Criminal Justice Training Assessment Project." *Law Enforcement Executive Forum* 4, 1.

Scott, Marian. 2011. "Cop had no licence to profile: Human rights commission recommends $20,000 in damages to comments at traffic stop." *The Gazette*, 5 February.

Scripture, Andrew E. 1997. "The sources of police culture: Demographic or environmental variables?" *Policing and Society* 7, 3, 163–76.

Seagrave, Jane. 1997. *Introduction to Policing in Canada*. Scarborough, ON: Prentice Hall.

Seagrave, Jane. 1996 "Defining community policing." *American Journal of Police* 15, 2, 1–22.

Sears, Robin V. 2006. "The old accountability shuffle." *Policy Options* June, 19–27.

Senge, Peter M. 2006. *The Fifth Discipline: The Art and Practice of the Learning Organization*. New York, NY: Doubleday.

Seymour, Andrew. 2012. "Judge to rule on Ottawa man's 'faint hope' appeal for murdering his stepfather." *The Ottawa Citizen*, 2 April.

Shafritz, J.M., J.S. Ott, and Y.S. Jang. 2005. *Classics of Organization Theory*. 6th edition. Toronto, ON: Thompson Wadsworth.

Shah, Chandrakant. 1990. *Public health and Preventive Medicine in Canada*. Toronto, ON: University of Toronto Press.

Sheldon, Randall. 2001. *Controlling the Dangerous Classes: A Critical Introduction to the History of Criminal Justice*. Boston, MA: Allyn and Bacon.

Sherman, Lawrence. 1998. "Evidence-based policing. Ideas in American policing." *Policing: Police Foundation*, 1–13. http://www.policefoundation.org/pdf/Sherman.pdf.

Sherman, L.W., and D. Weisburd. 1995. "General deterrent effects of police patrol in crime "hot spots": A randomized, controlled trial." *Justice Quarterly* 12, 625–48.

Silver, Jim. 2005. "The promise of investment in community-led renewal state of the inner city report: 2005. Part II: A view from the neighbourhoods." *Canadian Centre for Policy Alternatives* www.policyalternatives.ca.

Silver, Jim, Joan Hay, and Peter Gorzen. 2004. "Aboriginal involvement in community development: The case of Winnipeg's Spence neighbourhood." *Canadian Centre for Policy Alternatives* http://www2.brandonu.ca/library/cjns/25.1/cjnsv25no1_pg238-288.pdf.

Simeon, Richard. 2002. "Federalism and intergovernmental relations." In Christopher Dunn, ed., *The Handbook of Canadian Public Administration*, 204–23. Don Mills, ON: Oxford University Press.

Sinclair, Gordon. 2011. "We need a better plan to fight violent crime." *Winnipeg Free Press*, 3 November.

Size, John. 2012. "Manitoba a haven for drug traffickers: RCMP." CTV News ca. 28 January.

Skelton, Chad. 2005. "Missing persons unit 'beefed up.'" *Vancouver Sun*, 28 September. http://www.missingpeople.net/missing_persons_unit_beefed_up.htm.

Skolnick, Jerome. H. 1966. *Justice without Trial: Law Enforcement in a Democratic Society*. New York, NY: Wiley.

Skurka, Steven. 2007. "Top court rues police can be sued over wrongful convictions." Canada AM interview, 5 October.

Smith, Dale. 2012. *Maclean's* Politics on TV. Sunday, Sept. 30 edition.

Smith, Teresa. 2012. "Education just one of many priorities for aboriginals: Native leaders." *Postmedia News*, 27 March.

Solomon, Patrick, and Howard Palmer. 2004. "Schooling in Babylon, Babylon in school: When racial profiling and zero tolerance converge." *Canadian Journal of Educational Administration and Policy* 33, 1–16.

Souhami, Anna. 2007. "Understanding institutional racism: The Stephen Lawrence inquiry and the police service reaction." In Michael Rowe, ed., *Policing beyond Macpherson: Issues in Policing, Race and Society*, 66–87. Cullompton, UK: Willan.

Southwick, Lawrence Jr. 1998. "An economic analysis of murder and accident risks for police in the United States." *Applied Economics* 30, 593–605.

Speers, Kimberly. 2005. "Performance measurement in the Government of Alberta." *Revue Governance* 2, 1.

Speier, Susanna. 2011. "Did DNA analysis verify Osama Bin Laden's death?" *Scientific American*, 4 May.

Staples, David. 2003. "True Confession or con jobs? In the wake of notorious wrongful conviction cases in Canada." *Postmedia News*, Don Mills, ON, 30 June.

Statistics Canada. 2011a. "Police resources in Canada 2011." www.statcan.gc.ca.

Statistics Canada. 2011b. "Police-reported crime for selected offences, Canada." www.statcan.gc.ca/daily-quotidien.

Statistics Canada. 2010. "Police resources in 2010." www.statcan.gc.ca.

Statistics Canada. 2008. "Aboriginal Peoples in Canada in 2006: Inuit, Métis and First Nations, 2006 census." Catalogue No. 97-558-XWE2006002. Ottawa, ON: Statistics Canada.

Statistics Canada. 2001. *Canada Year Book 2001*. Ottawa, ON: Statistics Canada.

Stein, Karen, and Dan Antonowicz. 2001. "Section.745.6 – The Faint Hope Clause." www.canada.justice.gc.ca/en/ps/rs.

Stenning, Philip. 2011. "Isms and ists: A slightly personal but not intentionally trivial comment on racial profiling." *Canadian Journal of Criminology and Criminal Justice* 53, 1, 113–18.

Steve, Rennie. 2011. "Crime rate fell again in 2010, at lowest level since 1973: StatsCan: Crime rate continues to fall. *The Canadian Press* [Toronto], 21 July.

Stittle, Michael. 2007. "Project Kare: How a missing women's task force works." *CTV News*, 22 July. http://www.ctv.ca/ CTVNews/Canada/ 20070720/project_kare_070720/.

Stoney, Christopher, and Katherine A.H. Graham. 2009. "Federal-municipal relations in Canada: The changing organizational landscape." *Canadian Public Administration* 52, 3, 371–94.

Strick, John. 2002. "Regulation and Deregulation." In Christopher Dunn, ed., *The Handbook of Canadian Public Administration*, ch. 15. Oxford, UK: Oxford University Press.

Supreme Court of Canada. 2009. "R. v. McNeil SCC 3, [2009] S.C.R. 66." http://www.canlii.org/en/ca/scc/ doc/2009/2009scc3/2009scc3.pdf.

Supreme Court of Canada. 2007. *R. vs. Feeney.* http://csc .lexum. org/en/1997/1997scr2-13/1997scr2-13.html.

Supreme Court of Canada. 1991. *R. v. Stinchcombe*, [1991] 3 S.C.R.326." http://scc.lexum.org/en/1991.

Swol, Karen. 1997. "Private security and public policing in Canada." *Juristat* 18, 13.

Takagi, Paul. 1974. *The Correctional System. Social Justice* SocialJust@ aol.com.

Tanovich, David. 2006. *The Colour of Justice: Policing Race in Canada.* Toronto, ON: Irwin Law.

Taylor-Butts, Andrea. 2000. "Justice spending in Canada." Statistics Canada, *Juristat* 22, 11.

Templeton, Jack. 1998. *From Force to Service: The Winnipeg Police Service A Pictorial History.* Winnipeg, MB: Bunker to Bunker Books.

Theodore, Terri. 2012. "Many survivors are in terrible pain." *Winnipeg Free Press*, 25 February.

Thobani, Sunera. 2007. *Exalted Subjects: Studies in the Making of Race and Nation in Canada.* Toronto, ON: University of Toronto Press.

Thorne, Stephen. 2005. "Wrongful convictions continue to plague justice systems in Canada and elsewhere despite studies and reports on the issue, says a report by federal, provincial and territorial prosecutors and police." *Canadian Press*, 25 January.

Tibbetts, Janice. 2005. "Canada's system for detecting wrongful convictions inadequate, says UK official." *Postmedia News*, 23 October.

Time Magazine. 1969. "Canada: City without cops." www.time. com/ time/magazine/article/0,9171,840236,00.html.

Tindal, Richard, and Susan Nobes Tindal. 2004. *Local Government in Canada*. 6th edition. Scarborough, ON: Nelson. Thomson.

Tonry, Michael. 2004. *Punishment and Politics: Evidence and Emulation in English Crime Control Policy*. Cullompton, UK: Willan.

Toobin, Jeffrey. 2007. "The CSI Effect: The truth about forensic science." *New Yorker* 83, 11, 30–5.

Toronto Star. 2010. "Police evolving on race profiling." 15 February.

Totten, Mark. 2009. "Aboriginal youth and violent gang involvement in Canada: Quality prevention strategies." *IPC Review* 3 March, 135–56.

Totten, Mark. 2008. Promising Practices for Addressing Youth Involvement in Gangs. Vancouver, BC: British Columbia Ministry of Public Safety and Solicitor General, Victim Services and Crime Prevention Division.

Totten, Mark. 2000. *Guys, Gangs, and Girlfriend Abuse*. Peterborough, ON: Broadview Press.

Transportation Safety Board of Canada. 2006. "Annual Report to Parliament 2003–2004." www.tsb.gc.ca/rail.

Trevethan, Shelley, Sara Auger, John Patrick Moore, Michael MacDonald, and Jennifer Sinclair. 2002. The Effect of Family Disruption on Aboriginal and Non-Aboriginal Inmates. Research Report R-113. Ottawa, ON: Correctional Service of Canada.

Trott, Roger. 2006. "Training for law enforcement managers." *FBI Law Enforcement Bulletin*.

Truman, Harry S. 2011. "The buck stops here." from the Harry S. Truman Library, http://www.truman library.org/.

Truth and Reconciliation Commission of Canada Website. 2011. http://www.trc.ca/websites/trcinstitution/index.php?p=3.

Truxillo, Donald, M., Susanne R. Bennett, and Michelle L. Collins. 1998. "College education and police Job performance: A ten-year study." *Public Personnel Management* 27, 2, 269–79.

Tyler, Tracey. 2005. "Police, Crown target wrongful convictions; Report on justice urges change of attitude." *Toronto Star*, 26 January.

Tyler, Tom. 2005. "Policing in black and white: Ethnic group differences in trust and confidence in the police." *Police Quarterly* 8, 3.

Umbreit, Mark. 1995. *Mediation Interpersonal Conflicts: A Pathway to Peace*. West Concord, MA: CPI.

United States Department of Justice. 2005a. "Law enforcement officers killed and assaulted." United States Department of Justice. http://www2.fbi.gov/ucr/killed/2005/downloaddocs/federalnarrative.pdf.

United States Department of Justice. 2005b. "A review of the FBI's handling of intelligence and information related to the September 11 Attacks." Redacted, unclassified, and released to the public in June by the Office of the Inspector General.

United States Surgeon General. 2001. Youth Violence: A Report of the Surgeon General. Washington, DC: United States Department of Health and Human Services.

University College of the North. 2006. University College of the North, www.keewatincc.mb.ca.

University of Winnipeg. 2012. UWinnipeg names first director of indigenous inclusion. Release 2012/164, 4 October. http://www.uwinnipeg.ca/index/uw-news-action/story.883/title.-uwinnipeg-names-first-director-of-indigenous-inclusion.

Van Maanen, John. 1978. "The asshole." In P.K. Manning and Johan van Maanen, eds, Policing: A View from the Street, 221–38. Santa Monica, CA: Goodyear Publishing.

Van Maanen, John. 1974. "Working the street: A developmental view of police behavior." In H. Jacob, ed., The Potential for Reform of Criminal Justice, 83–130. Beverly Hills, CA: Sage,

Vermette, Heidi S., Debra A. Pinals, and Paul S. Appelbaum. 2005. "Mental health training for law enforcement professionals." Journal of the American Academy of Psychiatry and the Law 33, 42–6.

Vienneau, David. 1995. "Sale of RCMP rights to Disney denounced: Local firm can no longer make insignia rings." Toronto Star, 23 July.

Volkan, Vamik D. 1997. Bloodlines: From Ethnic Pride to Ethnic Terrorism. New York, NY: Farrar, Strauss and Giroux.

Waddington, Tank. 2010. "Policing with trust and confidence." Policing 4, 3, 197–8.

Waldfogel, Jane. 2006. What Children Need. Cambridge, MA: Harvard University Press.

Walker, Barrington. 2010. Race on Trial: Black Defendants in Ontario's Criminal Courts, 1858–1958. Toronto, ON: University of Toronto Press.

Wallis, Claudia, and Sonja Steptoe. 2006. "Help! I've lost my focus." Time Magazine, 16 January.

Walsh, P. J. Dermot, and Vicky Conway. 2011. "Police governance and accountability: Overview of current issues." Case Law Society and Change 55, 61–86.

Warren, Jennifer. 2008. "One in 100: Behind bars in America 2008." Washington, DC: The Pew Charitable Trusts. www.pewtrusts.org

Waters, Judeth, and William Ussery. 2007. "Police Stress: History, contributing factors, symptoms and interventions." *Policing: An International Journal of Police Strategies and Management* 30, 2, 169–88.

Waters, Judeth, N. Irons, and E. Finkle. 1982. "The police stress inventory: A comparison of events affecting officers and supervisors in rural and urban areas." *Police Stress* 5, 1, 18–25.

Weeks, Carly. 2007. "Canadians losing confidence in RCMP brass." *CanWest News Service* http://www.rcmpwatch. com /canadians-losing-confidence-in-rcmp-brass/.

Weisburd, David, Stephen D. Mastrofski, Marie Anne McNally, Rosanne Greenspan, and James J. Willis. 2003. "Reforming to preserve: COMPSTAT and strategic problem solving in American policing." *Criminology and Public Policy* 2, 421–56.

Weiss, Alexander. 2001. "Law enforcement executive education: Towards a paradigm for the 21st century." Illinois Law Enforcement Executive Forum 1, 2, 103–4.

Weitzel, Thomas. 2004. "Command School: The Education Process for Future Law Enforcement Leaders." Law Enforcement Executive Forum 4, 1.

Weitzer, Ronald, and Steven A. Tuch. 2005. "Determinants of public satisfaction with the police." *Police Quarterly* 8, 3, 279–97.

Welch, Mary Agnes and Mia Rabson. 2011. "Contentious cleanup." *Winnipeg Free Press*, 30 December.

Westmarland, Louise. 2010. "Dodgy customers? Can the police ever trust the public?" *Policing* 4, 3, 291–7.

White, Susan O. 1972. "A perspective on police professionalization." *Law and Society Review* 7, 1, 61–86.

Whittingham, Michael D. 1984. "Police/public homicide and fatality risks in Canada: A current assessment – serving and being protected." *Canadian Police Chief* 3, 10, 4–8.

Wilkinson, Vicki. 1994. "The marginalisation of women: Factors affecting the discontinuance of the careers of female police officers." Doctoral thesis, Edith Cowan University, Western Australia.

Willis, James J., Stephen D. Mastrofski, and David Weisburd. 2003. "Compstat in practice: An in-depth analysis of three cities." Police Foundation. http://www.policefoundation.org.

Wilson, Edward, and Joseph Davis. 1998. "Homicide or suicide: The killing of suicidal persons by law enforcement officers." *Journal of Forensic Sciences* 43, 1.

Wilson, James Q. 1968. *Varieties of Police Behavior: The Management of Law and Order in Eight Communities.* Cambridge, MA: Harvard University Press.

Wilson, James. Q., and Joan Petersilia. 2002. *Crime: Public Policies for Crime Control.* New York, NY: Oxford University Press.

Winnipeg Free Press. 2011. "Kyle Unger suing over wrongful conviction." 21 September.

Winnipeg Police Service. 2011. Auto theft suppression strategy website, http://www.winnipeg.ca/police/ TakeAction/WATSS.stm.

Winnipeg Police Service. 2008. WPS Missing Persons webpage. http://www.winnipeg.ca/police/div_41/missing_persons.stm

Winnipeg Police Service. 2006. "WPS collective working agreement." WPS internal document.

Winnipeg Police Service. 2005. "Annual reports 1999–2005." WPS website, policenet/police/AnnualReports/annual reports.stm.

Winnipeg Police Service. 2004. "The Winnipeg police service post-secondary reimbursement program." WPS internal document.

Woodcock, Connie. 2011. "Goodbye and good riddance to the long gun registry." *Toronto Sun*, 5 November.

Wood-Harper, A. Trevor, and Richard L. Baskerville. 1996. "A critical perspective on action research as a method for information systems research." *Journal of Information Technology* 11, 3, 235–46.

Wortley, Scot, and Akwasi Owusu-Bempah. 2011. "The usual suspects: Police stop and search practices in Canada." *Policing and Society* 21, 4, 395–407.

Wortley, Scot, and Julian Tanner. 2005. "Inflammatory rhetoric? Baseless accusations? Responding to Gabor's critique of racial profiling research in Canada." *Canadian Journal of Criminology and Criminal Justice* 47, 581–609.

Wortley, Scot, and Julian Tanner. 2003. "Data, denials and confusion: The racial profiling debate in Toronto." *Canadian Journal of Criminology and Criminal Justice* 45, 367–89.

Wright, David H. 2004. *Report of the Commission of Inquiry into the Matters Related to the Death of Neil Stonechild.* Regina, SK: Government of Saskatchewan.

York, Darlene Eleanor. 1994. *Cross-Cultural Training Programs.* Westport, CT: Bergin and Garvey.

York, Geoffrey. 1990. *The Dispossessed: Life and Death in Native Canada.* London, UK: Vintage.

Younging, Gregory. 2009. "Inherited history, international law, and the UN Declaration." In Gregory Younging, Jonathan Dewar, and Mike DeGagné, eds, *Response, Responsibility, and Renewal: Canada's Truth and Reconciliation Journey.* Ottawa, ON: Aboriginal Healing Foundation.

Zaccardelli, Giuliano. 2006. Letter from Commissioner Zaccardelli to Prime Minister Harper. Ottawa, Ontario, Government of Canada website. http://www. pm.gc.ca/eng /media.asp?id=1445.

Zartman, Jonathan. 2008. "Negotiation, exclusion and durable peace: Dialogue and peacebuilding in Tajikistan." *International Negotiation* 13, 1, 55–72.

Zwell, Michael. 2000. *Creating a Culture of Competence.* New York, NY: John Wiley and Sons, Inc.

Index